KV 5 *A Preliminary Report*

Publications of the
Theban Mapping Project
II

American University in Cairo Press
2000

KV 5

A Preliminary Report
on the Excavation of the
Tomb of the Sons of Rameses II
in the Valley of the Kings

Edited by Kent R. Weeks

 Theban
Mapping
Project

Publications of the Theban Mapping Project: II

First published in Egypt in 2000 by
The American University in Cairo Press
113 Sharia Kasr el Aini
Cairo, Egypt
http://aucpress.com

Dar el Kutub No. 17607/99
ISBN 977 424 574 1

Photography by Francis Dzikowski.
Wall reliefs, objects, and pottery drawn by Susan Weeks.
Hieroglyphic text set using Glyph for Windows 1.2.
Maps and illustrations by Walton Chan.
Additional illustrations by Ilka Schacht, Samar Zaki,
and Ashraf Salloum.
Designed by Walton Chan.

Typeset in Apollo MT and Frutiger.
Imagesetting by D & B Graphics, Cairo.
Printed in Egypt.

KV 5 / TMP Staff

Kent R. Weeks	1978 -	Director
Walton Chan	1996 -	Architect, Designer
Ashraf Salloum	1994 -	Architect
Samar Hafez Zaki	1998 -	Architect
Francis Dzikowski	1994 -	Photographer
Susan H. Weeks	1978 -	Artist
David A. Goodman	1978 -	Chief Surveyor
Nubie Abdel Basset	1982 -	Assistant Surveyor
Ahmed Mahmoud Hassan	1990 -	Foreman
Catherine H. Roehrig	1979 -	Egyptologist
Marjorie Aronow	1995 -	Egyptologist
Salima Ikram	1996 -	Egyptologist, Osteologist
Edwin C. Brock	1998 -	Egyptologist
Nathalie Walschaerts	1998 -	Egyptologist
Randa Baligh	1999 -	Egyptologist
Barbara Greene	1979, 1998 -	Ceramicist
Michael Jesudason	1996 -	Ceramicist
Lotfi Khaled Hassan	1997 -	Conservator
Lamia el-Hadidi	1994 - 1995	Conservator
Brendhan Hight	1997 -	Website Manager
Hans van den Berg	1997 -	Computer Consultant
John Bex	1997 -	Computer Consultant
Ilka Schacht	1999 -	Project Coordinator
Magdy Abu Hamed Ali	1999 -	Office Manager
Franklin Yates	1999	Intern

TABLE OF CONTENTS

Preface   1

Introduction   3

Archæological and Architectural Description
Kent R. Weeks   7

   The Entrance to KV 5   10

   Chamber 1   12

   Chamber 2   16

   Chamber 3   22

   Chamber 4   29

   Chambers 5 and 6   30

   Corridor 7   32

   Chamber 8   38

   Chamber 9   40

   Corridor 10   42

   Corridor 11   44

   Corridor 12   47

   Chamber 13   50

   Chamber 14   50

   Chamber 15   52

   Corridor 16   52

   Corridor 20   53

Wall Decoration   *Edwin C. Brock*   55

Inscribed Objects   *Edwin C. Brock and Nathalie Walschaerts*

   Shabtis   95

   Canopic Jars and Other Objects   104

Pottery   *Barbara Greene*   119

Fauna   *Salima Ikram*   127

Conservation, 1994 - 1999   *Lotfi Khaled Hassan*   135

Appendices

   I.   Mineralogical Analysis
      Advanced Terra Testing, Inc.   147

   IIa. Rock Mechanics Index Tests
      Hamza Associates   157

   IIb. Lithologic, Petrographic, and Mineralogic
      Identification of Two Surface Samples
      (Indurated Rocks)
      Hamza Associates   159

   III. Hydraulic Response of the Valley of the Kings
      Sherif M. A. El-Didy   161

   IV. Slope Deformations in the Valley of the Kings
      Michael Bukovansky and Donald P. Richards   167

   V.   Geotechnical Studies for KV 5
      Donald P. Richards, Michael Bukovansky, and John F. Abel, Jr.   173

   VI. KV 5 Tomb Stability and Rehabilitation
      John F. Abel, Jr.   189

Acknowledgments   201

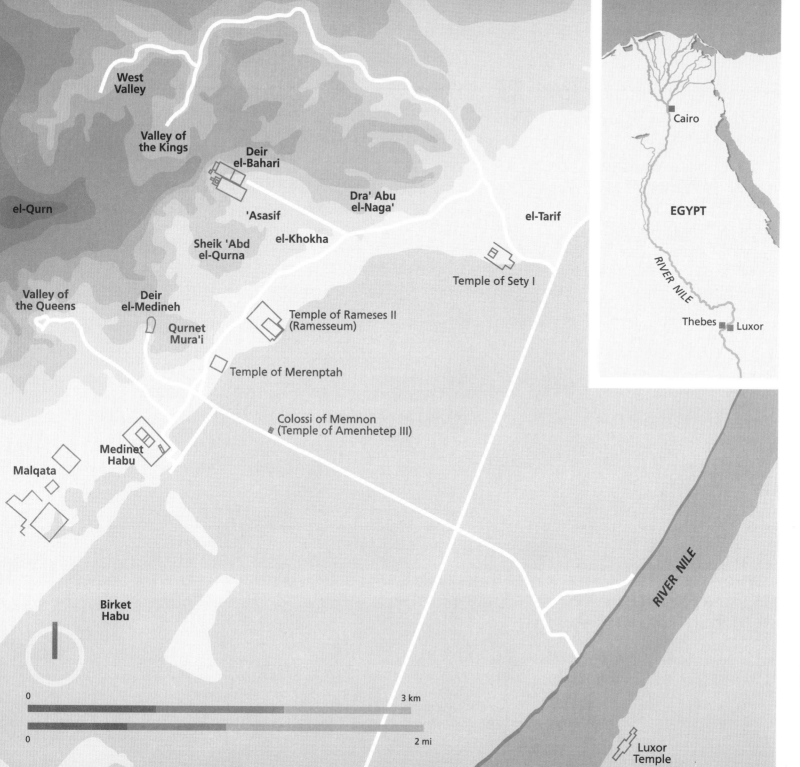

West Valley

Valley of the Kings

Deir el-Bahari

'Asasif

Dra' Abu el-Naga'

el-Tarif

el-Qurn

Sheik 'Abd el-Qurna

el-Khokha

Temple of Sety I

Valley of the Queens

Deir el-Medineh

Qurnet Mura'i

Temple of Rameses II (Ramesseum)

Temple of Merenptah

Colossi of Memnon (Temple of Amenhetep III)

Medinet Habu

Malqata

Birket Habu

RIVER NILE

Luxor Temple

0   3 km

0   2 mi

EGYPT

Cairo

RIVER NILE

Thebes   Luxor

Fig. 1: Maps of Egypt (inset) and Luxor/Thebes, showing location of the Valley of the Kings.

PREFACE

The Theban Mapping Project (TMP) was established in 1979 to prepare a detailed archæological map and database of the Theban Necropolis. The Necropolis, arguably one of the richest and most important archæological sites in the world, has suffered serious damage over time, and that damage is increasing in scope and intensity.

The TMP's goal is to establish a historical and contemporary record of all of the monuments in this ten-square-kilometer World Heritage Site, and to prepare detailed topographical maps, architectural plans, and surveys of their history and condition. The first of the final publications of this work is *The Atlas of the Valley of the Kings*, published in hard copy in Arabic and English, and on CD-ROM (2000). A second CD, *The Atlas of Ancient Thebes: An Archæological Database*, will appear in 2001. Several other, related works are in preparation.

In 1987, the TMP rediscovered KV 5 (King's Valley tomb number 5). Except for the fact that KV 5 lay at the entrance to the Valley of the Kings, all that was known about the tomb was from a brief comment and a partial plan of its first few chambers drawn by an English traveler, James Burton, in 1825. By 1995, the TMP's excavations had revealed what some scholars had long suspected: that KV 5 was the burial place of several sons of Rameses II. The tomb also turned out to be the largest ever found in Egypt — so far there are 110 corridors and chambers, with more to come. It is a tomb of unique plan, whose function as a family mausoleum for sons of a pharaoh is not known anywhere else in Egypt.

Fig. 2: TMP survey team working in the Valley of the Kings.

The following preliminary report is a technical summary of some of the work carried out in KV 5 from 1987 to 1999. Given the size of KV 5 and the amount of work still to be done, a final report is several years away. Not included here, for example, are reports of ongoing work on control marks in the tomb, commentary on epigraphic details, or more comprehensive analyses of objects and stratigraphy. That material will appear in articles and monographs during the next few seasons.

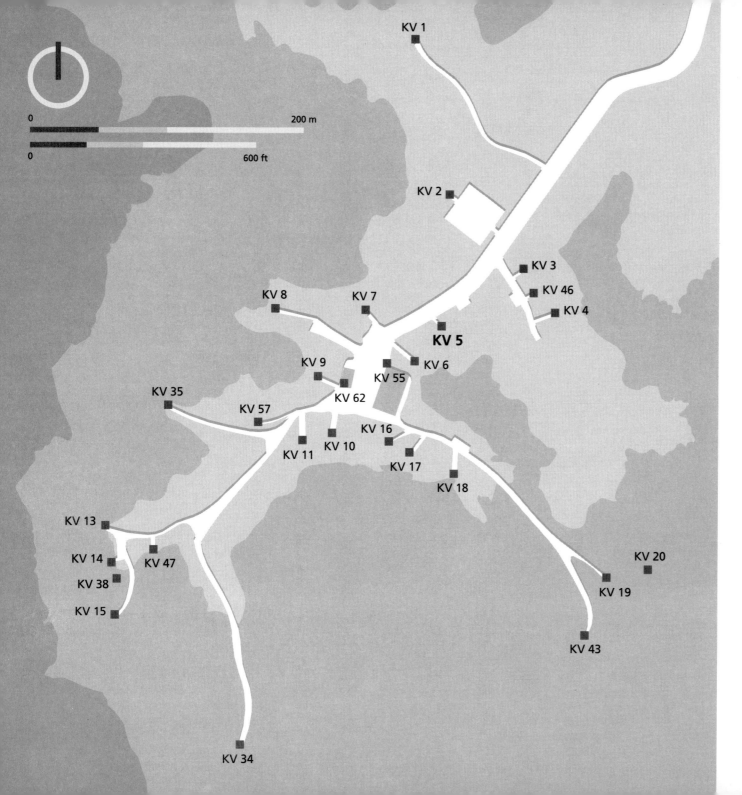

Fig. 3: Map of the Valley of the Kings, showing location of KV 5 and other major tombs.

INTRODUCTION

In July, 1987, the Theban Mapping Project rediscovered the entrance to a tomb in the Valley of the Kings that had been designated by John Gardner Wilkinson as 'KV 5'. Wilkinson's designation meant that it was the fifth tomb he had numbered as he moved southward into the Valley of the Kings (KV), cataloging its contents in 1827.

Wilkinson was one of the few nineteenth century travelers and explorers to see KV 5's entrance – or at least one of the few to refer to it in their journals. Indeed, were it not for Wilkinson's survey, and brief notes by such visitors as Robert Hay and Edward Lane, KV 5 might well have disappeared from history. In the three millennia before these nineteenth century visitors, KV 5 had suffered a dozen times from rare but heavy rains in the Valley of the Kings, and these had filled KV 5's chambers literally to their ceilings with stones, limestone chips, sand, and silts, and buried its entrance under several meters of debris.

The few nineteenth century explorers who ventured inside KV 5 did so by crawling along a narrow channel that had been cut through the top of the debris by James Burton in 1825. Burton's channel extended only about twenty-five meters into the tomb, and from it nothing could be seen of the tomb's walls or floor. Burton managed to make a sketch plan of the tomb's first few chambers, locating its walls and pillars by probing with a stick through the two or three centimeters of space separating the debris from the ceiling. His unscaled drawing showed eleven chambers in a peculiar arrangement, but gave little indication of their functions or what type of tomb KV 5 might have been.

James Burton, unpublished journals, British Museum Add. MSS 25613-75, 1825:

This tomb is all in a state of ruin. On the ceiling alone which has in general fallen in vast masses are to be seen some small remains here and there of colouring. The substance of the rock between the small chambers and the large ones above cannot be more than 18 inches. Being full of mud and earth the descent from the pillared room to those underneath is not perceptible. The Catacomb must have been excavated very low in the valley or the valley much raised by the accumulation of earth, stones and rubbish brought down by the rains. I found a large piece of breccia verd'antico, evidence of those quarries having been used in this king's time and of some sarcophagus having been in the tomb of this material. It is possible there is some passage leading from below the center of the pillared chamber into that where the sarcophagus stood.

Edward Lane, unpublished journals, British Museum Add. MSS 34080-8, 1827:

Returning, and proceeding along the central branch, we arrive at the Fifth Tomb, on the left side; the direction of which is towards the south-east. Its entrance is at the base of the slope, and is surrounded by rubbish which has been taken out. The passage has been quite filled up by detritus washed in by rains, and by fragments of the rock which have fallen in consequence of the damp on such occasions: but a way has been cut through this mass of rubbish and stones; leaving part all along to support the loosened portions of rock above. As we proceed, the destruction becomes greater; and at length it is impossible to trace any plan: nothing is seen but rubbish and fragments of stone, through which a passage has been made with difficulty and danger.

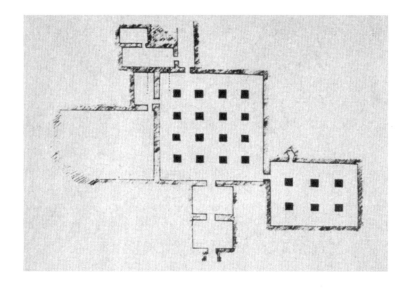

Fig. 4: Burton's sketch plan of KV 5 (top) and a computer reconstruction (bottom) of the exploratory trenches he dug inside the tomb.

Later explorers who ventured into Burton's channel concluded that KV 5 was an unimportant, undecorated, uninscribed, and uninteresting hole in the ground of only minor archæological interest. Indeed, early in the twentieth century, Howard Carter began to clear the entrance to KV 5, but abandoned the work after digging less than a meter into the doorway. He had found no artifacts, exposed no decorated walls, and apparently became convinced that further excavation would be a waste of time.

In the 1960s, Egyptologist Elizabeth Thomas reviewed the available material on KV 5 for her masterful study, *The Royal Necropoleis of Thebes*. She did not explore Burton's channel herself – Howard Carter had reburied the tomb entrance under three meters of debris dumped from his other excavations, making it completely inaccessible. But it is a tribute to Ms Thomas's knowledge of the Valley of the Kings that she concluded from the scanty observations of Burton, Lane, Hay, and Lepsius, that KV 5 was perhaps an Eighteenth Dynasty tomb, enlarged by Rameses II as the burial-place "for more than one member of his family." We now know that Ms Thomas was correct.

Knowledge of the general location of KV 5 was never lost. Several early maps showed its approximate position, at the base of a hill immediately adjacent to the main path into the Valley. The area otherwise contained only two tombs, KV 6 and KV 55.

KV 5 was finally probed in the summer of 1987 because of a government plan to widen the roadway into the Valley of the Kings to ease traffic congestion. This required digging into the adjacent hillsides. We knew that KV 5 lay somewhere in the vicinity and could be threatened by it. Our attempts to pinpoint the tomb using geophysical devices were unsuccessful, so we dug a ten–meter–long trench along the base of the hill through Carter's dump, and relocated the entrance in a matter of days.

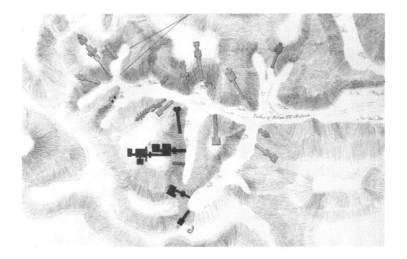

Fig. 5: Early maps of the Valley of the Kings, by (clockwise from above) Pococke, the *Description d'Egypte*, and Belzoni.

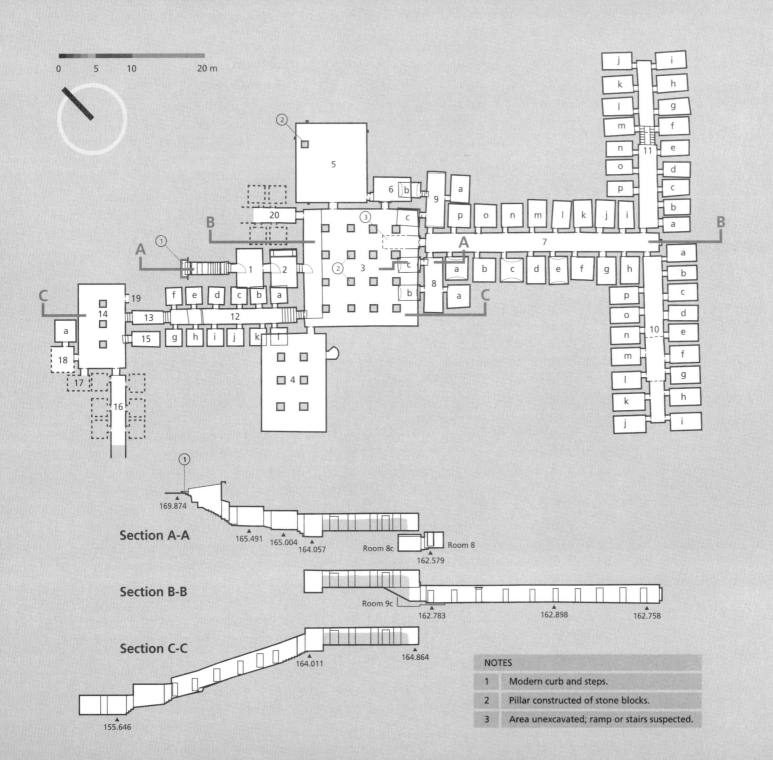

Section A-A

169.874
165.491 165.004
164.057
Room 8c   Room 8
162.579

Section B-B

Room 9c
162.783   162.898   162.758

Section C-C

164.011   164.864
155.646

NOTES

1	Modern curb and steps.
2	Pillar constructed of stone blocks.
3	Area unexcavated; ramp or stairs suspected.

Fig. 6: Plan and longitudinal sections of KV 5.

ARCHÆOLOGICAL AND ARCHITECTURAL DESCRIPTION

Kent R. Weeks

Following the rediscovery of KV 5, we made several exploratory visits along Burton's channel and into the tomb's few accessible chambers. This meant slithering through a crawl space between the debris and the ceiling that was rarely more than seventy centimeters high, an uncomfortable and sometimes painful experience, and we could gain only vague notions of what KV 5's plan might have looked like from these visits. But we did confirm the accuracy of Burton's sketch plan – he saw the chambers we have labeled 1, 2, 3, 4, 5, 6, 7 (first 1.5 meters only), 9, 9a, 9b, and 9c – and, although clearly incomplete, it showed that KV 5's plan was unlike any other tomb in the Valley of the Kings.

Early in our clearing of Chamber 1, we had found traces of carved and painted plaster still adhering to chamber walls. As we exposed these walls, it also became clear that KV 5's decoration was as unusual as its plan. The names of two sons of Rameses II were carved on the walls, suggesting that the tomb was, uniquely, the burial place of several princes.

Over the next six years, as we slowly dug our way through chambers 1 and 2, we were increasingly fascinated by what Chamber 3 might reveal and what might lie beyond it. Chambers 1 and 2 were small rooms, nineteen and eighteen square meters, respectively. Chamber 3 covered 244 square meters. Unfortunately, our engineers warned against major clearing in Chamber 3 until more geotechnical studies could be conducted. We therefore decided to crawl across the

Fig. 7: The entrance to the Valley of the Kings, with KV 5 at center.

chamber and explore the doorway Burton had seen in its eastern wall.

We began clearing that doorway late in 1994. By February, 1995, we had progressed 2.5 meters into the room beyond. On the morning of February 2, our workmen noted that debris no longer filled the room to its ceiling, but had begun to slope gradually downward. Peering into this larger crawl space, we realized that we had not entered a chamber but a corridor that extended deep into the bedrock. Crawling into the corridor, thirty-two meters from its entrance, we found a statue of Osiris cut into the eastern end wall. To its left and right, transverse corridors, each twenty-two meters long, extended north and south. At intervals along all three corridors, doorways led into other rooms or suites of rooms, a total of forty-eight of them. Suddenly KV 5 had become the largest tomb ever found in the Valley of the Kings.

Over the next four years, KV 5 continued to grow: from Burton's eleven chambers to 67 in 1995, 110 in 1999, and a likelihood of at least 150 in a coming season. KV 5 is not only the largest tomb in the Valley of the Kings, it is one of the largest ever found in Egypt. It is unique in plan. It is unique in its function as a family mausoleum for a still-unknown number of sons of Rameses II. By any standard, it is a remarkable example of dynastic architecture, and a physical reflection of what must have been significantly-altered views of the roles of princes, of the nature of kingship, and of funerary practices in the reign of Rameses II.

Areas of Selected KV Tombs

Tomb	Tomb Owner	Area
KV 5	sons of Rameses II	> 1800 m²
KV 7	Rameses II	853 m²
KV 8	Merenptah	833 m²
KV 11	Rameses III	722 m²
KV 17	Seti I	658 m²
KV 14	Tausert / Setnakht	632 m²
KV 9	Rameses V / VI	491 m²
KV 57	Horemheb	471 m²
KV 6	Rameses IX	363 m²
KV 62	Tutankhamen	112 m²

KV 5 Corridor, Chamber, and Object Designations

The numbering system we have used to identify corridors and chambers in KV 5 still must be considered temporary. Chambers are necessarily numbered in the order of their discovery; that means that an architecturally-logical system cannot always be followed. The decision whether to assign a number to a chamber (e.g., Chamber 9) or give it a letter designation as a side-chamber (e.g., 9a) is also one that perforce is arbitrary.

We already have had to re-number several rooms and may find it necessary to do so again. In such cases, a tabular summary of old and new designations in the final report will hopefully prevent confusion.

Pillars are identified alphabetically in parentheses following their chamber designator, e.g., 3(a), 4(f).

Objects are numbered in order of discovery within each chamber or corridor: 1.25 is the 25th object from Chamber 1; 3.2a-d are the four pieces of object 2 from Chamber 3.

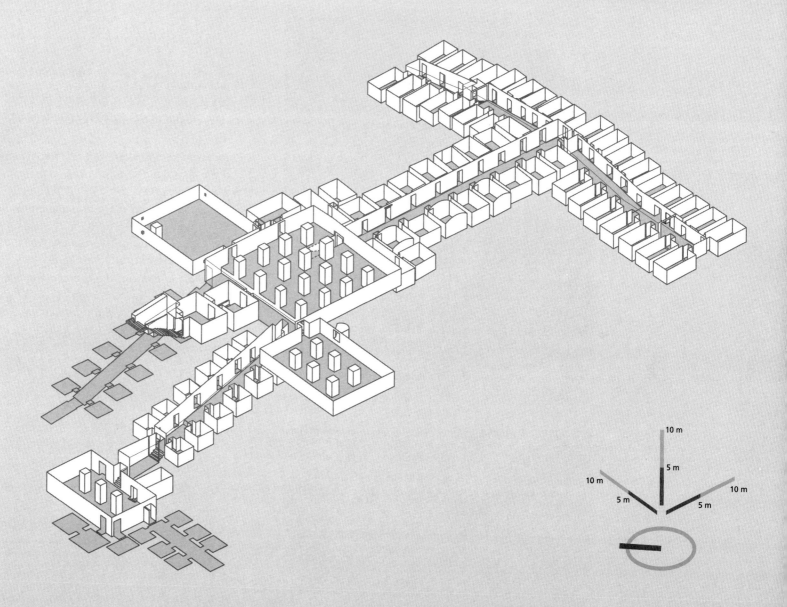

Fig. 8: Isometric drawing of KV 5.

10 m
5 m
10 m
5 m
10 m
5 m

The entryway to KV 5 was cut into the limestone bedrock, and measured 4.46 meters deep, 2.84 meters wide and 4.17 meters long. A staircase formed its steeply-sloping base. Only six steps are preserved today, although originally there were perhaps twice that number. The steps led to the 1.23 meter-wide, 2.54 meter-high door of the tomb. There is an inwardly-sloping overhang before Gate 1.

After another few days of clearing at the entrance, a cartouche of Rameses II was found on the door's left reveal. It had been noted by Burton in 1825 and remarked upon by Carl Richard Lepsius three decades later. On the left door jamb was carved a kneeling figure of Ma'at and another cartouche of Rameses II. This doorway had been recut 0.20 meters wider in antiquity, after the west wall of Chamber 1 had been decorated. Such recutting is characteristic of many of the major doorways in KV 5 (e.g., those between chambers 1 and 2, 2 and 3, 3 and 7, 3 and 12, and 3 and 20).

Fig. 9: (Top) The area in of KV 5 in 1920 (from the Carter MSS I.J.337). The tomb entrance is covered with debris and a water shed for donkeys. KV 6 is on the right. We should like to thank the Griffith Institute for permission to publish this photograph. (Center) The same area in 1987 prior to the tomb being re-located by the TMP (photograph by David Goodman). Note the souvenir vendors' stalls in front. (Bottom) The same view in 1997, after the entrance was cleared and the retaining walls around it was built.

Carl Richard Lepsius, *Denkmäler*, 1849-1859:

Dies Grab is mit Schnutt angefüllt. Ein schmaler Weg ist ausgebrochen und führt bald in einen grossen Pfeilersaal und viele, an 8 oder 9, Nebenkammern, noch weiter hinten [ist das Grab] verschüttet. Links ist eine gewölbte Kammer, wo noch etwas gemalter Stuck zu sehen ist, wie auch anderswo. An der Thüre aber, am linken Pfosten ist noch deutllich das mit Salz überzogene Schild Ramses' II (User-ma-Re setep-en-re) zu sehen vor einer knieenden geflügelten Göttin. Es war also ein von ihm angefangenes und dann verlassenes Grab. Auch bis hinten ist Regenschutt bis fast an die Decke. Der Eingang ist auch schlecht gelegen. (Vol. 3, p. 197)

[This tomb is filled with debris. A narrow path is cut out and leads to a great pillared hall and many – 8 or 9 – side-chambers. Further chambers are buried. On the left is a vaulted chamber where one can still see painted plaster, as is also found elsewhere. At the door, however, on the left jamb one can still clearly see the cartouche of Ramses II (User-ma-Re setep-en-Re), covered with salt, in front of a kneeling, winged goddess. We deal with a tomb that was constructed for him, then abandoned. Also up to its far end, there is flood debris. The entrance is badly located.]

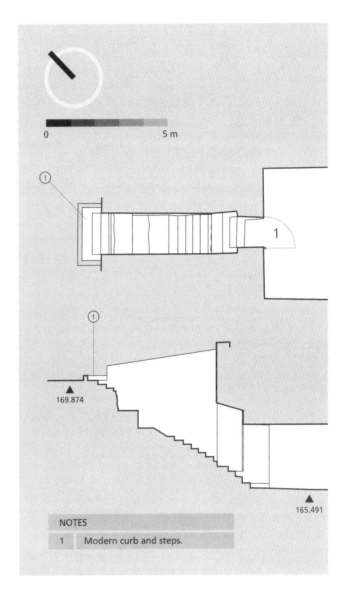

Fig. 10: Plan and section of the entrance to KV 5.

Chamber 1

Our study of Chamber 1 began in July, 1988, with an examination of Burton's channel. It contained only a few objects, all of them washed or carried into the tomb within the last hundred years: a broken champagne goblet, a piece of an early twentieth-century newspaper, and some broken mammal bones, mostly donkey.

In the late nineteenth or early twentieth century, a shelter for tourists' donkeys had been erected directly over the entrance to KV 5. In the 1950s, at the same time as a paved road was laid down, a sewer line to the rest house beside the entrance to KV 6 was installed, also directly above the tomb entrance. Both shelter and sewer contributed to the organic material we found in the channel.

It was not until 1989 that we began to clear the debris that completely filled Chamber 1, and not until ten years later, in 1999, that the last of the debris was removed. This long process was made necessary by the debris itself. The material that filled Chamber 1 was washed into the tomb by at least twelve major floods in KV over the past 3,000 years. These floods were the result of sudden, heavy rainstorms pummeling the slopes surrounding the Valley, when several centimeters of rain might be dumped in a matter of minutes on a few hectares of hillside. Such quantities of water could not be absorbed by the Valley's thin overburden of sand and silt, and it therefore roared down the hillside, carrying with it tons of limestone chips, chert, silt, and sand.

By the time these floodwaters reached low-lying parts of the Valley, they were traveling at over fifteen kilometers per hour with sufficient force to carry stones weighing fifteen to twenty-five kilograms. This flood-borne debris surged into the entrances of low-lying tombs like KV 5, filling them with many cubic meters of debris. The nature of these floods

Dimensions of Chamber 1	
Floor Elevation	165.49 msl
Length	3.60 m along N wall, 3.69 m along S wall
Width	5.17 m along W wall, 5.28 m along E wall
Height	2.60 m
Area	19.08 m²
Volume	49.61 m³
Width of Gate 2	1.17 m
Height of Gate 2	2.54 m

was the subject of a hydrological study we conducted in 1994; it is summarized in Appendix III.

Inside the tomb, the floods did substantial damage. Water-borne stones were hurled against painted and plastered walls, and any decoration not knocked off was so softened by the water that it turned to mush and fell away. Objects in the tomb were tossed about to such an extent that we frequently found pieces of the same pot scattered a hundred meters apart in different chambers of the tomb.

The flood quickly slowed as it moved through the tomb. We can see clearly the pattern of its decline: heavier stones were dropped relatively near the tomb entrance, where the force of the floodwaters had only begun to diminish; further inside, where the waters had slowed considerably, chambers were filled with layers of tiny stone chips and silt; at the rear of the tomb, where the flood waters were thin and weak, only the finest silts were deposited.

In Chamber 1, the force of the flood deposited relatively large pieces of stone, and densely packed the silts it carried. The debris here had dried to such concrete-like hardness that the picks of strong workmen were needed to cut into it. But embedded in the debris were objects – potsherds, ostraca, fragments of stone sarcophagi, canopic jars, animal bones,

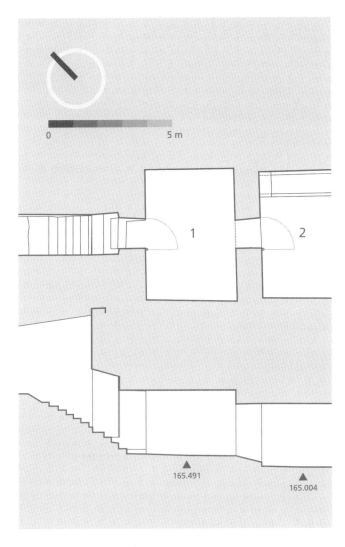

Fig. 11: Plan and section of Room 1.

and pieces of decorated plaster. To remove these fragile objects from the dense matrix was a time-consuming and delicate operation.

Since stratigraphic control has rarely been maintained in the clearing of KV tombs, we were anxious to establish such a record in KV 5. We had hoped that it might be possible to tie together the stratigraphic records of several KV tombs and compile a hydrological history of the Valley. However, given the floods' different intensities, the complexity of their locations and paths, and the similarity of flood debris in every stratum, this cannot yet be done. The stratigraphy of Chamber 1 revealed eleven principal layers of silts or limestone chips, or a combination of both, each of different thickness, each deposited by floods of different force and duration.

Many of the artifacts found in the debris had been washed into tomb from various areas of the valley, but there is no indication that they came from one particular part of the valley. The churning of debris by the floods tossed objects about in an almost random fashion, and there appears to be no stratigraphically or architecturally significant pattern to the distribution of intrusive objects in the tomb. The objects found directly on the floor were frequently (but by no means always) indigenous to KV 5, but very few were found *in situ*. We found no evidence that KV 5 had been re-used in later times (i.e., after the New Kingdom, as several other KV tombs had been), as a storeroom, campsite, or hermitage.

The ceiling of Chamber 1, originally cut horizontally, was badly damaged during the past forty years by the vibrations of tourist buses parked immediately adjacent to the tomb entrance. Blocks were shaken loose from the overlying bedrock causing an almost dome-like void to be created. This process is discussed in greater detail in Appendix V.

The discovery that Chamber 1 had been extensively decorated with elaborately carved and painted plaster scenes demanded special care be taken to protect and stabilize the walls. The remaining decoration, together with the fragments found in the debris, enabled us to begin the arduous task of restoring on paper the scenes and texts with which the tomb was originally filled. To date, we have found no wall in any part of KV 5 devoid of carved or painted plaster decoration.

The artisans who carved and decorated Chamber 1 were forced to deal with limestone bedrock that had fractured and cracked many thousands of years ago because of geological pressures in the hillside. These extended many meters horizontally through the tomb and often continued vertically to the surface of the hillside above. The ancient craftsmen chinked these cracks with limestone chips and thick plaster in order to create a smooth surface to decorate. Unfortunately, they also produced a wall that was often seriously unstable because of the weight of the repairs. Virtually every crack and fracture that we see today in the bedrock was present when the ancient Egyptians dug KV 5, and any fractures of significant size were repaired by the masons. Indeed, there is scant evidence of any recent damage to KV 5 except in chambers 1 and 5, which lie at a shallow depth beneath the paved road for tourist buses. The fractures and fissures in the KV 5 hillside are discussed in Appendix IV.

Objects from Chamber 1

Chamber 1 produced seven shabtis, six canopic jar fragments, and two possible sarcophagus fragments. These will be discussed further in the chapter on Inscribed Objects.

Objects from Chamber 1

Shabtis

1.3	inscribed	blue faïence	NW quadrant, floor
1.4	inscribed	blue-green faïence	NW quadrant, floor
1.5	inscribed	blue-green faïence	NW quadrant, floor
1.6	inscribed	calcite	SE quadrant, floor
1.21	inscribed	faïence	SW quadrant, floor
1.24	inscribed	calcite	NE quadrant, 0.10 m above floor
1.25	uninscribed	calcite	NE quadrant, 0.10 m above floor

Canopic Jars

1.10	inscribed	calcite	S of center, floor
1.11	inscribed	calcite	S of center, floor
1.12	inscribed	calcite	S of center, from fill (joins 2.11)
1.13	uninscribed	calcite	S of center, floor
1.23	inscribed	calcite	NE quadrant, 0.10 m above floor
1.26	uninscribed	calcite	NE quadrant, floor

Possible Sarcophagus or Canopic Box Fragments

1.9	inscribed	red granite	S half, from fill
1.22	uninscribed	basalt (?)	NE quadrant, 0.50 m above floor

Other Objects

1.7	hand from an anthropoid sarcophagus	wood	S quadrant, top of fill
1.8	round drawer pull with dowel	wood	S half, 2.00 m from ceiling
1.15	painted scepter fragment (21 x 3 cm)	wood	SW quadrant, 2.00 m from ceiling

In addition, four 'wiglets', sometimes also called 'wig curls', perhaps from coffins or furniture, were found: one of glass, two of faïence, one of glazed but uncertain material. Two are from the NW quadrant, 2.0 meters below the ceiling; one from NW quadrant, floor; one from the SE quadrant, 2.0 meters below the ceiling. Forty tubular faïence beads were found in the NW quadrant, 1.80 meters below the ceiling; thirty-four faïence tubular beads were found in the NE quadrant, 1.80 meters below the ceiling.

On the floor in the northwest corner of Chamber 1 lay a Canaanite amphora base that had been re-used by one of the artists decorating the chamber walls. It still had traces of blue paint in it, and that paint had spilled onto the floor immediately below a scene in which blue paint had been used.

Pottery from Chamber 1

The pottery from Chamber 1 is a mixture of types and periods. The sherds had been thoroughly tossed about by floodwaters and there is no significant stratigraphic or geographical distribution. We find Ramesside, New Kingdom, Late Period, Coptic, and Roman sherds scattered throughout the debris. Note that several sherds from this chamber came from vessels other sherds from which were found as far afield as chambers 11 and 14. See the chapter on Pottery for more details.

Fig. 12: Object 1.7, hand from an anthropoid sarcophagus.

Chamber 2

The excavation of Chamber 2 continued from 1990 until 1998, first in the southern half of the room, then the northern. It was not until 1998 that we discovered a large pit in the floor of the chamber, immediately below the north wall.

As in Chamber 1, there is stratigraphic evidence for perhaps twelve floods, but the strata are more regular and more nearly horizontal, probably the result of a reduction in the strength of the flood after it had passed through chambers 1 and 2. The debris contains more fine silts and small limestone chips, fewer stones, and no boulders. The ceiling of the chamber was flat, just slightly broken; only a few small pieces of limestone from it or the walls were found in the debris.

The gates from Chamber 1 into 2 and Chamber 2 into 3, like the gate at the tomb entrance, were recut in antiquity and made about 0.20 meters wider.

Dimensions of Chamber 2

Floor Elevation	165.00 msl
Length	3.63 m along N wall, 3.60 m along S wall
Width	5.01 m along W wall, 5.13 m along E wall
Height	2.53 m
Area	18.32 m²
Volume	46.35 m³
Width of Gate 3	1.21 m
Height of Gate 3	2.34 m

Objects from Chamber 2

Shabtis

2.36	uninscribed	wood	E end of pit, 0.20 m below chamber floor
2.39	inscribed	calcite	E end of pit, 0.10 m below chamber floor
2.44	inscribed	faïence	NE quadrant, floor

Canopic Jars

2.9a-d	inscribed	calcite	SW quadrant, 0.50 m above floor
2.10	inscribed	calcite	SW quadrant, 0.25 m above floor
2.11	inscribed	calcite	SW quadrant, floor (piece joins 1.12)
2.12a-b	uninscribed	calcite	SW quadrant, 0.50 m above floor
2.13	uninscribed	calcite	SW quadrant, floor
2.14a-b	uninscribed	calcite	E of center of room, floor
2.28	inscribed	calcite	N of center, 0.20 m above floor
2.29	inscribed	calcite	NE quadrant, 0.20 m above floor
2.30a-c	inscribed	calcite	NE quadrant, 0.20 m above floor
2.31a-e	uninscribed	calcite	NE quadrant, 0.20 m above floor
2.32	uninscribed	calcite	N third, floor
2.33a-b	uninscribed	calcite	N third, floor
2.34a-b	uninscribed	calcite	N third, 0.20 m above floor
2.35a-d	uninscribed	calcite	E end of pit, 0.20 m below chamber floor
2.45	uninscribed	calcite	N third, 0.10 m above floor

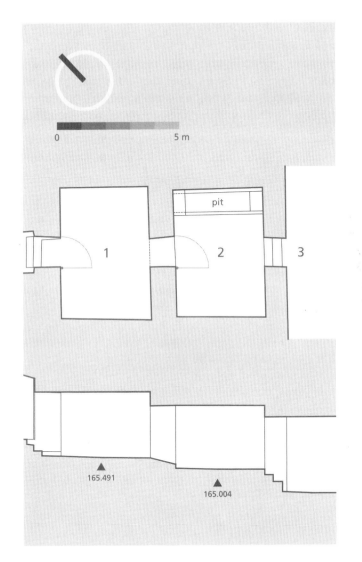

Fig. 13a: Plan and section of Room 2.

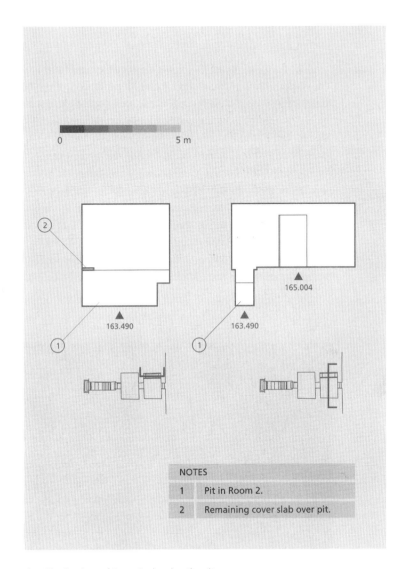

Fig. 13b: Sections of Room 2, showing the pit.

NOTES	
1	Pit in Room 2.
2	Remaining cover slab over pit.

17

Other Objects from Chamber 2

A faïence ring bezel (2.48) with the cartouche of either Thutmes III or IV (Men-kheper-Ra or Men-kheperu-Ra) was found lodged in an ancient crack in the west wall of the chamber, 0.50 meters above the floor. Eleven 'wiglets', three of faïence, eight of an unidentified glazed material, were found: three in the SW quadrant, 2.00 meters below the ceiling; five from the NW corner, 2.50 meters below the ceiling; the remainder from the east end of the pit, 0.50 meters below the chamber floor. Fragments of two amulets, one an *ankh* sign, the other a goddess, both of faïence (2.1, 2.2), were found in the SE quadrant, 0.50 meters below the ceiling. Fragments of two light green faïence vessels came from the top of the debris in the SW quadrant. Several light green faïence, flat tile inlay fragments were found in the north

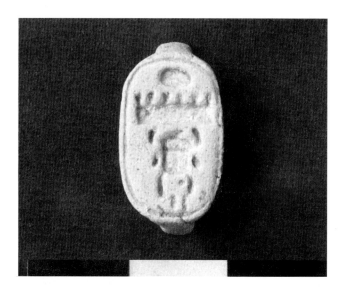

Fig. 14: Object 2.48, faïence ring bezel.

third of the chamber, 1.00 to 1.50 meters below the ceiling, and in the east end of the pit, top of the fill. A limestone ostracon, written on both sides, came from the SW quadrant, 2.20 meters below ceiling (2.8). One small piece of multi-colored glass (2.38), a vessel rim with handle, came from the east end of the pit, 0.20 meters below the chamber floor.

Pottery from Chamber 2

There is no discernable distribution of potsherds in the debris; at every level, it is a mix of New Kingdom (Ramesside) and Coptic and, from 2.00 meters below the ceiling to the floor, Late Period. Debris in the pit in Chamber 2 also contained a mix of New Kingdom, Late Period and Coptic sherds. See the chapter on Pottery for more details.

The Pit in Chamber 2

In 1998, we cleared the debris from the northern third of Chamber 2. We had left this there during several previous seasons in order to maintain a record of the room's stratigraphy. Upon reaching the level of the chamber floor, we found a large rectangular pit that had been cut into the floor. It extended from the east to the west wall of the chamber along the base of the north wall. A small ledge (0.15 meters wide on the north side, 0.09 to 0.12 meters wide on the south) ran along the two sides of the pit to enable sealing blocks to be installed, and one of these, still *in situ*, lay at the western end of the pit. It measured 1.01 x 0.49 meters, and was 0.09 meters thick. There were probably six such sealing blocks over the pit, but no trace remains of the other five. The total volume of the pit is 4.17 cubic meters.

Fig. 15a (above): The pit in Chamber 2.
Fig. 15b (above right): The sealing block over the pit.

As we removed the debris that filled the pit, it seemed increasingly possible that we might find archæological material of some interest, and therefore we mounted a camera on a tripod directly over the pit to photograph our progress. A QTVR of this operation may be seen on our web site, www.kv5.com.

At the east end of the pit, there was a shelf, 0.52 meters below the chamber floor and 0.52 meters deep, 0.78 meters wide, perhaps for a canopic box. To its west, the pit continued downward. At the western end, at a depth of about one meter, we began uncovering bones: first the articulated foreleg of a cow, originally mummified and wrapped as a food offering, then a human skull with cervical vertebrae and bits of mummified tissue and linen attached. A total of three human skulls were found, and beneath them lay a fully articulated adult male skeleton, arms crossed on his chest, traces of mummified tissue and wrappings adhering to his skull and long bones. The body lay with its head up against the west wall of the pit. Several pieces of limestone lay beneath its thigh and pelvis. Bits of mummified tissue

with linen bandaging attached lay in the debris adjacent to it. It seems certain that none of the top three human skulls or the cow's foreleg originally came from this pit, and it is likely that the body, too, was intrusive. We believe all of the bones might have been brought from burial chambers deeper inside KV 5 by ancient tomb robbers who wanted to search them for precious metals and amulets here, near the tomb entrance, where the light was better. They then dropped the bodies onto the floor of chambers 1 and 2, where later floods washed some of them back inside the tomb, and others into the pit.

It is possible that chambers 1 and 2 of KV 5 together originally constituted a small, Eighteenth Dynasty tomb that was later usurped and enlarged by Ramesses II. We base this upon the location of the tomb within the Valley of the Kings, the design of its entrance, the proportions of the first two chambers, and the dimensions of their doorways. This idea had earlier been voiced by Elizabeth Thomas in *The Royal Necropoleis of Thebes* (1966), p. 150. This would very likely mean that the pit in Chamber 2 also dated from the Eighteenth Dynasty. This is discussed in more detail in Kent Weeks' *The Lost Tomb* (1998).

Note that eight of the fifteen canopic jar fragments found in this chamber were found in debris directly above the east end of the pit. There is a ledge at this end of the pit on which a canopic chest might have been placed.

The Human Remains from the Pit in Chamber 2

Skull 1 The uppermost and easternmost of the skulls in the pit. Robust adult male, middle aged; dolichocephalic; four cervical vertebrae attached; dentition only moderately worn; healed scar above right eye on frontal bone, ca. 0.03 m long (perhaps a battle scar).

Skull 2 More delicate muscle attachments; adult male, middle-aged; three cervical vertebrae attached; teeth are small, heavily worn.

Skull 3 Also of delicate build; adult male, middle-aged; badly damaged.

Skull 4 This skull is attached to a fully articulated adult male skeleton, ca. 50 years old; almost perfect dentition with surprisingly little wear; arms folded on chest; right tibia, several bones of feet missing. The position of the arms suggests that this skeleton was not washed into the tomb or tossed about.

Fig. 17: Skull 1, found in the pit of Chamber 2.

21

Chamber 3

By almost any standard, Chamber 3 is one of the most intriguing parts of KV 5. It is the largest room known so far in the tomb and one of the largest in the Valley. Its flat ceiling is supported by sixteen pillars, a number not equalled in any other KV tomb. Seven doorways lead through its walls to other rooms and corridors. These doors lie at three different floor levels, evidence of the several architectural changes that Chamber 3 underwent during the reign of Ramesses II.

To date, we have cleared only a portion of Chamber 3: the area between the west wall and the row of pillars 3(a) through 3(d); a strip between the south wall and pillars 3(d), 3(h), 3(l) and 3(p); a strip between the east wall and pillars 3(n) - 3(p), extending from the south wall to the doorway to Corridor 7; the area between pillars 3(b) - 3(c) and 3(f) - 3(g). It is not yet possible to understand fully the functions of this unusual chamber or why it underwent several changes in plan.

Stage 1

The carving of the doorway from Chamber 2 and those leading into chambers 4, 5, and 6 presumably was done early on, since the thresholds of their doors lie at this (164.85 msl) floor level. The decoration of Chamber 3's walls was also done then.

Stage 2

Some time after this, the floor level between the western wall and the first row of pillars was lowered by 0.80 meters. Steps were cut from the higher floor of Chamber 2 through the doorway into the now-lowered Chamber 3. The doorway was also widened by about 0.20 meters (and 0.20 meters of the relief decoration to its immediate north was cut away).

Dimensions of Chamber 3

Floor Elevation	averages 164.05 msl at front of chamber, 164.85 m at rear
Length	15.72 m along N wall, 15.55 m along S wall
Width	15.54 m along W wall, 15.34 m along E wall
Height	from 2.97 to 3.02 m in front of chamber; 2.24 to 2.31 m in back
Area	244.16 m² including pillars, 228.68 m² excluding pillars*
Volume	582.94 m³ including pillars, 547.68 m³ excluding pillars
Doors	
from Chamber 2	1.15 m wide (recut from an original width of about 1.00 m); 2.98 m high (originally 2.08 m)
into Chamber 4	1.00 m wide, 2.01 m high (threshold lies 0.70 m above recut floor of Chamber 3)
into Chamber 5	1.22 m wide, 1.92 m high
into Chamber 6	1.00 m wide, 1.98 m high
into Corridor 7	1.11 m wide, 2.05 m high (threshold lies 1.83 m below floor of Chamber 3)
into Corridor 12	1.04 m wide, 2.24 m high
into Corridor 20	1.02 m wide, 2.25 m high
Pillars	vary from 0.89 m to 1.20 m per side
length (N-S)	0.91 - 1.20 m
width (E-W)	0.89 - 1.05 m
Pillar Height	varies from 2.24 m to 2.30 m

* For comparison, the burial chamber (J) of Merenptah (KV 8) covers 206.68 m²; that of Seti I (KV 17), 126.23 m².

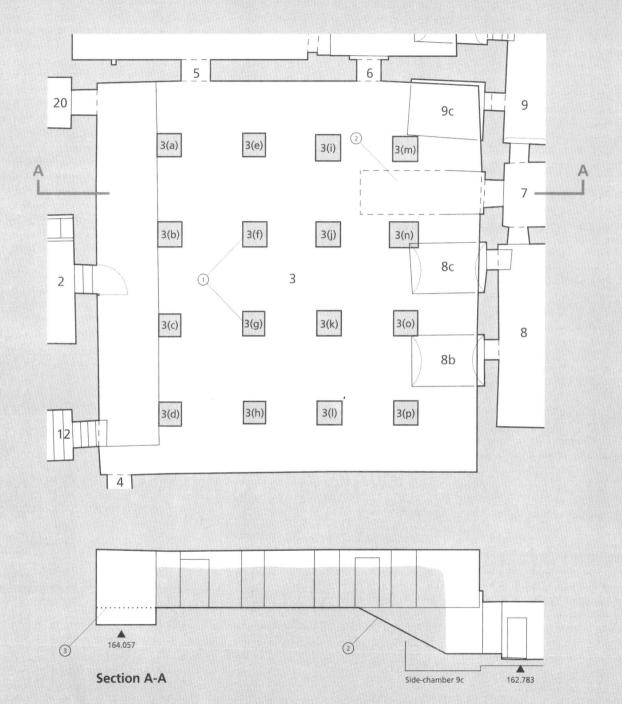

NOTES

1   Pillar constructed of stone blocks.

2   Area unexcavated; ramp or stairs suspected.

3   Original floor level.

0   5 m

Fig. 18: Plan and section of Chamber 3.

Section A-A

164.057

Side-chamber 9c   162.783

The cutting of the new floor level produced a relatively flat surface, but along the pillar line, the edges of the cut are jagged and, in front of the doors into chambers 4 and 20, were left rough.

Stage 3

At this stage, the doorways into corridors 12 and 20 were cut through the ends of the decorated north wall of Chamber 3. The threshholds of these two doors lie at the lower Chamber 3 floor level and lead into steeply-sloping corridors. Perhaps at this same time, the door into Corridor 7 was cut into the east face of a pit dug 1.83 meters below the floor of Chamber 3. Excavations have not yet exposed all of that pit so it is not known whether it contains steps or a ramp (or both).

What is the reason for the lower levels of the doorways into corridors 7, 12, and 20? We do not yet have an explanation. It did permit side-chambers 8b, 8c, 9b, 9c, 12a, 12b, 12c, 12d, and 12f to be cut beneath the floors of chambers 1, 2, 3, 4 and 6, but that does not seem an especially compelling justification. Only further clearance and continued study of the tomb's decoration are likely to provide an answer.

Stage 4

Whatever the reason for lowering the floor level at the front of Chamber 3, sometime after it was completed the floor level was raised back to its former height by laying down 0.80 meters of clean limestone. Most pieces weigh about 500 grams. They were placed over the lowered floor, then covered with a thick layer of hard, white gypsum plaster. There is evidence of this plaster in front of the doorway from Chamber 2, and it extends about three meters to the left and right. But beyond that, traces vanish and the layer of limestone chips slopes suddenly down to the lower floor and stops, leaving the areas in front of corridors 12 and 20 un-

Fig. 19a (top): The recut floor of Chamber 3. The original floor level is visible on the west wall at right.
Fig. 19b (bottom): Detail of limestone chips and plaster layer used to rebuild original floor level.

changed. Again, it is difficult to explain why the floor was raised.

Of the sixteen pillars in Chamber 3, fourteen were cut from the living rock. Two, however, pillars 3(f) and 3(g), were partly built of cut stone: the bottom meter of each was cut from bedrock, but the upper 1.20 meters was constructed from roughly hewn blocks, then plastered over. There seems to be no geological reason for this; indeed, the bedrock here is of better quality and freer of cracks than almost anywhere else in the room. Where the pillars are in contact with the ceiling, the stone is smoothly cut and devoid of any defects.

A hieratic graffito was found on one of the roughly cut blocks on the western face of pillar 3(g). It is extremely faint and so far has defied reading.

Stratigraphy of Chamber 3

There is little to distinguish the kind of floodborne debris in Chamber 3 from that in Chamber 2. But because of the lowering of the floor at the front of Chamber 3, most of the larger stones were immediately deflected upon entering, as the floodwaters moved left and right into the doorways of corridors 12 and 20. The pillars, of course, caused the flood-waters and the debris to swirl about and move in wildly different directions. As a result, the chamber's stratigraphy is much more complicated and chaotic than elsewhere in the tomb. Indeed, except for the clearly-defined, man-made layer of limestone on the lowered floor at the front of Chamber 3, it is almost impossible to identify individual strata in the chamber.

Fig. 20: Pillar 3(g) of Chamber 3.

Every wall and every pillar face in Chamber 3 was originally decorated, but most of it was paint on plaster and, because of the several major fractures and fissures in the bedrock here, the ancient artisans first had to patch deep cracks with thick plaster that soon fell from its own weight and the effects of flooding (the location of fissures and fractures is discussed in Appendix V). Every significant flaw, whether in the ceiling, walls, or pillars, contains traces of ancient plaster. But Chamber 3, far away from the road, shows none of the effects of heavy tourist buses found in chambers 1 and 2.

There is enough of this ancient repair work evident here to show that virtually all of the damage to the chamber's ceiling occurred at least three millennia ago and has remained

Fig. 21: Fissure in ceiling of Chamber 3, anciently filled with plaster.

unchanged since. Evidence of fallen ceiling blocks is confined to the lower (hence, earlier) layers of debris in the room, except for a small section defined by pillars 3(c), 3(d), 3(g), and 3(h) and another around pillar 3(m).

Only the western wall of Chamber 3 shows extensive traces of relief carving: on each side of the central doorway from Chamber 2 there are four sons of Ramesses II, seated in a row, facing a standing *sem*-priest. Figures to the north of the doorway face south, those on the south face north.

There are traces of plaster on the other walls of the chamber and on each of the sixteen pillars. Pillar 3(e), especially, has extensive painted relief carving preserved. There are traces of blue painted plaster on the ceiling.

Also on the ceiling, between pillars 3(h) and 3(l) and the southern wall, the name and date, "BURTON 1825" was written in lampblack. Between it and the wall is a hieratic graffito, graciously translated for us by French Egyptologist Yvan Koenig:

r3-ʿ ḥ3t-sp 19

"This graffito may have a double meaning whether 'extremity, limit' (cf. *Wb* II, 394, 1-8 and Coptic ra) meaning the 'limit' reached by the workers of the tomb during the Year 19 of an unknown king, probably Ramses II, or 'activity, work' (cf. *Wb* II, 395, 12-13 and 396, 4). The two meanings may converge in the meaning of 'limit of the work which was reached during the nineteenth year of the reigning king'."

Fig. 22: Burton's graffito (top), and ancient graffito (bottom) on the ceiling of Chamber 3.

Objects from Chamber 3

Shabti Fragments

3.78	inscribed	faïence	0.10 m S of 3(c), 0.50 m above floor
3.79	uninscribed	calcite	adjacent S side of 3(c), 1.50 m above floor

Canopic Jars

3.7	uninscribed	calcite	N jamb door into 12, 0.20 m from floor
3.8a, b	inscribed	calcite	same location
3.20	uninscribed	calcite	between doors into 2 and 20, 0.20 m above floor
3.30a, b	uninscribed	calcite	same location
3.42	uninscribed	calcite	SW corner of 3(b), ceiling to 1.00 m below it
3.50	inscribed	calcite	between 3(b) and 3(c), ceiling to 1.00 m below it
3.58	inscribed	calcite	0.10 cm S of 3(b), on floor

Possible Sarcophagus or Canopic Box Fragments

3.6	incised bands	calcite	between 3(c) and 3(d), ceiling to 0.50 m below it
3.25	uninscribed	calcite	between 3(c) and 3(g), ceiling to 0.50 m below it
3.74	uninscribed	calcite	between 3(a) and 3(b), 1.40 m below ceiling

Other objects from Chamber 3

Two pieces of glass vessels (3.10, 3.86), the first, light blue-green, lay adjacent to the west wall, north of the door into Corridor 12, 0.50 meters above the floor; the latter, light blue with a dark blue core, found between 3(e) and the north wall, 1.00 meters below the ceiling. A third (3.91), light blue, yellow and brown, was found between 3(c) - 3(g), ceiling to 1.00 meters below the ceiling.

A calcite vessel rim (not a canopic jar) was found adjacent to the west wall, north of the door into Corridor 12, 1.00 meters above the floor.

What appears to be a granite door socket (3.32) lay north of the door into Chamber 2, 1.00 meters above floor; pieces of gold leaf (3.45, 3.49) lay west of 3(b), 100 meters below the ceiling; a piece of sandstone (3.71, measuring 5 x 3 x 1.5 centimeters) lay between 3(g) - 3(h), 1.00 meters below the ceiling. There is a worn groove on one side of it, suggesting that it might have been used as a tool to sharpen implements.

Two pottery ostraca, written in hieratic, came from between 3(e) and the north wall, 0.15 meters above the floor (3.89), and from between 3(b) - 3(f), on the floor (3.66). An alabaster box fragment (3.77) was found between pillars 3(c) - 3(g), 0.20 meters above the floor.

Pottery from Chamber 3

There is no discernable distribution of sherds, except that the layer of limestone chips lying between the plaster floor and the lowered floor at the front of Chamber 3 contained none. There were a few objects found adjacent to the west wall (e.g., 3.20) below the level of the original floor, but these lay in places where the plaster floor had been broken through in ancient times. Although less than a quarter of Chamber 3 has been cleared so far, we have already catalogued twelve thousand pot sherds, more than from any other single chamber in KV 5. See the chapter on Pottery for more details.

Chamber 4

Because the floods that coursed through Chamber 3 were largely deflected into Corridor 12 by the pillars and changes in floor levels in Chamber 3, the floodwaters entering Chamber 4 were of low intensity. The result is that Chamber 4 contains only about one meter of floodborne material, most being fine silt with only a few small limestone chips. At the time of writing, we have dug only about a quarter of Chamber 4, exposing a strip between the east wall and pillars 4(a), 4(c) and 4(e). The only objects found were three small fragments of blue faïence (4.2a-c). What might have been a small side-chamber was begun at the northern end of the eastern wall. Chamber 4 contains six pillars.

Dimensions of Chamber 4	
Length	12.83 m along W wall; 13.02 m along E wall
Width	8.83 m along N wall; 8.86 m along S wall
Height	2.00 m
Area	114.63 m² incl. pillars, 108.6 m² without
Volume	229.26 m³ incl. pillars, 217.21 m³ without
Width of Gate	1.03 m
Height of Gate	2.01 m
Pillar Size	from 0.97 to 1.05 N-S; 0.94 to 1.10 E-W

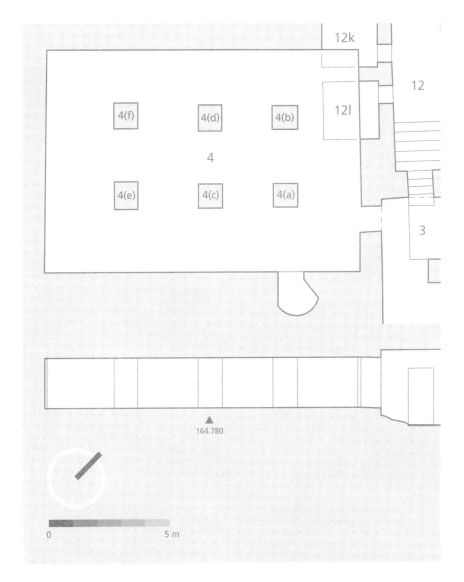

Fig. 23: Plan and section of Room 4.

Chambers 5 and 6

Chambers 5 and 6 have not yet been cleared, and will not be for some time. Chamber 5 is the most poorly-preserved of all the chambers in KV 5: its ceiling is so badly damaged (largely, we think, from the vibrations of tourist buses on the road immediately adjacent), that it probably can only be cleared by digging into it through the overriding bedrock and installing an entirely new roof. Its condition is unfortunate, because Chamber 5 promises to be especially important in understanding KV 5. The chamber is the third largest in the tomb (101.85 cubic meters) after chambers 3 and 4. It may originally have contained several pillars. Today, only one pillar remains standing. It is made of cut stones, and is so oddly placed in the northwestern-most corner of the chamber that it may be a later addition, perhaps added to support the ceiling. Four small niches cut high up in each of its four walls suggest that the room might have served as a burial chamber.

Chamber 6 is smaller, better preserved, and joined by doorways to both chambers 3 and 5. It lies directly above Chamber 9b.

Fig. 24a (top): View of Chamber 5.
Fig. 24b (bottom): One of the niches in Chamber 5.

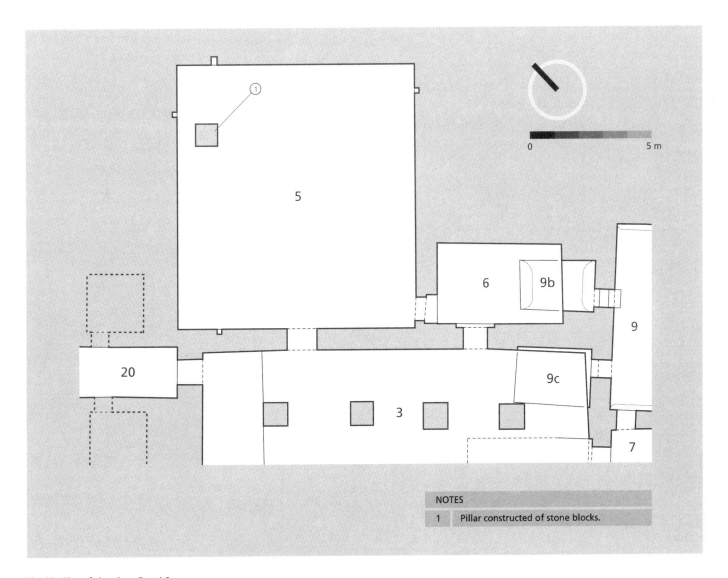

Fig. 25: Plan of chambers 5 and 6.

NOTES

| 1 | Pillar constructed of stone blocks. |

Corridor 7

It was the discovery of this corridor, on 2 February 1995, that thrust KV 5 into the archæological spotlight. Until then, it had seemed to be a tomb of unusual plan, small and presumably of little importance. But with the discovery of Corridor 7, its side-chambers and other corridors at its end (10 and 11), KV 5 became the largest tomb ever found in the Valley of the Kings – containing 67 chambers. Today, with the discovery of corridors 12 and 20 and their many side-chambers and extensions, the number of chambers is 110 and is still growing.

The entrance to Corridor 7 was clogged with debris from the earliest floods, and therefore later floods did not reach the corridors and chambers beyond. About two meters into Corridor 7, the level of the debris dropped significantly, from ceiling height (about 2.30 meters) to a depth of about 1.80 meters. Debris in the entrance included some sizeable blocks of limestone, some of them almost certainly from the ceiling of Chamber 3. Farther into the corridor, however, the debris consisted of silts and small limestone chips, similar to that in Chamber 4. The side-chambers were filled to the same depth with similar material. Control marks are common on both side walls and on the ceiling.

The walls of Corridor 7 are penetrated by twenty doorways. Two of them, at the beginning of the corridor, lead to suites of rooms (chambers 8a-c and 9a-c). The next sixteen (eight on each side) appear to be single side-chambers (designated 7a-p). Of these side-chambers, we have partially cleared only 7a, 7l and 7o. The last two gates lead into two further corridors, 10 and 11, each also containing sixteen side-chambers.

Dimensions of Corridor 7

Floor Elevation	162.78 msl
Length	32.13 m
Width	from 2.46 to 2.54 m
Height	from 2.27 to 2.43 m (2.34 at midpoint)
Area	81.2 m²
Volume	190.81 m³
Width of Gate 7	1.11 m
Height of Gate 7	2.07 m

Width of Doorways Leading to Corridor 7 Side-Chambers

7a	0.74 m	7i	0.73 m*
7b	0.76	7j	0.93*
7c	0.68	7k	0.77*
7d	0.79	7l	0.68*
7e	0.72*	7m	0.69
7f	0.75*	7n	0.76*
7g	0.95*	7o	0.76
7h	0.66*	7p	0.75

* Door jambs and intervening walls are broken and measurements are approximate.

Width of Doorways Leading from Corridor 7 to Other Chambers

to chamber 3	1.11 m
to chamber 8	0.78 m
to chamber 9	0.79 m
to corridor 10	0.91 m
to corridor 11	0.88 m

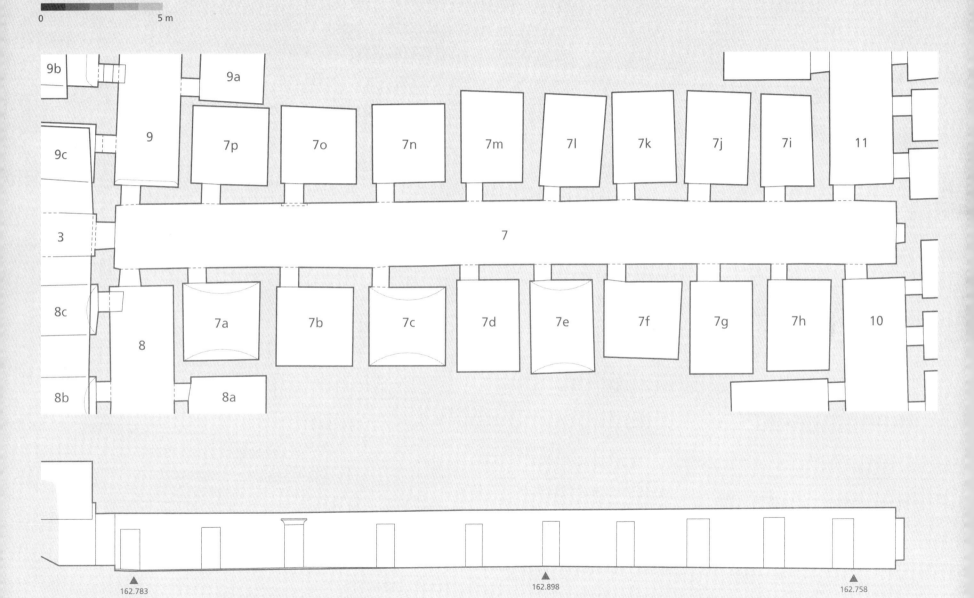

Fig. 27: View of Corridor 7, partially cleared. The statue of Osiris is at the rear of the corridor.

Dimensions of Excavated Corridor 7 Side-Chambers			
	Side-Chamber 7a	Side-Chamber 7l	Side-Chamber 7o
Length	3.08 m	3.67 m	3.09 (2.98) m*
Width	3.05 (3.15) m	2.51 m	3.07 m
Height	n/a	n/a	1.94 m
Area	9.55 m²	9.14 m²	9.33 m²
Volume	n/a	n/a	18.88 m³
Door Width	0.74 m	0.68 m	0.76 m
Door Height	n/a	1.79 m	1.83 m

* The first measurement is taken along the east wall; the other is taken along the west.

Basic Dimensions of Other, Unexcavated Corridor 7 Side-Chambers					
	Length (m)		Width (m)		Area (m²)
	E wall	W wall	N wall	S wall	(approx.)
7b	3.12	3.14	3.12	3.12	9.77
7c	n/a	n/a	n/a	n/a	n/a
7d	3.65	3.64	2.57	2.60	9.41
7e	3.64	3.68	2.57	2.62	9.52
7f	2.97	3.07	3.13	3.07	9.36
7g	3.67	3.68	2.62	2.61	9.62
7h	3.58	3.63	2.60	2.55	9.25
7l	3.59	3.69	2.05	1.88	7.12
7j	3.66	3.68	2.63	2.60	9.58
7k	3.64	3.63	2.53	2.61	9.39
7m	3.56	3.67	2.59	n/a	9.35
7n	3.10	3.14	2.95	n/a	9.20
7p	3.08	3.09	3.10	3.11	9.55

Note that the two widest doorways, 7g and 7j, lie directly across from each other near the end of the corridor. Most of the doorways of the side-chambers are of similar design. Their lintels are about 0.22 meters thick, their jambs vary from 0.60 to 0.79 meters wide (the average being 0.65 meters). Only the lintel of 7o differs from the others: instead of being flat, the side facing Corridor 7 is a well-cut cornice.

The side-chambers are of a basically similar, rectangular plan, but their dimensions and door widths vary. Some of the chambers were much less carefully cut than others: 7f and 7i seem to be the result of hasty or inaccurate measuring. Three of the chambers – 7a, 7c and 7e – have slightly vaulted ceilings. These chambers, together with 8a, 8b, 9 and 9b, have the only vaulted ceilings found so far in KV 5.

Fig. 28: Lintel above doorway to Side-Chamber 7o. Note the relief of Hathor to the left.

All chambers were filled with flood debris similar in composition to Corridor 7, although it contained slightly more fine silts, especially chambers near the end of the corridor. The three partially-cleared side-chambers contained relatively few sherds (7a had 250 sherds, 7o had about 200, 7l only fifty). No objects were found, but there were fragments of mammal bones. Minute traces of decorated plaster adhere to all the chamber walls, and substantial pieces of decorated plaster lay in the lowermost layers of the debris. These will require considerable time and patience to remove and study, and that work has only just begun.

Objects from Corridor 7

The few objects found in Corridor 7 include a fragment (7.22) of calcite, possibly from a sarcophagus, incised with what might be the drawing of an eye; a faïence 'wiglet' (7.1); the neck and handle of a multi-colored glass vessel (7.9a-b); a rim fragment from a dark blue glass vessel (7.17); and two tear-drop shaped blue-green glass beads (7.2a-b).

At the end of Corridor 7, cut into its eastern end wall, was a niche with a carving of the figure of Osiris or, more probably, of Ramesses II as Osiris. It wears a *shebyu*-collar and holds both a flail and scepter in each hand. The face is missing. It was probably broken in antiquity. A natural crack runs through the bedrock at this point, and traces of mud plaster suggest that the face had broken off and the ancient artisans were forced to plaster it back into position. The figure was originally covered entirely with plaster; black paint may still be seen on the feet and legs. Such depictions are unusual; the only other example was found in 1997 by Christian LeBlanc while clearing in the tomb of Ramesses II (chamber Ja) in the Valley of the Kings. Like the floor before the figure of Osiris in the tomb of Rameses II, the floor here was also deliberately cut in an irregular fashion. At the foot of the Osiris statue was found an offering of what appear to be modeled clay sycamore figs.

Figure 29a (top): The floor in front of the Osiris statue.
Figure 29b (bottom): Clay sycamore figs.
Figure 29c (right): The Osiris statue.

Chamber 8

This large, rectangular room has a flat ceiling. There are traces of carved relief on the western wall, but these are so faint they must have been made inadvertently when artisans, who were decorating a layer of plaster applied to the wall, exerted enough pressure that their tools cut into the underlying rock. The east wall of the chamber was decorated with this type of carved and painted plaster. Part of the wall between chambers 8 and 7a collapsed in the distant past (the fallen blocks lay directly on the chamber floor). Several of them show traces of fine decoration.

No objects were found in Chamber 8, but there were many pieces of decorated plaster fallen from the walls, and several small mammal bones lay on the floor.

Chamber 8 has three side-chambers, but so far only one (8c) has been cleared. This small room is vaulted (the curve of the vault rises 0.13 meters from the walls to the midline of the chamber). Side-chamber 8c lies 0.43 meters below the floor of Chamber 8, and is reached through an 0.80 meter-wide doorway with a 1.08 meter-long sloping threshold. The room lies beneath the floor of Chamber 3. It was filled almost entirely with floodborne silt. In the lower levels we recovered about 750 sherds and numerous animal bones.

The thickness of the bedrock between the ceiling of Side-chamber 8c and the floor of Chamber 3 is only 0.49 meters. Side-chamber 8b also has a vaulted ceiling; it has not yet been cleared. Side-chamber 8a, also uncleared, has a flat ceiling.

Dimensions of Chamber 8

Floor Elevation	162.54 - 162.58 msl
Length	2.28 m
Width	2.63 m
Height	2.07 m
Area	18.88 m²
Volume	39.09 m³
Door Width	0.78 m
Door Height	1.83 m

Dimensions of Side-Chambers 8a, 8b, and 8c

	Side-Chamber 8a	Side-Chamber 8b	Side-Chamber 8c
Floor Elev.	162.337 msl	162.345 msl	162.149 msl
Length	3.07 m (E wall), 3.15 m (W wall)	3.00 m	2.97 m (S wall), 3.19 m (N wall)
Width	3.12 m (N wall), 2.96 m (S wall)	2.04 m	2.00 m (W wall), 2.00 m (E wall)
Height	n/a	n/a	1.68 m
Area	9.15 m²	6.11 m²	6.16 m² (approx)
Volume	n/a	n/a	10.80 m³ (approx)
Door Width	0.70 m	0.80 m	0.80 m
Door Height	n/a	1.36 m	1.40 m

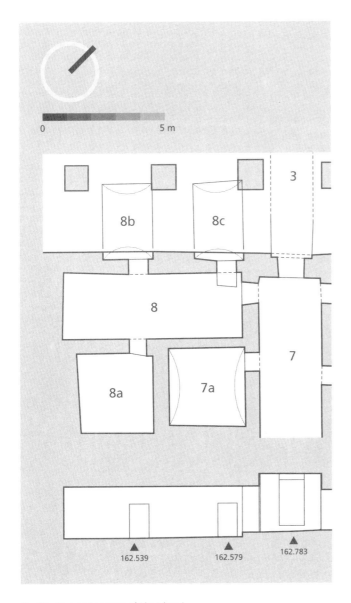

Fig. 30: Plan and section of Chamber 8.

Fig. 31a (top): View of Chamber 8, looking out to Corridor 7 and across to Chamber 9. The doorway to Side-chamber 8a is at front right (the opening behind is a breakthrough into Side-chamber 7a where the intervening wall has partly collapsed). The doorway to Side-chamber 8c is at left.
Fig. 31b (bottom): Fragments of decorated plaster found in Chamber 8.

Chamber 9

Chamber 9 was apparently cut in two stages: the shape of the vaulted ceiling at the front of the chamber is noticeably different from that at the rear. The change occurs just beyond the door into Side-chamber 9c. It would appear that Chamber 9 was originally a room with a single side-chamber (9c). Then it was enlarged – its size nearly doubled, in fact – and two additional side-chambers (9a and 9b) added. Chamber 9 is roughly similar to Chamber 8 except for its vaulted ceiling and the fact that only one side-chamber (9b) was also vaulted (both 8a and 8b were vaulted).

Carved decoration is still visible on the east door jamb leading into Chamber 9 and on its southern wall. But, as in Chamber 8, it is faint and represents only the traces of cutting originally done through a plaster overlay. Numerous control marks in red paint can be seen on all walls and the ceiling in the front half of the chamber. A fragment of calcite (9.5), possibly part of a sarcophagus, was found on the floor adjacent to the door into the chamber; nearby lay three 'wiglets' (9.4a-c) and three broken tubular faïence beads.

Side-chamber 9b has a vaulted ceiling of a form very similar to that in 8a. It resembles the vaulting in the first part of Chamber 9, not that at the rear.

The distance between the ceiling of Side-chamber 9b and the floor of Chamber 6 cannot yet be determined. The bedrock between the ceiling of Side-chamber 9c and the floor of Chamber 3 is 0.66 meters thick.

Dimensions of Chamber 9

Floor Elevation	162.49 to 162.53 msl
Length	7.26 m (E wall), 7.27 m (W wall)
Width	2.57 m (N wall), 2.52 m (S wall)
Height	2.30 m
Area	18.54 m²
Volume	42.65 m³
Door Width	0.79 m
Door Height	1.61 m

Dimensions of Side-Chambers 9a, 9b, and 9c

	Side-Chamber 9a	Side-Chamber 9b
Floor Elevation	162.298 msl	161.843 msl
Length	2.60 m	3.00 m (S wall), 3.12 m (N wall)
Width	3.65 m (E wall), 3.59 m (W wall)	2.00 m (E wall), 1.94 m (W wall)
Height	n/a	n/a
Area	9.41 m²	6.06 m²
Volume	n/a	n/a
Door Width	0.71 m	0.68 m
Door Height	n/a	1.70 m

	Side-Chamber 9c
Floor Elevation	162.329 msl
Length	3.12 m (S wall), 3.05 m (N wall)
Width	2.31 m (E wall), 2.22 m (W wall)
Height	n/a
Area	6.94 m²
Volume	n/a
Door Width	0.70 m
Door Height	n/a

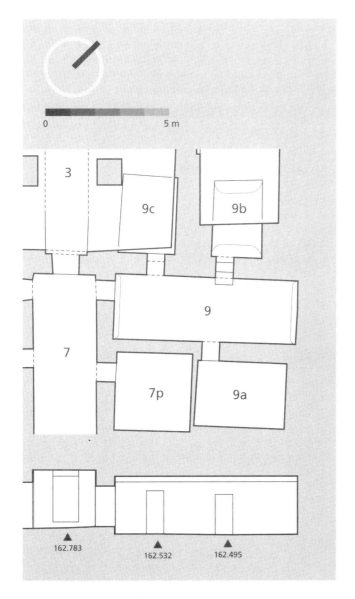

Fig. 32: Plan and section of Chamber 9.

Fig. 33: View of Chamber 9, looking out to Corridor 7 and across to Chamber 8. Doorways to side-chambers 9b (front) and 9c (rear) are at right, the doorway to 9a is at left.

Corridor 10

Beginning at the southeast corner of Corridor 7, Corridor 10 extends southward over twenty-two meters, and runs beneath the rear chambers of KV 6. It is about ten meters shorter than Corridor 7, although we are not yet certain that we have actually reached the corridor's end. As with Corridor 7, Corridor 10 also has sixteen side-chambers (10a-p), but here, seven lie on the west side of the corridor, nine on the east. None appears to be vaulted, and none is preceeded by suites of rooms as in Corridor 7 (i.e., chambers 8 and 9). From its entrance to just beyond the doorway of Side-chamber 10e, the corridor ceiling slopes downward at a 9.6° angle; beyond that point, it runs horizontally until, beyond 10g, it drops 0.17 meters and then continues horizontally. The corridor varies from 2.58 to 2.62 meters wide between the entrance and Side-chamber 10g; beyond, it narrows to 1.96 meters. No part of Corridor 10 or its side-chambers has yet been excavated. Traces of red painted control marks can be seen on the walls.

Dimensions of Corridor 10

Floor Elevation	n/a
Length	22.63 m
Width	2.58 m at entrance; 2.62 m below ceiling change; 1.99 m to 1.96 m at end
Height	n/a
Area	57.0 m^2 (approximate)
Volume	n/a
Door Width	0.91 m
Door Height	n/a

Width of Doorways Leading to Corridor 10 Side-Chambers

10a	0.70 m	10i	0.70 m
10b	0.76	10j	0.69
10c	0.95	10k	0.80
10d	1.15	10l	0.73
10e	0.80	10m	1.21
10f	1.09*	10n	0.78
10g	1.79*	10o	0.97
10h	0.73	10p	*

* Doorway damaged or destroyed and measurement approximate or unavailable.

Note that the first side-chamber, 10a, and the last two, 10l and 10j, have the narrowest doorways.

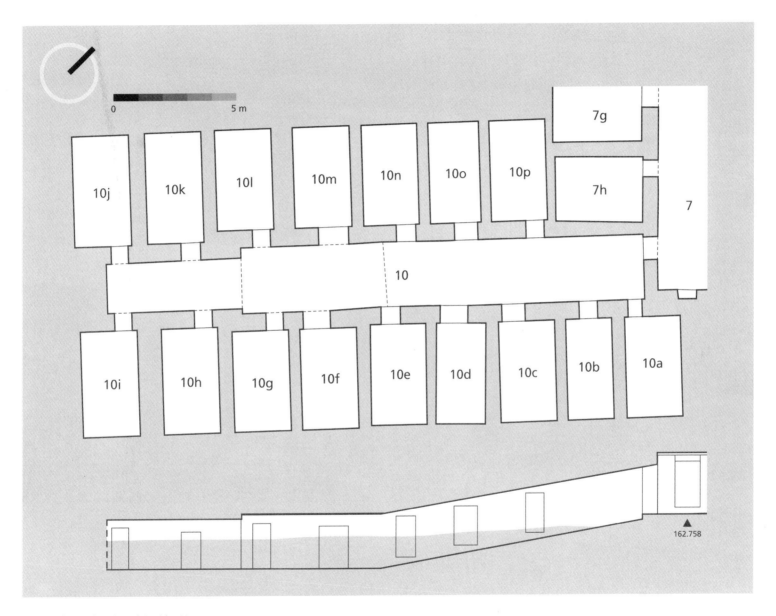

Fig. 34: Plan and section of Corridor 10.

Corridor 11

Almost a mirror image of Corridor 10, Corridor 11 extends northward from the northeast corner of Corridor 7. Like corridors 7 and 10, it too has 16 side-chambers. The floor and ceiling slope downward for 11.05 meters at a 5.07° angle until, immediately beyond doorways 11e and 11n, the ceiling drops 0.81 meters and a staircase-ramp combination leads downward 2.45 meters. Beyond, the corridor slopes for 8.72 meters at 10.58°. We have excavated most of the corridor to bedrock.

Dimensions of Corridor 11	
Floor Elevation	162.70 msl at entrance; 159.03 msl at end
Length	22.22 m long (22.83 m including the entrance gate)
Width	2.5 m to 2.63 m before stairs; stairs are 2.03 m; beyond stairs it is 1.97 m
Height	2.1 m at entrance; beyond it is from 2.18 m to 2.27 m
Area	50.99 m² (approx)
Volume	120 m³ (approx)
Door Width	0.79 m
Door Height	1.61 m

Fig. 35a (top): View down Corridor 11.
Fig. 35b (bottom): View of staircase in Corridor 11, looking back towards doorway from Corridor 7.

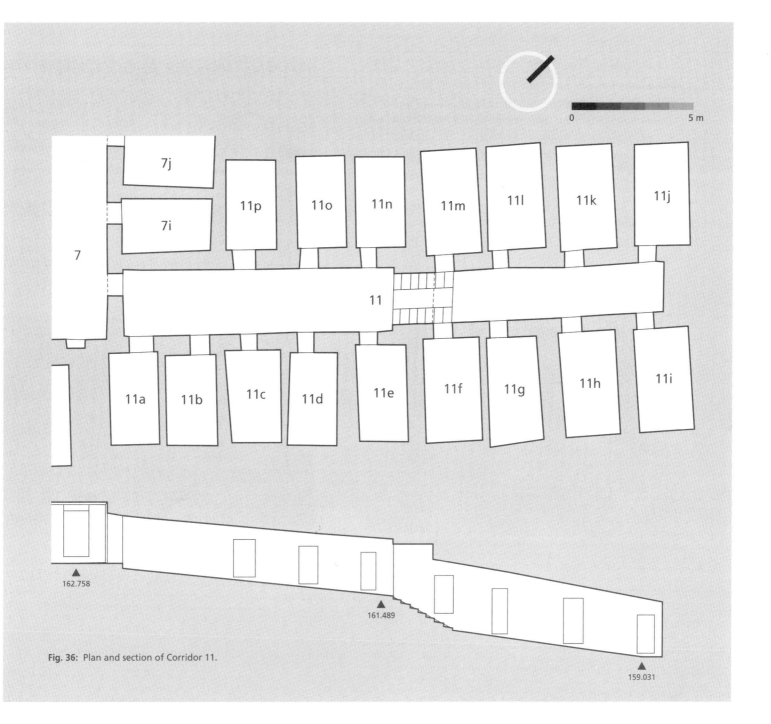

Fig. 36: Plan and section of Corridor 11.

Only two 'wiglets' and a fragment of a faïence vessel with a lotus flower design (11k.1) were found in the corridor or the two side-chambers we have so far cleared. The floor at the end of Corridor 11 was covered with a thick layer of blue plaster extending from the doors of 11h - 11k to the rear wall. We have cleared two side-chambers, 11j and 11k. Both were filled with almost pure silt. There was no plaster on the floor of 11j, but the floor of 11k had three one-centimeter-thick plaster layers, each a different color, laid down directly atop each other. Plastered floors are not common in Egyptian tombs, and I am unaware of any with multiple layers.

Dimensions of Side-Chambers 11j and 11k		
	Side-Chamber 11j	Side-Chamber 11k
Floor Elevation	158.972 msl	159.356 msl
Length	4.69 m	4.82 m
Width	2.22 m (E wall),	2.28 m (E wall),
	2.29 m (W wall)	2.32 m (W wall)
Height	1.32 m	2.00 m
Area	9.61 m²	10.07 m²
Volume	12.69 m³	20.14 m³
Door Width	0.73 m	0.79 m
Door Height	1.52 m	1.80 m

Fig. 37a (top): View into Side-chamber 11k.
Fig. 37b (bottom): Detail of layers of plaster on the floor of Side-chamber 11k.

Corridor 12

Corridors 12 and 20, which extend from Chamber 3 toward the front of KV 5 and under the paved road beyond it, were completely unexpected discoveries. We know of no tomb in KV with corridors or chambers cut back toward the entrance. Although only a part of Corridor 20 has yet been excavated, it seems to be a mirror image of 12. If that proves true, and there are also the equivalents of chambers 13 - 19 at the end of 20, then the total number of chambers in KV 5, currently 110, will exceed 150.

The early flood debris that poured through chambers 1, 2 and 3 was deflected by the lowered floor in Chamber 3 and channelled into corridors 12 and 20. As a result, the stones in the debris here are as large as those in KV 5's entrance chambers. Since corridors 12 and 20 slope steeply downward, the speed of the flood resulted in the debris being even more densely packed here than in other chambers. Corridor 12 slopes dramatically downward at an angle of 19.86° at its entrance, 17.23° at its end.

Corridor 12 has 12 side-chambers (12a - l). There is a steep set of stairs at the entrance to the corridor that leads to a roughly-cut floor. Two-thirds of the way along, just before the doorways of side-chambers 12e - 12h, there is a badly broken set of stairs, now resembling a roughly-cut, 0.47 meter-high ledge. The elevation at the top of this ledge is 159.34 msl, compared to 164.01 msl at the beginning of the corridor (top of the steps). At its end, there is a 0.75 meter drop in the level of the ceiling and another set of four steps — without a central ramp as in Corridor 11 — that are well-carved and well-preserved.

An uninscribed calcite shabti (12.29) was found in the doorway of Corridor 12. Nearby, about a meter lower in the debris, lay an uninscribed fragment of a calcite vessel (12.1).

Dimensions of Corridor 12	
Floor Elevation	159.343 msl, at top of stairs before 12e-h
Length	18.42 m
Width	1.99 m at front of chamber, 2.04 m at end
Height	2.32 m at entrance, 2.73 m at top step, end
Area	36.65 m² (approx)
Volume	97.10 m³ (approx)
Door Width	1.04 m
Door Height	2.32 m

Fig. 38: Object 12.1, fragment of a vessel.

A fragment of a red granite sarcophagus (12.16) lay on the corridor floor beside the doorway of Side-chamber 12c. In the upper levels of the debris just inside the corridor were found three blue faïence tubular beads (12.4a-c); a fragment of a blue-green faïence vessel decorated in black paint with a lotus design (12.20); a blue-green faïence 'tile' with the cartouche of either Thutmosis III or IV (12.3); a small blue-

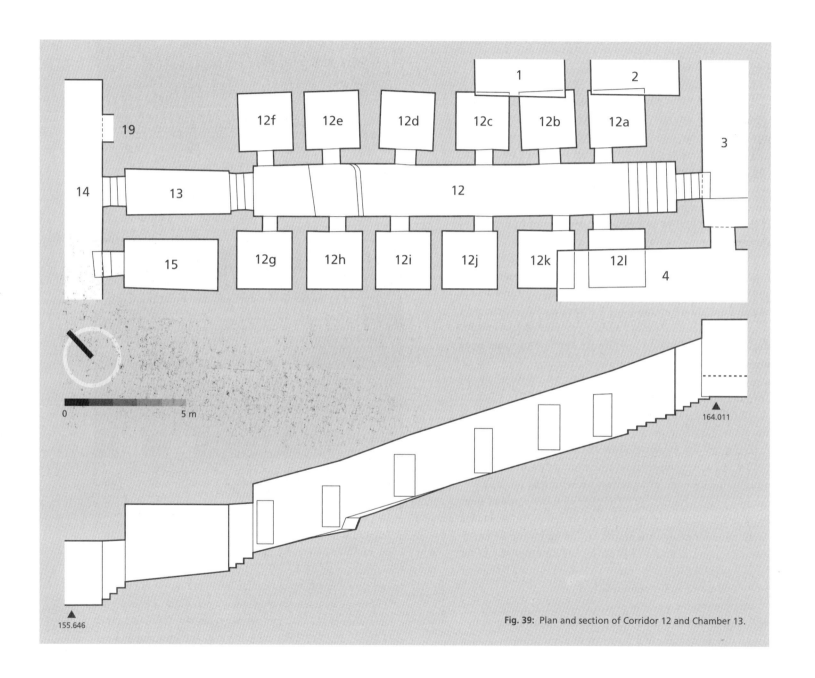

Fig. 39: Plan and section of Corridor 12 and Chamber 13.

green faïence plaque pierced by one small hole (12.12); and two sherds of dark blue glass vessels (12.14, 12.19).

Two side-chambers (12a, 12b) lie beneath the floor of Chamber 4; three others (12j, 12k, 12l) lie beneath the floors of chambers 1 and 2. The distance between the ceilings of two of these chambers and the floor of the chambers above is as follows: from the ceiling of Side-chamber 12a to the floor of Chamber 4: 0.73 meters; from the ceiling of Side-chamber 12l to the floor of Chamber 2: 0.94 meters. Had Corridor 12 not been cut at so steep an angle, the placement of these five chambers would not have been possible, and one wonders if that was a reason for its unusual slope.

Only one side-chamber, 12b, has been cleared so far.

Dimensions of Side-Chamber 12b	
Length	2.89 m
Width	2.30 m
Height	2.01 m
Area	5.70 m²
Volume	11.37 m³
Door Width	0.71 m
Door Height	1.81 m

Fig. 40: View from Chamber 13 to Corridor 12, looking up towards the doorway from Chamber 3.

Chamber 13

This is an extension of Corridor 12, preceded and followed by four steps. Between the stairs, the corridor's floor slopes downward at an angle of 3.49°, but the ceiling is horizontal. The doorway at the entrance to Corridor 13 has a 0.75 meter lintel; the door at the end, into Chamber 14, has a 1.42 meter lintel. The floor elevation is 157.017 meters above sea level at the bottom of the entrance stairs; 156.797 msl at the center of the room; and 156.576 msl at the top of the stairs into Chamber 14.

The only objects found in the corridor were fragments of conglomerate breccia, perhaps part of a sarcophagus (13.3, from the floor at entrance); and two light blue faïence 'wiglets' (also from the entrance).

Dimensions of Chamber 13	
Length	6.20 m
Width	1.50 m at entrance; 1.70 m at end
Height	1.98 m at entrance, top of steps; 2.64 m at base of steps; 3.08 m at end
Area	10.12 m²
Volume	27.51 m³

Chamber 14

This chamber, with three pillars along its north-south axis, has been only partially cleared. The floodborne debris it contains includes many large (five- to ten-kilogram) blocks of limestone, as well as chips and silt, tossed here with great force as the flood waters cascaded down the steep slope of corridors 12 and 13. A substantial number of potsherds were washed in as well. The room has several doorways cut through its walls, into small rooms such as 15 and 17, into suites of rooms such as 18, and into corridors with numerous side-chambers, such as 16. Nothing is yet known about 19.

In Chamber 14 lay several light blue faïence 'wiglets'; one tubular faience bead and two faience disk beads; three pieces of glass vessels, blue or blue-green in color; a blue glass bead; and two blue-green faïence vessel fragments with a scale-pattern in black.

Dimensions of Chamber 14	
Floor Elevation	155.65 msl
Length	6.40 m
Width	11.12 m
Height	2.55 m
Area	71.57 m² with pillars; 69.14 m² without
Volume	182.49 m³ with pillars; 176.30 m³ without
Door Width	1.20 m
Door Height	2.31 m
Pillars	0.90 ± 0.02 m on each side

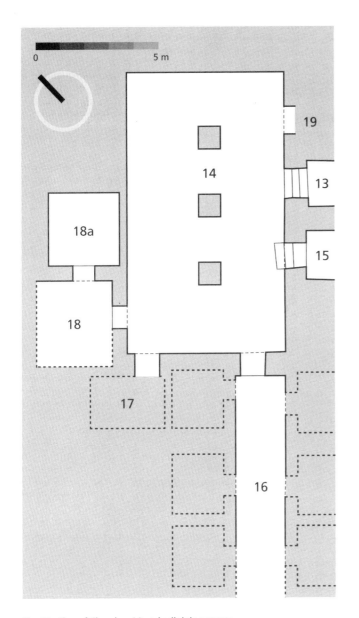

Fig. 41: Plan of Chamber 14 and adjoining rooms.

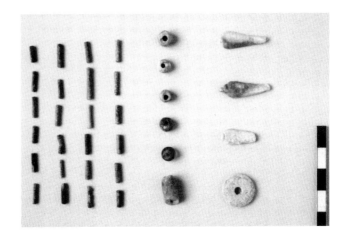

Fig. 42a (top): Faïence 'wiglets' from various locations inside KV 5.

Fig. 42b (bottom): Stone, glass, and faïence beads, both tubular and disk-shaped, from various locations inside KV 5.

Chamber 15

This small room was filled with silt and some limestone chips. It contained no objects. Its only unusual feature is its doorway, whose steps were cut into the floor of Chamber 14, over 0.36 meters in front of the door jamb.

Dimensions of Chamber 15	
Floor Elevation	155.006 msl
Length	4.74 m
Width	1.93 m (W wall), 2.04 m (E wall)
Height	2.20 m
Area	8.54 m²
Volume	18.50 m³
Door Width	0.95 m
Door Height	1.88 m

Corridor 16

This horizontal corridor has not yet been completely cleared. We do know, however, that it has a minimum of eight side-chambers (apparently similar in size to those in Corridor 7), and that it extends at least 18 meters southward into the Valley of the Kings.

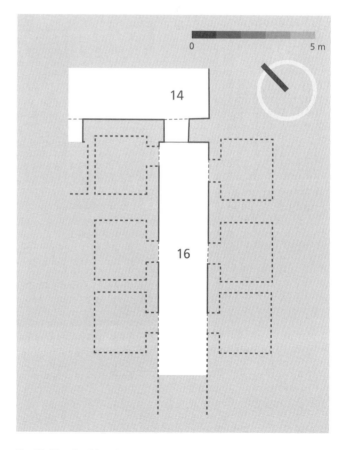

Fig. 43: Plan Corridor 16.

Corridor 20

So far, we have dug only twelve meters down Corridor 20, but the layout of side-chambers and the steep slope of its floor and ceiling suggest that its plan will be a mirror image of the chambers 12-19 complex, whose entrance lies on the other side of Chamber 3.

Four gates and side-chambers have so far been found, none of which lie beneath chambers 1 or 2.

Dimensions of Corridor 20	
Floor Elevation	161.608 msl (at entrance)
Length	n/a
Width	2.03 m (S wall), 2.08 m (N wall)
Height	n/a
Area	n/a
Volume	n/a
Door Width	0.99 m
Door Height	2.25 m

WALL DECORATION
Edwin C. Brock

Technique of Decoration

The walls of KV 5 are decorated in raised relief cut into lime plaster applied to the prepared rock surface. The surface preparation may render the wall completely smooth, as in the beginning of corridor 7, or it may be 'keyed' (left rough), for better adhesion of the plaster. In areas where plaster has fallen away, traces of texts and figures may survive where the artisans cut through the plaster into the stone surface. Where the plaster is still intact, there are traces of color, and evidence of decoration can be found on every wall. What follows are the more complete and recognizable examples of KV 5's decoration.

Entrance

North Jamb, Reveal: The exterior surface of the entrance, beneath the overhang, is damaged with only traces of a text column visible on the left (north) reveal.
Text:

... [wsr-m3ʿt-rʿ stp]-n-[rʿ] ... [rʿ-]ms.s [mri-imn] m3ʿ [ḥrw] ...
... [User-ma'at-Ra setep-en-Ra Ra]meses [Mery-Amen] true of voice ...

North Jamb, Thickness: A winged figure of Ma'at kneels on a basket above two *ḏd*-pillars and two *tyt*-knots. Between the wings of Ma'at is a *šn*-sign, its base directed toward the cartouche of Rameses II. Traces of text give her speech; the lacunae in columns 1 and 2 may have contained: "she protects her beloved son" or "I come before" or "she receives her beloved son" by analogy with other examples of this motif.

Fig. 44a (above Left): Entrance, North Jamb, Reveal.
Fig. 44b (above Right): Entrance, North Jamb, Thickness.

55

In other examples, the basket is placed over the heraldic plants of Upper and Lower Egypt. Pairs of *ḏd*'s and *tyt*'s do appear beneath figures in contemporary tombs in the Valley of the Queens (QV 66: antechamber, entry wall, left side; QV 71: door to east side-room, north jamb). These emblems also appear on the left jamb thickness of the door to Corridor 12 in KV 5.

1:

... *nb.t   pt* ...

2:

... *nb [t3wy] wsr-m3ʿt-rʿ stp-n-rʿ di ʿnḫ*

3:

... *mi rʿ ḏt*

4+x:

... *s3 ḏd w3s ḫ3 s nb*

1:    [Recitation by Ma'at, daughter of Ra] Lady of heaven …
2:    … Lord of the Two Lands Userma'at-Ra-setepen-Ra, given life
3:    like Ra forever …
4+x: … all [life] protection, stability dominion behind her

South Jamb, Thickness (not shown): Traces of a pair of *ḏd*-pillars and at least one *tyt*-knot. The south jamb presumably mirrored the better-preserved scene on the north.

Chamber 1

West Wall, South Half: Beneath a frieze formed by the cartouches of Rameses II surmounted by solar disks and flanked by uraei, the king, followed by Prince Amenherkhepeshef, offers wine to Sokar and Hathor. The prince holds the *ḥw*-feather fan and a sash in one hand. Both deities are seated on thrones; Hathor embraces Sokar with one arm and holds an *ꜥnḫ* in the other hand. Sokar, in his hawk-headed guise and wearing the *ꜣtf* crown, holds a *wꜣs*-scepter in one hand and an *ꜥnḫ* in the other. A similar scene is found in QV 68, where the god is named Ptah-Sokar-Osiris.

Above king and prince:

x+1:

sꜣ rꜥ n ḫt.f nb ḫꜥw

x+2:

rꜥ-ms.s mri-imn

x+3:

mꜣꜥ ḫrw ḫr wsir

x+4: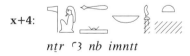

nṯr ꜥꜣ nb imntt

x+5:

sꜣ nsw tpy n ...

Fig. 45: Chamber 1, West Wall, South Half.

Fig. 46: Chamber 1, West Wall, South Half.

x+6:

iry-pꜥt ...

x+7:

mḥ ib mn[ḫ n nb ?].f

x+8:

imn-ḥr-ḫpš.f

x+9: ![glyphs]

... mꜣꜥ ḫrw ḥr wsir ...

x+1: Bodily son of Ra, Lord of Appearances,
x+2: Rameses Mery-Amen,
x+3: true of voice with Osiris,
x+4: the great god, Lord of the West.
x+5: king's first son of [his body],
x+6: hereditary prince [royal scribe?]
x+7: king's confidant ...,
x+8: Amenherkhepeshef,
x+9: true of voice with Osiris ...

Behind king:

![glyphs]

... ḥr ...

South Wall: Beneath a frieze of the king's cartouches (with glyphs oriented towards the entrance), three scenes are preserved. The westernmost shows Prince Rameses standing before Nefertem-Horhekenu who grants the prince a position as one pre-eminent in the realm of the dead (*st m ḫnty iw-grt*). This deity combines guardian aspects of the Memphite deity with a form of Horus from Bubastis. Both deities have some association with precious ointments as well. In the middle scene, Rameses stands before a god. Only the legs and feet of the deity are visible, although there are traces of what may be the edge of the top of his head beneath the texts. No surviving text names the god, but there are of traces of a place-name as part of his epithet (ending in *nt*, followed by the city glyph). The god grants a position as one pre-eminent in the Necropolis (*st m ḫty tꜣ ḏsr*). In the eastern-most scene, which continues on the south side of the east wall, the king, accompanied by his ka, with the Horus name above, consecrates an offering of meat and a lotus bouquet on an altar.

West End:

1: ![glyphs]

sꜣ nsw tpy ...

2: ![glyphs]

n ḫt.f imy-r mšꜣ ...

3: ![glyphs]

rꜥ-ms.

4: ![glyphs]

s mꜣꜥ [ḫrw] ...

5: ![glyphs]

nfr-tm ...

Fig. 47: Chamber1, South Wall, West End.

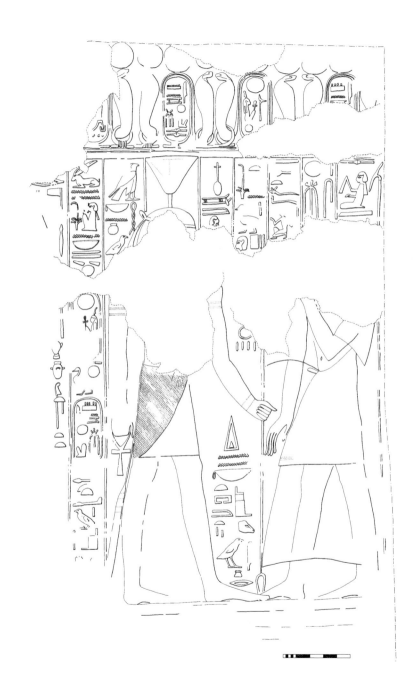

6:

ḥr ḥknw

7:

[ḏd mdw] sp 4

8:

di.n.i n.k st m ḫntyt iw-grt

1: king's first son
2: of his body, overseer of the army ('general') …
3: Rameses,
4: true of voice …
5: Nefertem
6: Horhekenu
7: [recitation ?] 4 times:
8: "I have given to you a place in the necropolis"

Center:

1: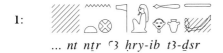

… nt nṯr ʿ3 ḥry-ib t3-ḏsr

2:

… w

3: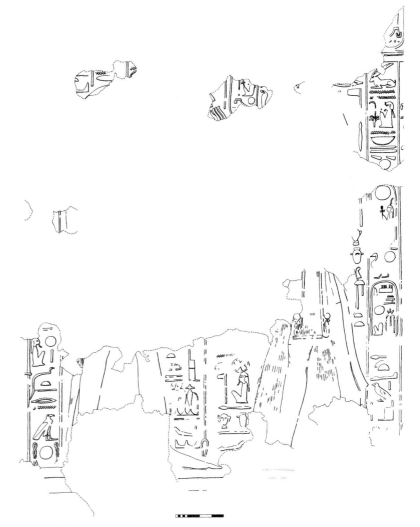

… wsr-m3ʿt-rʿ stp-n-rʿ

Fig. 48: Chamber 1, South Wall, Center.

61

4:

5:

... *i* ...

6:

7:

[*ws*]*ir nṯr ꜥꜣ ḥry-ib imntt*

8:

wnn nsw nb tꜣwy [*wsr*]*-mꜣꜥt-rꜥ* [*stp-n-rꜥ*] *sꜣ rꜥ*

rꜥ-m[*s.s*] *mri-imn* [*mꜣꜥ*] *ḫrw ḫꜥꜥ w ḥr st ꜥnḫ*[*w*]

9:

... *n*[*t*] ...

10: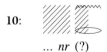

... *nr* (?)

11:

... *t* ...

12:

... *f rꜥ ḏt r nḥḥ*

13:

... *st m ḫnty tꜣ-ḏsr*

1: ... the great god dwelling in the necropolis
2: ... (?) ...
3: User-ma'at-Ra setep-en-Ra ...
4: ... (?) ...
5: ... (?) ...
6: ... [true of voice with?]
7: Osiris the great god dwelling in the West
8: May the king, the Lord of the Two Lands, User-ma'at-Ra setep-en-Ra the son of Ra, Rameses-Mery-Amen, true of voice, appear on the throne of the living.
9: ... (?) ...
10: ... (?) ...
11: ... west/western
12: ... Ra forever eternally
13: ... a place as one pre-eminent in the necropolis

East End:

1:

2: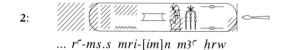

... *rꜥ-ms.s mri-*[*im*]*n mꜣꜥ ḫrw*

3:

Fig. 49: Chamber 1, South Wall, East End.

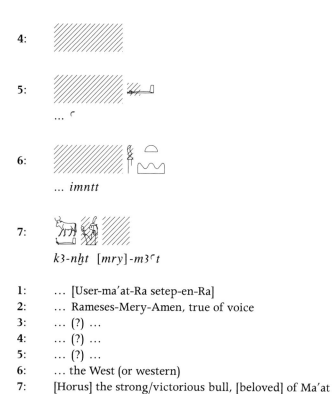

4:

5:

... ʿ

6:

... *imntt*

7:

k3-nḫt [mry]-m3ʿt

1: ... [User-maʾat-Ra setep-en-Ra]
2: ... Rameses-Mery-Amen, true of voice
3: ... (?) ...
4: ... (?) ...
5: ... (?) ...
6: ... the West (or western)
7: [Horus] the strong/victorious bull, [beloved] of Maʾat

East Wall, South Half: This scene depicts the god to whom the offering was being made on the east end of the south wall. Only the foot of the deity is preserved. The remains of four small mummiform figures on a standard probably represent the Four Sons of Horus and suggest that the deity was Osiris, seated in a kiosk. The presence of this structure is also indicated by the upright at the corner of the south wall. It has a banded edge decoration and a horizontal base with cavetto cornice striations (in red, yellow, and blue) beneath the matting on which the standard and the god's foot rests.

1:

ḏd mdw di.n.i n.k ḥʿʿ rʿ m pt

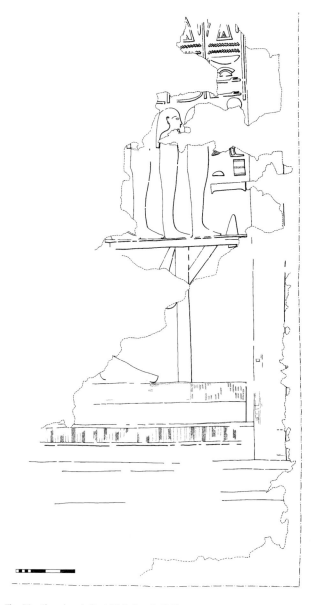

Fig. 50: Chamber 1, East Wall, South Half.

2:

ḏd mdw di.n.i n[k] ...

3:

... st ...

1: Recitation : "I have given to you the appearance of Ra in the sky"
2: Recitation: "I have given to [you] ..."
3: .... seat/place(?)

West Wall, North Half: A prince and the king stand before a seated god and goddess. The figures are preserved only from their torsos down, and no identifying texts or iconographic elements are preserved. The king may hold the prince's hand and both figures seem crowded together. When the door was widened, part of the prince's figure was cut away.

North Wall, West Half: At the west end of the wall, a prince and the royal *k3*, crowned with the king's Horus name, accompany the king, who stands before Ptah, offering a censer. The god stands in a kiosk with jars of ointment/unguent before it. Traces of glyphs above and behind the head of the king suggest the reading:

x+1:

... [nb] t3wy

x+2:

... m3ᶜ [ḫrw ḫr] wsir ...

x+1: ... [Lord of the] Two Lands
x+2: [Userma'at Ra setep en Ra] true [of voice with] Osiris ...

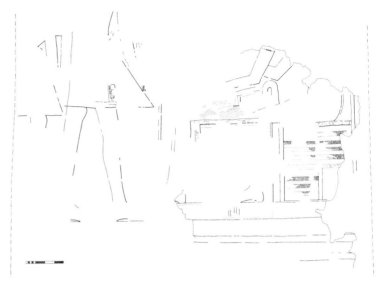

Fig. 51: Chamber 1, West Wall, North Half.

Fig. 52: Chamber 1, North Wall, West Half. Detail of Ptah.

Fig. 53: Chamber 1, North Wall. Drawing of east (right) section on opposite page is a 'hand-copy', not a collated tracing.

Before Ptah:

x+3:

... *t* ...

x+4:

... *nfr*

Behind Ptah:

... *ḥ3.f nb ʿw[t] ib nb* ...
... all ... behind him, all joy ...

North Wall, East Half: At the east end the king, followed by a prince, stands before three *mrt*-chests, distinguished by a crossed pair of ostrich feathers over each chest. The prince carries the single feather *ḥw*-fan over his right shoulder and holds the king's *ḥḳ3*-scepter in his left hand. The curving tail hanging by his leg suggests that he wears a priest's leopard skin.

Before king:

... *t ʿ* ...

Behind king:

... [ʿnḫ] *ḏd w3s*
... [life] stability, dominion

Behind prince:

... [*m3ʿ ḫr*]*w ḫr nṯr* [ʿ]*3 nb* ...
... [true of] voice with the great god, lord of ...

East Wall, North Half (not shown): The god receiving the offerings on the north wall was most likely Osiris, mirroring the scene on the south half of the east wall. Traces of the uprights of a shrine near the northeast corner followed to the south by the *imy-wt* symbol and a standard showing the feet of four small mummiform gods provide details of the scene and clues to the identity of the god. Osiris's feet appear on a mat placed over a blue cubit-shaped podium. The position of the feet in relation to the stand with the Four Sons of Horus suggests that Osiris was seated.

Chamber 2

West Wall, South Half: A prince and the king, preserved mainly from the legs down, stand before a large heap of offerings. These include a cow, vessels, and baskets of fruit. Traces of glyphs at the bottoms of text columns can be seen before and above the head of the king (not on drawing):

   ... *s3* ...,   ... *s* ...,   ... *n* ...

and some signs survive at the south end of the wall, above the offerings:

   ... *nn* ...
   ... these (?) ...

Fig. 54: Chamber 2, West Wall, South Half.

South Wall: The Hathor cow stands in her bark, on the west half of the wall, the recipient of a pile of offerings that is depicted on the south half of the west wall. She is shown wearing a *mnᶜt* necklace with the counterpoise at the back of her neck. The solar disk and two colorful plumes are placed between her horns, and a pattern of red with white streaks behind her suggests a canopy or shrine covering. Before her is a small figure of Rameses II and a standard bearing a sphinx. Similar scenes are found in contemporary tombs in the Valley of the Queens, including QV 40 and QV 73. The east half of the wall shows a prince holding a *ḥw*-fan and a scepter (perhaps the *ḥk3*-scepter), accompanying the king, who offers cloth to the gods shown on the south half of the east wall.

x+1:   

   ... *wsir nsw*

x+2:

   ... *wsr-m3ᶜt-rᶜ stp-n-rᶜ* ...

x+3:

   ... *snb* [*nb*] *ḥ3 st*

x+4:

   ... *rᶜ* ... *ᶜnḫ ḏd w3s ḥr.i* ...

x+5:

   ... *n rᶜ rnpwt tm ḥr.i*

x+6:

   ... *nš*

Fig. 55: Chamber 2, South Wall, West Half.

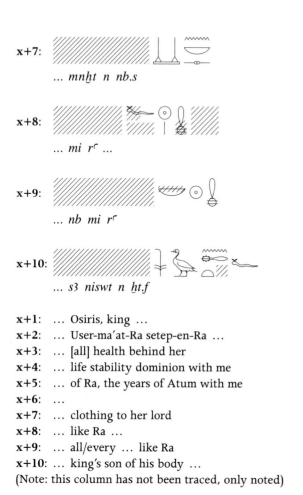

x+7: ... *mnḫt n nb.s*

x+8: ... *mi rꜥ* ...

x+9: ... *nb mi rꜥ*

x+10: ... *s3 niswt n ḫt.f*

x+1: ... Osiris, king ...
x+2: ... User-ma'at-Ra setep-en-Ra ...
x+3: ... [all] health behind her
x+4: ... life stability dominion with me
x+5: ... of Ra, the years of Atum with me
x+6: ...
x+7: ... clothing to her lord
x+8: ... like Ra ...
x+9: ... all/every ... like Ra
x+10: ... king's son of his body ...
(Note: this column has not been traced, only noted)

Fig. 56: Chamber 2, South Wall, East Half.

Fig. 57: Chamber 2, South Wall, East Half.

Fig. 58: Chamber 2, South Wall, West Half.

East Wall, South Half: The recipients of the offering of cloth are a seated god and goddess, but all that remains of the two deities are their lower legs and feet, part of a throne and the forked bottom of the *w3s*-scepter held by the god. A vertical line to the right may be part of the upright of a kiosk.

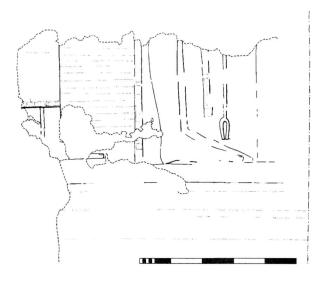

Fig. 59: Chamber 2, East Wall, South Half.

West Wall, North Half: The king stands before a god and the goddess Hathor, identified by her bovine head. Although the identity of the god before Hathor is uncertain, traces of text in front of the legs of the king mention Anubis. The remains of a text column behind the god is probably the conclusion of the god's statement of what he gives to the king. Behind the goddess are traces of the phrase "… all life, [stability, prosperity,] all joy behind her".

x+1: … *n* [*i*]*npw* [*ḫnt*?]*y* …

x+2: … [*ḫ*ʿ]ʿ *r*ʿ *m pt dt sp* 2

x+3: … *s*[*nb*] *nb 3wt-ib nb ḥ3* …

x+1: [Recitation ?] by Anubis pre-eminent in the Divine Booth
x+2: I have given to you the appearance of Ra in heaven forever and ever
x+3: … all life, [stability, prosperity,] all joy behind her

Fig. 60: Chamber 2, West Wall, North Half.

North Wall: The western half shows a prince and the king standing before a god. The upper part of the wall is poorly preserved, and no identification of the prince or the god is possible. A prince and the king are shown on the eastern half of the wall with offerings on a shrine-shaped altar topped with four semicircular projections.

Fig. 61a: Chamber 2, North Wall, West Half, before excavation (left) and after excavation but prior to conservation (right).

Fig. 61b: Chamber 2, North Wall, West Half, after conservation. Note the pit at the foot of the wall.

Fig. 61c: Chamber 2, North Wall, West Half.

Fig. 62: Chamber 2, North Wall, East Half.

East Wall, North Half: Two deities seated on thrones and facing the corner are the recipients of the offerings presented on the east half of the north wall. Not enough is preserved to identify these figures, but the northern-most is likely a male, suggested by the forked bottom of the *wȝs*-scepter shown before him. The bottoms of three text columns framing the north edge of the door into Chamber 3 are preserved to the right of the gods.

1: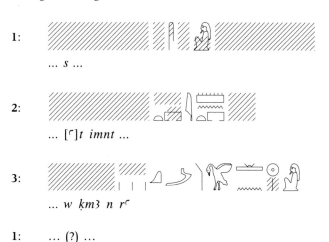

... *s* ...

2:

... [ꜥ]*t imnt* ...

3:

... *w ḳmȝ n rꜥ*

1:      ... (?) ...
2:      ... the Hidden Chamber
3:      ... which Ra created

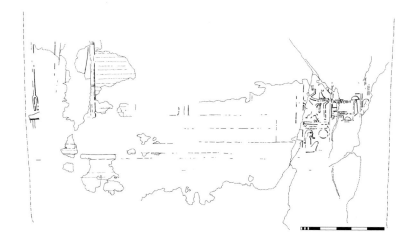

Fig. 63: Chamber 2, East Wall, North Half.

Pit: Traces of decoration and text survive on the north side of the pit near its upper edge. They were painted on plaster applied to the stone surface. It is possible to detect the head of a goddess facing west and wearing on her head the symbol for the West, *imtt* (minus the feather). Traces of a text column in front of the goddess preserve too few fragments of signs to be read. The goddess could be Hathor in her role as goddess of the West. Behind her head are the remains of two short columns of glyphs giving the name of the god Anubis and part of one of his epithets, *ḫnty sḥ-nṯr*. This is followed in a third column by the glyph of a man holding a staff. No traces of the figure of Anubis survive. The orientation of the figure and of the glyphs toward the west end of the pit suggests that it was decorated like a coffin or sarcophagus with figures facing the head end, just as the skeleton was aligned.

Behind Hathor:

x+1:

inpw ...

x+2:

ḫnty ...

x+3:

wr(?) *n* ...

x+1: Anubis ...
x+2: Pre-eminent [in the divine booth ?] ...
x+3: great one (?) of ...

Fig. 64: Chamber 2, Pit, North Wall.

Plaster Fragments: Fragments of painted plaster fallen from the walls were discovered among the layers of debris. Among these were pieces with remains of glyphs from the top fill of the northwest quadrant including such groups as

 and

(both oriented to the right). Among fragments in the south-west quarter are part of the pre-nomen of the king

,

and such glyph groups as

.

Plaster fragments from the southeast quadrant, illustrated at right, include such signs as

.

Figurative elements include the detailed roundel with lotus flower decoration from the counterpoise of the *mn*ᶜ*t* worn by the Hathor cow from the southwest quadrant. An eye and fingers were found in the northern part of the room. Plaster fragments recovered from the debris in the north third of this chamber show the shoulder, wig, and corselet strap of a god (so identified by the red skin). This might belong to the scene on the northern half of the east wall or to the unidentified god on the north wall.

Fig. 65: Plaster fragments from Chamber 2.

Chamber 3

Door Jambs, North Thickness (not shown): All that remains are traces of the feet of a standing figure; since the feet are close together with an ankle length hem-line showing, it is a goddess, probably Ma'at. Similar figures are found on the doorways leading to inner chambers in other Ramesside tombs, including that of Nefertari (QV 66), Sety I (KV 17), and Horemheb (KV 57).

South Thickness (not shown): As with the north jamb, only traces of the lower legs and feet of a goddess facing into Chamber 2 remain at the lower part of the jamb. There are possible traces of a large ostrich feather near the upper part of the thickness that suggest the presence of Ma'at.

West Wall, South Half: Four seated figures of princes face the door leading from Chamber 2. Before the northern-most prince is an offering stand and a pair of wine jars. A figure identifiable by his leopard skin cloak as the *Iun-mutef* priest stands on the other side of the offering table and faces the princes. Each prince wears a long-sleeved tunic and ankle-length robe. Enough of the head of the second prince is preserved to show a short wig and side-lock. In the depictions of the second and third princes, the left arm is bent over the chest and holds a *sḫm*-scepter; the extended right hand holds a folded cloth. The first prince appears to hold a scepter in his extended right hand.

Before the priest:

x+1: ... *t3*

x+2: ... *ib. tn* ...

Above the second prince:

y+1: ... *y* ...

y+2: ... *wsir wsr* ...

y+3: ... *ꜥ* ...

Above the third prince:

z+1: ... *mr.f*

z+2: ... *r ḫtw*

West Wall, North Half: Traces of four seated figures of princes face the door leading from Chamber 2, and the scene is basically a mirror-image of that on the west wall, south. An offering table with a pair of wine jars is placed before the southern-most seated figure. A *Iun-mutef* priest faces the princes from the other side of the offering table. A painted plaster fragment recovered from the debris near the north wall shows the curled end of a side lock and a broad color. It may belong to one of the sons, as those on the south side of the west wall are shown wearing the side-lock.

Fig. 66: Chamber 3, West Wall, South Half.

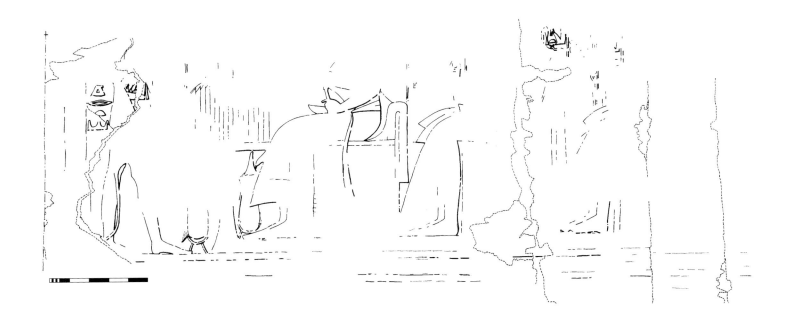

Fig. 67: Chamber 3, West Wall, North Half.

Behind the priest:

... [*iw*-]*grt*

Before the second prince:

Before the third prince:

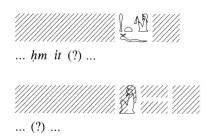

... *ḥm* *it* (?) ...

... (?) ...

Pillar 3(e) (not shown): One face of this broken pillar shows a mummiform figure with a large ꜥnḫ carved diagonally across the chest. The
bottoms of two text columns identify the figure as Shu. Traces of a
ḥkr frieze appear above the text columns, and another ꜥnḫ is carved
below the first text column.

x+1:

šw

x+2:

s3 rꜥ nṯr ꜥ3

x+1:   Shu,
x+2:   the son of Ra, the great god.

South Wall (not shown): At a point about three meters east of the
door to Chamber 4, the feet of a goddess are represented by traces of
yellow paint on plaster.

Ceiling (not shown): Traces of blue still can be seen on the ceiling, but
with no indication of stars.

Plaster Fragments (not shown): Some plaster fragments from the
area of the south wall include groups of glyphs such as:

In the west wall area fragments with glyphs include:

(all oriented to the right). Other fragments from the room include
shrines, the rear of a goddess's head with the knot of her red fillet,
and an ear.

Chamber 4

East Wall (not shown): Although no decoration was found on the walls during the clearance of the east side of this room, numerous fragments of painted plaster were found in the debris near the walls. In the northeast corner, several pieces from a figure of a *Iun-mutef* priest were collected, showing the shoulder, collar and side-lock. Other fragments include the wig and shoulder of a god facing right, parts of a throne, and a pleated gown with a red sash. Pillar 4(b) has the remains of a large ꜥnḫ on one face. Another large ꜥnḫ was found in the debris in the northeast quadrant. Very few textual fragments have been found. One example is:

There are traces of blue on the ceiling and red architectural layout lines are visible on the walls.

North Wall, between the doors to Chamber 9 and Side-chamber 7p:
This scene is nearly identical to that on the rear wall of the first pillared
hall (F) in the tomb of Sety I (KV 17). Beneath a frieze of *ḥkrw*, there is
a kiosk surmounted by a row of uraei. Osiris is seated within the kiosk
and Hathor, Mistress of the West, stands behind him. At the front of
the kiosk, a standing figure of the falcon-headed Horus, son of Isis,
wears the crowns of Upper and Lower Egypt and presents Rameses II
to Osiris. Unfortunately, the figure of the king is not preserved, although traces can be seen of the flail over his shoulder. To the west
of this scene there are traces of what may be a winged sun disk on the
lintel of the door to Chamber 9.

Lintel of Chamber 9 door (not shown):

x+1: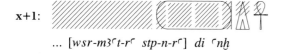

  ... [*wsr-mȝˁt-rˁ stp-n-rˁ*] *di ˁnḫ*

x+2:

  ... *rˁ-ms.s mri-imn mi rˁ*

x+1: ... User-ma'at-Ra setep-en-Ra
x+2: ... Rameses mery-Amen, given life like Ra

Fig. 68a: Corridor 7, North Wall, between the doors
to Chamber 9 and Side-chamber 7p. Detail of Horus.

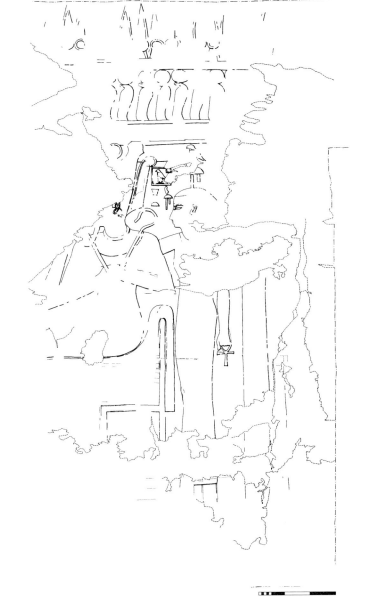

Fig. 68b: Corridor 7, North Wall, between the doors
to Chamber 9 and Side-chamber 7p.

East Jamb of Chamber 9 door (not shown):

... *r ͨ-ms.s mri-imn*
... Rameses mery-Amen,

mry wsir ḫnty [imntt nṯr] ⸢3⸣
beloved of Osiris, pre-eminent in the west, the great god

Between Chamber 9 and Side-chamber 7p:

Behind Horus:

[ḥr s3] 3st
[Horus son of] Isis

Before Hathor:

ḥwt.ḥr ḫnt imntt
Hathor, Mistress of the West

North Wall, between the doors to side-chambers 7p and 7o: From west to east, a prince (name gone) stands behind the king, holding a *ḫw*-fan. The king holds up an offering of cloth over a tapering offering stand. A *nmst*-vessel and a lotus bouquet are placed on the stand. On the eastern half of the wall, a seated ram-headed god, followed by the goddess Hathor, face the king and prince. No texts survive to identify either the prince or the ram-headed god. As to the god, we probably can rule out a solar deity, because there is no trace of a sun disk on the god's head, which would be expected if the sun god were represented

Fig. 69a: Corridor 7, North Wall, between the doors to side-chambers 7p and 7o. Detail of Hathor.

Fig. 69b: Corridor 7, North Wall, between the doors
to side-chambers 7p and 7o.

in his ram-headed form. The other likely ram-headed deity is Khnum, but it could also be an unusual form of Anubis with a ram's head. This is found primarily during the time of Rameses II, and examples include the Valley of the Queens tombs of his daughters Meryetamen (QV 68) and Bent'anta (QV 71), where a ram-headed Anubis is accompanied by Hathor. There is a representation of a ram-headed Osiris in the tomb of Merenptah (KV 8).

Between 7p and 7o (not shown):

Before and above Hathor:

x+1: ... *imn*[*t*]*t*

x+2: ... *nbt pt*

x+1: the West
x+2: Lady of heaven

North Wall, between the doors to 7o and 7n (not shown): Unlike the north walls to the west, where the raised relief was cut into the smoothed rock surface, the walls from here eastward were left rough with the decoration cut into the plaster coating that has now largely disappeared. Only scattered traces of decorated plaster remain on this stretch of the wall. A goddess wearing a red gown stands facing east while behind her stands a figure wearing a pleated robe.

Side-chamber 7l - Plaster Fragments (not shown): Many plaster fragments in the debris cleared from this room bore a feather pattern.

South Wall, between the doors to chambers 8 and 7a: Traces of the arms of two figures facing each other were cut to the left of the inscription. The figure facing east, probably the king rather than a prince, raises one arm in greeting while holding up an uncertain object

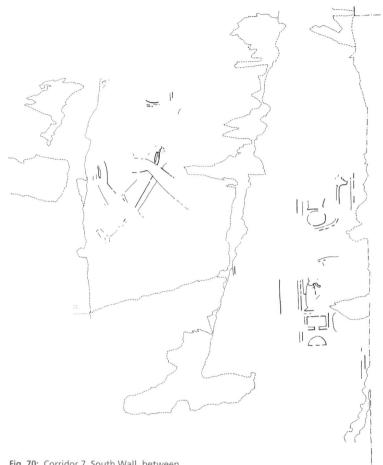

Fig. 70: Corridor 7, South Wall, between the doors to chambers 8 and 7a.

with the other. The arm of the deity he faces is raised to present the sign of life to the nose of the king.

East Jamb of Chamber 8 door:

... *wsr-mꜣꜥt-rꜥ stp-n-rꜥ* [*mry*]
... User-ma'at-Ra setep-en-Ra [beloved of]

wsir ḫnty imntt ...
Osiris pre-eminent in [the West] ...

Above crossed arms:

... *nb tꜣ* ...

7a Lintel (not shown):

... *ꜥnḫ* [*ws*]*ir nsw* ...
... May the Osiris, the king ... live ...

South Wall, between the doors to side-chambers 7a and 7b:
Beneath a frieze of uraei, indicating the presence of a kiosk, Thoth stands facing east with arm outstretched in the gesture of summoning or invoking. The cartouches of Rameses II lie to the left of Thoth, indicating that the god was addressing the king. A figure behind Thoth, with one arm raised either holds up an *ꜥnḫ*, or possibly performs the rite of offering Ma'at (*fꜥi mꜣꜥt, rdi.t mꜣꜥt*). There are traces of a small squatting figure with the base of the *ꜥnḫ* touching its knee, suggestive of how the Ma'at figure is shown as the offering in this rite. There are traces of the long yellow garment with pleats shown as red lines worn by the offering figure.

Before Thoth:

x+1: *ḏd mdw in ḏḥwty nb* ...

x+2: ... *t* ...

x+3:

Fig. 71: Corridor 7, South Wall, between the doors to side-chambers 7a and 7b. Detail of cartouches.

x+4:

nb t3wy wsr-m3ʿt-rʿ stp-n-rʿ

x+5:

nb ḫʿw rʿ-ms.s mri-imn

x+1: Recitation by Thoth, Lord of …
(A similar writing of Thoth's name, with *t* above and *y* below the standard, is found in Nefertari's tomb - Room G, left wall, first line of BD 94, a spell for begging water pot and palette from Thoth).

x+2: …

x+3: …

x+4: Lord of the Two Lands, User-ma'at-Ra setep-en-Ra,

x+5: Lord of appearances, Rameses mery-Amen

Fig. 72: Corridor 7, South Wall, between the doors to side-chambers 7a and 7b.

West Wall: Traces of relief near the top of the wall show the head of the king (as indicated by the uraeus) wearing an elaborate head-dress of ram's horns and a disk with two plumes flanked by a pair of large uraei. Behind the king is a winged goddess, perhaps Meretseger or Hathor, enclosing him protectively with her outspread wings.

Over the winged figure's arm:

x+1:

...

x+2:

imntt

x+3:

...

Fig. 73: Chamber 8, West Wall.

East Wall: Two fragments of relief found in the floor debris near the break in this wall show the lower torso and forearm of a prince facing right on one piece, and part of a column of text on the second:

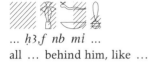

... *ḫȝ,f nb mi* ...
all ... behind him, like ...

Plaster Fragments (not shown): In addition, several fragments of painted plaster were found in the floor debris in the northeast quadrant of this room. Among these were part of an ostrich feather plume, several pieces of pleated garments, and traces of glyphs:

Some fragments show a shrine's cavetto cornice and one of these has a cursive hieroglyphic graffito:

... *n nfr r* ... *kn* ... *ir.n* ...

From the area of the south end of the east wall adjacent to the door to 8a, fragments include the multicolored stripes of a throne, and part of a male figure with traces of these glyphs:

Fig. 74: Chamber 8, East Wall, relief fragments.

92

Chamber 9

Doorway, East Thickness: Remains of a scene show the Anubis canine facing out from the room, recumbent on a shrine. The animal is depicted with a sash looped around its neck, but without any of the other regalia such as the *sḫm*-scepter or the flail that are often seen in other depictions. Traces of text columns read, in part:

x+1:

     ḏd mdw [in inp]w ḫnty

x+2: ▨▨

     ...

x+3: ▨▨

     [ḏd mdw di.] n.i n.k

x+1: Recitation by Anubis, pre-eminent in [the Divine Booth?]
x+2: ...
x+3: [Recitation: "I have given to] you ..."

Faint traces of a winged sun disk can be seen at the top of the south wall of the room, to the south of the door. Plaster fragments found among the debris layers include part of a collar and the stripes on the cornice of a shrine, as in Chamber 8.

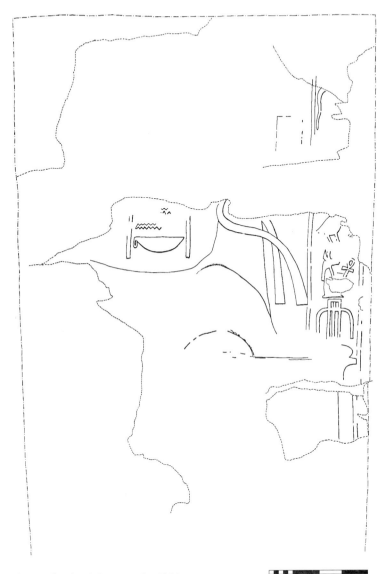

Fig. 75: Chamber 9, Doorway, East Thickness. The Anubis canine (its head missing) with a sash around its neck is at center.

Corridor 12

Several traces of decoration (not shown) have been noted on the walls of this passage descending westwards from the southwest corner of Chamber 3. Traces of $\underline{d}d$-pillar can be seen on the south thickness of the doorway. On the north wall, near the corridor entrance, the legs and feet of two figures facing each other can be discerned. That on the right can be identified as the king by the uraei flanking the apron of his kilt. Traces of the king's nomen are found to the right of the door to 12e.

INSCRIBED OBJECTS

Edwin C. Brock and Nathalie Walschaerts

Shabtis

Object: 1.3

Provenience: Chamber 1; northwest quadrant; 2.00 m below ceiling. (1989)

Material: Faïence

Dimensions: 4.70 x 2.50 x 1.50 cm

Description: Shabti fragment (legs) with three bands of inscription; body light blue. Typical of Sety I shabtis.

Date: Nineteenth Dynasty (?)

Text:

x+1:

  i[m] ḥr-nṯr ist ḥwi [dnyw] i[m m] s [ḫ]rw[t].f [m]k.s[w]

x+2:

  k3.tw ir ḥsb.tw nw nb rˁ nb ir.w im.s r smḥt

x+3:

  wḏb r s[rd] sḫt [r] ḥni šˁ.t n imnty r i3bty [r] ḥni

x+1: … in the Necropolis, indeed, obstacles are imposed therewith, as a man at his duties, here he is,

x+2: you shall say: if one reckons, at any time, daily, which has to be done there, to irrigate

x+3: the riparian lands, to cultivate the fields, to transport sand of the East to the West, to ship …

Fig. 76: Object 1.3.

Object: 1.4
Provenience: Chamber 1; northwest quadrant; floor, corner (1989).
Material: Faïence
Dimensions: 2 x 1 x 1 cm
Description: Shabti fragment, foot, with traces of last line of inscription; body light blue-green, surface eroded in places.
Date: (?)
Text:

... *r* ...   ... *ḫn* ...

Fig. 77: Object 1.4.

Object: 1.5
Provenience: Chamber 1; northwest quadrant; floor, corner (1989).
Material: Faïence
Dimensions: 2 x 1 x 5 cm
Description: Shabti fragment, legs and feet, with traces of two lines of inscription; body blue-green, surface eroded.
Date: (?)
Text:

x+1:

... *r ir.t*

x+2:

k3[t]   ... *k r* ...

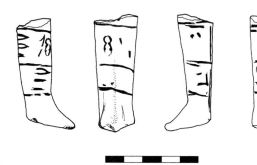

Fig. 78: Object 1.5.

Object: **1.6**
Provenience: Chamber 1; southeast quadrant; floor, near door (12/6/89).
Material: Calcite
Dimensions: 12 x 4 x 3 cm
Description: Complete 'lost contour' shabti with traces of text column, face, wig, beard, crossed arms and tools in black.
Date: Twentieth Dynasty

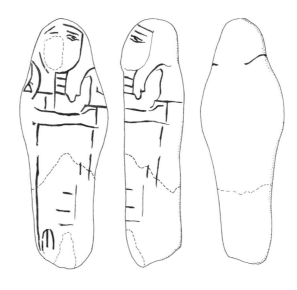

Fig. 79: Object 1.6.

Object: **1.21**
Provenience: Chamber 1; northwest quadrant; 2.20 m below ceiling, between 0.80 and 0.50 m above floor (24/1/99).
Material: Faïence
Dimensions: 7.20 x 4.50 x 2.70 cm
Description: Body fragment of shabti of Sety I, Nineteenth Dynasty, with inscription; body light blue-green.
Date: Nineteenth Dynasty
Text:

1: *shḏ wsir mn-m3ʿt-rʿ pw m3ʿ ḫrw ḏd.f i*

2: *šbty pt ir ʿš[t] [i]r ḥsb.t wsir sty-mry-n-ptḥ*

3: *... [r ir.t] k3.t nb irr m ḫr-nṯr r srd*

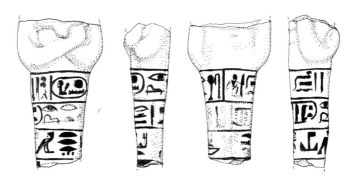

Fig. 80: Object 1.21.

1: The illuminated one, the Osiris, Men-maʾat-Ra, the Justified, he speaks: O,

2: this shabti, if one calls, if one reckons, the Osiris, Sety Mery-en-Ptah

3: [to do] all the work which is to be done in the Necropolis, to cultivate …

97

Fig. 81: Top left: Object 1.21. Top center: Object 2.39. Top right (from left to right): Objects 1.6, 13.4, 12.29. Bottom left: Object 3.78. Bottom right: Object 3.79.

Object: **1.24**

Provenience: Chamber 1; northeast quadrant; between 0.10 and 0.50 m above floor (25/1/99).

Material: Calcite

Dimensions: 10.23 x 3.50 x 3.90 cm

Description: 'Lost contour' shabti, feet broken away; inscribed - text, wig, face, crossed arms in black.

Date: Twentieth Dynasty

Text:

sḥḏ wsir nb tꜢwy [N]
The illuminated one, the Osiris, Lord of the Two Lands, [N]

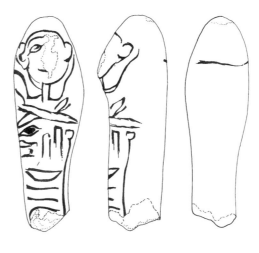

Fig. 82: Object 1.24.

Object: **1.25**

Provenience: Chamber 1; northeast quadrant; 0.10 m to 0.50 m above floor (25/1/99).

Material: Calcite

Dimensions: 8.58 x 4.44 x 2.86 cm

Description: 'Lost contour' shabti, lower legs and feet missing, no inscription or painted decoration.

Date: Twentieth Dynasty

Object: **2.36** (not shown)

Provenience: Chamber 2; pit, east end; 0.20 m below floor (16/9/96).

Material: Wood

Dimensions: 8.5 x 3 cm

Description: Shabti fragments without inscription.

Date: (?)

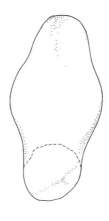

Fig. 83: Object 1.25.

Object: 2.39

Provenience: Chamber 2; northeast quadrant in pit; 0.10 m below floor (16/9/96).

Material: Calcite

Dimensions: 10.50 x 3.70 x 3.10 cm

Description: 'Lost contour' shabti with inscription, face, wig, arms, and text borders in black.

Date: Twentieth Dynasty

Text:

šḥḏ Wsir [N] …

The illuminated one, the Osiris [N] …

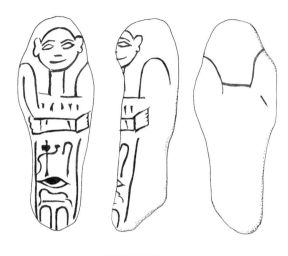

Fig. 84: Object 2.39.

Object: 2.44

Provenience: Chamber 2; north third, 0.70 m from the north wall, 0.45 m from the west wall; 2.25 m below the ceiling (2/10/96).

Material: Faïence

Dimensions: 3.40 x 2.40 x 1.60 cm

Description: Shabti legs and feet with incised inscription.

Date: (?)

Text:

x+1:

… w … ty s … t.s [ḥn]i [š]ʿ.t … i3btt imntt

x+2:

mk.t[w] k3.tw mi sp nb nfr m ḥr-nṯr

x+1: … ship [sand from] the East to the West

x+2: … here (?), so shall you say, like every good deed in the Necropolis

Fig. 85: Object 2.44.

Object: **3.78**

Provenience: Chamber 3; 0.10 m south of pillar 3(c); 1.50 m below ceiling (27/2/99).

Material: Faïence

Dimensions: 3 x 2.50 x 1.80 cm

Description: Shabti fragment of Sety I with inscription.

Date: Nineteenth Dynasty

Text:

1:

... t i[r ꜥ]š [t]w [wsir] sty-mry-n-ptḥ   m3ꜥ ḥrw

2:

r ir.t k3.t irrw.t m ḥr-nṯr r srd

3:

sḫt r smḥ.t wḏbwt [r] ḥni

1:     [The Osiris] Sety Mery-n-Ptah, justified,
2:     to do all the work which is to be done in the Necropolis, to cultivate
3:     fields, to irrigate the riparian lands, to ship ...

Fig. 86: Object 3.78.

Object: **3.79**

Provenience: Chamber 3; pillar 3(c), south side; 2.30 m below ceiling (27/2/99)

Material: Calcite

Dimensions: 7 x 4.50 x 2.70 cm

Description: 'Lost contour' shabti, upper half; text, face, wig, crossed arms in black.

Date: Twentieth Dynasty

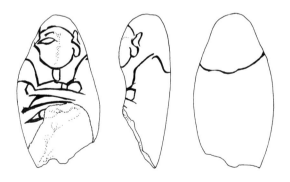

Fig. 87: Object 3.79.

Text:

[*sḥd*] [*Ws*]*ir* [*N*]
[The illuminated one], the Osiris, [N]

Object: **12.29**
Provenience: Corridor 12; beside Side-chamber 12e; 0.20 m above
floor (4/11/95).
Material: Calcite
Dimensions: 12.30 x 4.40 x 3.50 cm
Description: 'Lost contour' shabti without inscription, but with
traces of vertical borders, beard and wig in black.
Date: Twentieth Dynasty

Fig. 88: Object 12.29.

Object: **13.4**
Provenience: Chamber 13; floor, between gate and doorway (16/11/95).
Material: Calcite
Dimensions: 17.50 x 6 cm
Description: Shabti without text, but with black vertical text borders;
sculpted crossed arms, wig lappets, face, ears, wig outline,
collar, crossed arms, hoes, and basket rendered in black.
Date: Nineteenth/Twentieth Dynasty (?)

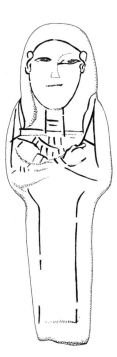

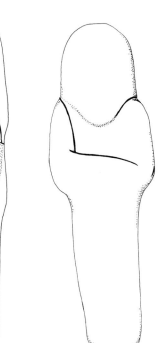

Fig. 89: Object 13.4.

Object: **17.1**

Provenience: Chamber 17; entrance; 0.00 to 0.50 m below ceiling (18/3/97).

Material: Calcite

Dimensions: 5.50 x 5 x 4 cm

Description: Broken lower part of painted and inscribed shabti of Setnakht.

Date: Twentieth Dynasty

Text:

x+1:

· ... *wsr-ḫꜥw-rꜥ stp-n-rꜥ* ...

x+2:

r ir k3.t nb.w irr m ḫr-nṯr r swdi sḫt

x+3:

[*r sm*]*ḥy wḏb r ḫni šꜥ.t n i3bt.t*

x+1: ... Setnakht ...

x+2: to do all the works which are to be done in the Necropolis, to cultivate fields

x+3: [to irrigate] the riparian lands, to ship the sand of the East ...

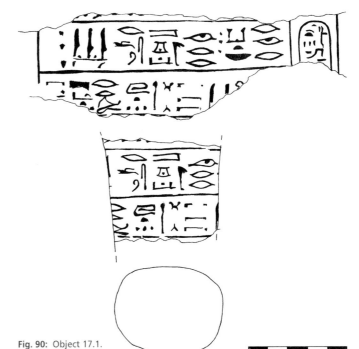

Fig. 90: Object 17.1.

Canopic Jars

Object: **2.9a**

Provenience: Chamber 2, southwest quadrant, 1.50 to 2.00 m below ceiling.

Material: calcite

Dimensions: 4.2 x 3.4 cm

Text:

x+1:

… [*i*]*nḳ. n* …

[I] have brought together …

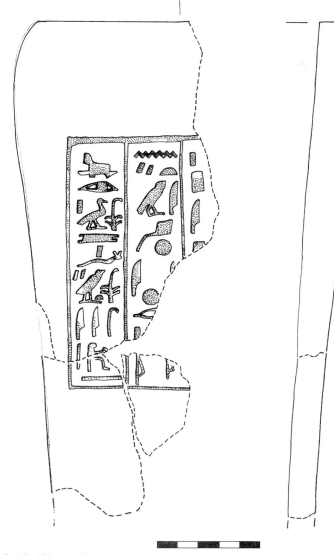

Fig. 91:
Object 2.9a.

Object: **2.9b**

Provenience: Chamber 2, southwest quadrant, 1.50 to 2.00 m below ceiling.

Material: Calcite

Dimensions: 4.3 x 2.1 cm

Owner: (?) (this fragment might complete the third text column on **3.31a, b, c** which belongs to Suty)

Fig. 92:
Object 2.9b.

Text:

x+1:

… *ḳbḥ-*[*snw*].*f* …

… Qebehsenuef …

Object: **2.10, 2.11, 1.12**

Provenience: **1.12:** Chamber 1, south half of chamber, 0.10 to 0.20 m above floor; **2.10:** Chamber 2, southwest quadrant, 2.25 m below ceiling; **2.11:** Chamber 2, southwest quadrant, 2.50 m below ceiling.

Fig. 93: Objects 2.10, 2.11, 1.12.

Material: Calcite
Dimensions: **2.10**: 15 x 9 x 2 cm; **2.11**: 4.2 x 3.1 cm; **1.12**: 5 x 3 cm
Owner: Suty (Swty)
Text:

2:

[ḥr ḥ]py [st]p ...

3:

nty im im3ḫy ḥr [ḥ]py

4:

wsir s3 nsw mr.f swty m3ꜥ ḫrw

2:     [over Ha]py ... [I] have extended ...
3:     he who is within, revered with [Ha]py
4:     the Osiris, king's son, whom he loves, Sety, true of voice

Object: **2:28**
Provenience: Chamber 2, north third, corner, 2.30 m below ceiling.
Material: Calcite
Dimensions: 10 x 6 x 2 cm
Owner: Amenherkhepeshef
Text:

1:

ḏd mdw in nbt.ḥt ḥp.t ...

2:

ḥr ḥpy stp.n.i s3w[.i] ḥr ...

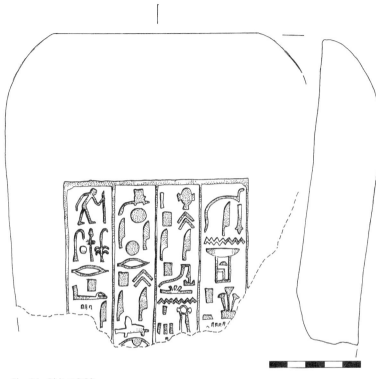

Fig. 94: Object 2.28.

3:

im3ḫy ḥr ḥpy wsir [s3 nsw]

4:

smsw sš nsw iry-pꜥt imn[-ḥr-ḫpš.f] ...

105

1: Recitation by Nephthys: "[I] embrace …

2: over Hapy, I have extended [my] protection over …

3: revered with Hapy, the Osiris, [king's]

4: eldest [son], royal scribe, hereditary prince, Amen-[her-khepeshef …]"

Object: 2.29

Provenience: Chamber 2, northeast quadrant, 2.30 cm below ceiling, 0.50 m from north and east walls.

Material: Calcite

Dimensions: 14 x 16 x 2 cm (largest)

Owner: Rameses Mery-Atum

Text:

1:

… s[ẖ]n.n.ꜥwy …

2: [stp.]n.i sꜣw.i ḥr nty im …

3: … ḳbḥsnwf wsir sꜣ nsw n ẖt [.f] …

4: … rꜥmss mry-itm …

1: … My arms embrace … [Note: the writing of sẖn is a metasthesis]

2: I have [extended] my protection over he who is within

3: … Qebhsenuef, the Osiris, king's bodily son

4: … Rameses Mery-Atum …

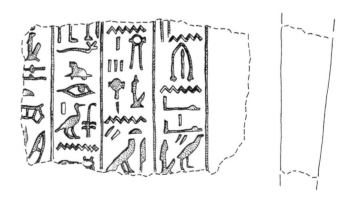

Fig. 95: Object 2.29.

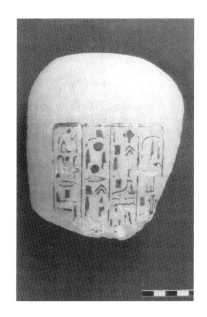
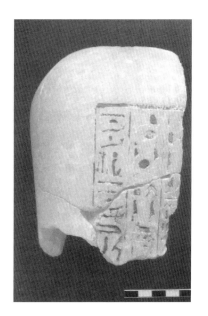
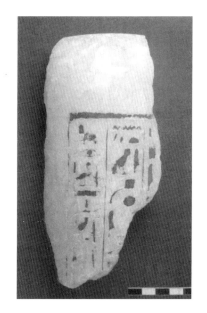
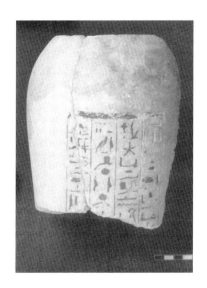
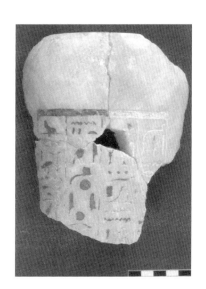

Fig. 96: Top left: Object 2.28. Top centre: Object 2.30. Top right: Object 2.10. Bottom left: Object 2.47. Bottom right: Object 3.31.

Object: **2.9; 2.30a, b, c**

Provenience: **2.9**: Chamber 2, southwest quadrant, 1.50 to 2.00 m below ceiling; **2.30a, b, c**: Chamber 2, northeast quarter, 2.30 m below ceiling, 0.70 m from north and east walls.

Material: Calcite

Dimensions: 17.4 x 11.5 x 3.2 cm

Owner: Rameses Mery-Atum

Text:

2: ![hieroglyphs]

ḥr ḥpy stp.n.i s3w.i.ḥr ...

3: ![hieroglyphs]

im3ḫy ḥr ḥpy wsir š⸢ nsw ...

4: ![hieroglyphs]

n it.f r⸢mss mryitm ...

2: over Hapy, I have extended my protection over ...

3: one revered with Hapy, the Osiris, king's bodily son ...

4: of his father, Rameses Mery-Atum ...

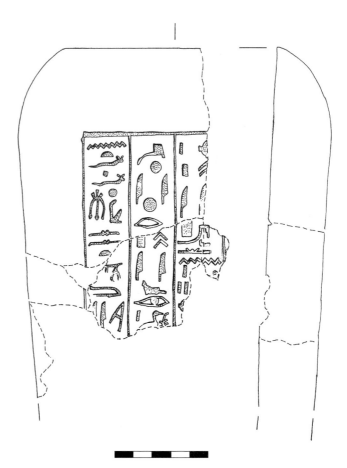

Fig. 97: Objects 2.9, 2.30a, b, c.

Object: 2.47a, b

Provenience: Chamber 2, pit.

Material: Calcite

Dimensions: 18.9 x 17.4 x 2.6 - 3.5 cm

Owner: Suty (?) or Mery-Amen (?) (Suty is consistently written
swty; there is no space for

before the *y*. If fragment **3.58** does join below the
fourth text column, then the owner is Mery-Amen)

Text:

1: *ḏd mdw in nt ink .n. ˹[wy]*

2: *i ḥr dw3-mwt.f stp.n.i s3[w] ...*

3: *nty im im3ḫy ḥr dw3[mwtf]*

4: *wsir s3 nsw n ẖt.f mry.f [?]y ...*

1:    Recitation by Neit: "I have brought my arms together
2:    over Dwamutef, I have extended [my] protection …
3:    he who is within, one revered with Dwa[mutef]
4:    the Osiris, king's beloved bodily son, [?]y …"

Fig. 98: Objects 2.47a, b.

Object: **3.31a, b, c**

Provenience: Chamber 3, 0.50 m east of door from Chamber 2, on floor.

Material: Calcite

Dimensions: **3.31a:** 10 x 7 x 2 cm; **3.31b:** 9 x 9 x 2 cm; **3.31c:** 14 x 6 x 3 cm

Owner: Suty

Text:

1:

... ḏd mdw in srḳt in[ḳ] ...

2:

ḥr ḳbḥ-snw.f stp.n.i s3[w.i] ...

3:

nty im im3ḫy ḥr [ḳbḥ-snw.f]

4:

wsir s3 nsw n ḫt.f sw[ty m3ꜥ ḫrw] ...

1: Recitation by Serqet "... brought together ...
(for: "[I] have brought [my arms] together")

2: over Qebehsenuef, I have extended [my] protection ...

3: he who is within, revered with [Qebehsenuef],

4: the Osiris, king's bodily son Su[ty] ..."

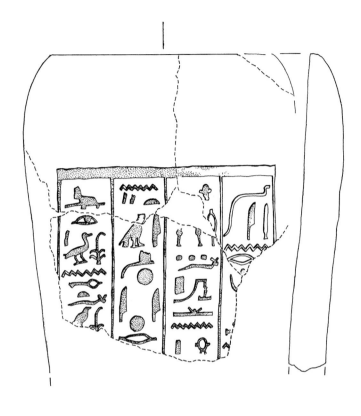

Fig. 99: Objects 3.31a, b, c.

Object: 3.58

Provenience: Chamber 3, 0.70 m south of pillar 3(b), 2.70 m below ceiling on plaster floor.

Material: Calcite

Dimensions: 7 x 8 x 3 cm

Owner: Mery(?)-Amen (may join **2.47a, b**)

Text:

... *imn m3ᶜ ḫrw*

... Amen, true of voice.

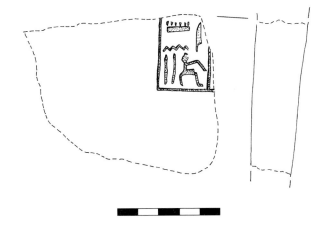

Fig. 100: Object 3.58.

111

Object: 12.10 - Offering Table

Material: Limestone

Provenience: Corridor 12, south side fill 1.00 to 2.00 m below ceiling.

Dimensions: 14 x 11 x 4 cm

Description: Two-thirds of an offering table in the form of a *ḥtp* sign with triangular areas flanking top bearing the first line of text. The remainder of the text is inscribed on the rectangular frame surrounding the sunken central portion inscribed with images of offerings, mostly lost.

Owner: (?)

Text:

1:

... *s3.f s'nḫ rn.f pn t*

2:

... *nṯr '3 mry.ty di.f šsp.i*

mw ... tp t3 ... i m3'ty n k3 n wsir ...

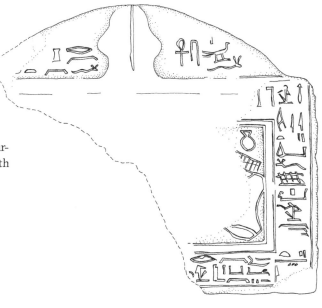

Fig. 101a: Object 12.10.

1: ... his son who causes his name to live, Pen ... t ...

2: ... beloved of (?) ... the great god, may he let me receive the water ... on earth ... Ma'aty, for the ka of the Osiris ...

Fig. 101b: Object 12.10.

Object: **1.9** (not shown)
Provenience: Chamber 1.
Dimensions: 14 x 12 x 15 cm
Material: Red granite
Description: Fragment of a sarcophagus with the head and shoulder of an anthropoid god in sunk relief, facing right. Stylistic features and dimensions of the figure suggest that it might be from the outer sarcophagus box of Merenptah, although there is no textual evidence for this supposition.

Object: **3.48**
Provenience: Chamber 3.
Dimensions: 22 x 22 x 10.7 - 15 cm
Material: Calcite
Description: Fragment of a sarcophagus lid with remains of two incised anthropoid figures facing left. The hand of a third figure can be seen to the right. Traces of blue and green pigment remain on the figures. Each figure is shown bent slightly forward at the waist. The figure on the left is higher than the right-hand one, suggesting that they stood on a sloping or stepped surface that rises to the left. Perhaps they form part of the scene in the fifth gate of the Book of Gates, representing the judgement hall of Osiris. If this is the case, they would be part of the group of nine figures ascending steps to the podium on which Osiris is enthroned before the balance of judgement. The exterior surface has a convex curve from top to bottom, the interior surface has a concave curve and the thickness of the fragment is greater at the top than the bottom.

Fig. 102: Object 3.48.

Inscribed Faïence Objects

Object: **2.48** (not shown)

Provenience: Chamber 2, crack in west wall, 0.50 m above floor.

Dimensions: 1 x 1.5 x 0.25 cm

Material: Faïence

Description: Flat oval ring bezel with broken ends of ring attached, light blue-green glaze, incised with pre-nomen of either Thutmes III or Thutmes IV. The uncertainty arises from the presence of two short vertical lines incised below the scarab. Three lines would be expected for Thutmes IV and no lines for Thutmes III.

Text:

Fig. 103: Object 12.3.

Object: **12.3**

Provenience: Corridor 12, entry, 0 - 0.50 m below ceiling.

Dimensions: 4 x 2.9 x 1 cm

Material: Faïence

Description: Fragment of a plaque(?), light blue glaze on two sides, partial cartouche of Thutmes III or Thutmes IV in black. Note: three faïence plaques from the tomb of Thutmes III (KV 34) of similar dimensions, JdE 32232 a, b, c.

Text:

Ostraca

Object: 2.8
Provenience: Chamber 2, southwest quadrant, 2.20 m below ceiling.
Dimensions: 10 x 8 x 1 cm
Material: Limestone
Description: Flake with part of four lines of text on one side and part of two lines of text on the other.

Object: 3.21
Provenience: Chamber 3, 1.00 m north of door to 12, 2.00 m below ceiling.
Dimensions: 8 x 3 x 2 cm
Material: Limestone
Description: Flake with traces of bird glyph in red.

Object: 3.66 (not shown)
Provenience: Chamber 3, southeast corner of pillar 3(b), between plaster floor and rock floor.
Dimensions: 4.2 x 2.4 x 0.6 cm
Material: Nile silt
Description: Sherd with part of one line of hieratic in black, whose beginning, end, and lower edge of text are missing.

Object: 3.89
Provenience: Chamber 3, area between pillar 3(e) and north wall, 0.15 m above floor.
Dimensions: 7.5 x 7.8 x 0.8 cm
Material: Imported marl
Description: Sherd with part of first three lines of hieratic text in black.

Object: 7.14
Provenience: Corridor 7, floor.
Dimensions: 4.23 x 3 cm
Material: Pottery
Description: Sherd with part of one line of hieratic text.

Object: 11.5
Provenience: Side-chamber 11g, near rear wall, 1.00 - 2.00 m.
Dimensions: 15 x 13 x 3 cm
Material: Limestone
Description: Flake inscribed on two sides in black ink. Stern of boat on one side and two columns of cursive hieroglyphs on the other side.

Text:

x+1:
...itm...

x+2: alternately
...n b3... ...nw...

Object: 12.11
Provenience: Corridor 12, south side 1.00 m below ceiling.
Dimensions: 3.54 x 3.5 x 0.25 cm
Material: Nile silt, cream slip
Description: Sherd with part of hieratic text in black.

Fig. 104: Top row, left to right: objects 2.8 (obverse and reverse), 3.21, 3.89.
Bottom row, left to right: objects 7.14, 11.5 (obverse and reverse), 12.11.

P O T T E R Y

Barbara Greene

The pottery selection presented here comprises a small sample of the pottery recovered from the fill in KV 5 and studied by the author during two weeks in November 1997.[1]

Flood debris (layers of packed mud, sand, and gravel) has penetrated all of the many rooms examined up to the present time. Twentieth Dynasty, Late Period and Coptic pottery have been washed in with the flood debris and mingled with the original contents of the tomb. Weathered sherds and sherds from the Coptic Period have been found in every context examined so far, from Chamber 1 to Chamber 17. Chamber 2 was filled with three meters of flood debris; when cleared, a rectangular pit was revealed along the north wall. There was a concentration of New Kingdom marl clay (Marl D) amphora sherds with numerous joins from within the pit and in the fill over the pit. These are not weathered and are probably original to the tomb, indicating that other material in the pit may be also. There was a concentration of Nile silt footed beakers of Twenty-fifth to Twenty-sixth Dynasty date (minimum count of nineteen) in chambers 1 and 2 which had been used as lamps. Perhaps these were brought by plunderers and abandoned in the outer rooms on their way out of the tomb.

Of the pottery assigned to the Nineteenth Dynasty, and therefore likely to be original to the tomb, some, such as the dishes, beer jars, and meat jars have a date range which extends from the late Eighteenth to the Twentieth Dynasty. The sharp-shouldered Canaanite jars with heavy bases

Sherd Count From Excavated Chambers of KV 5		
Chamber	Number of sherds	Comments
1	3,025	many whole vessels
2	4,235	many whole vessels
3	14,326	only partially cleared
4	660	
7	2,712	
8	450	
8c	240	
9	684	
9b	104	
11	794	only partially cleared
11j	105	
11k	140	
12	3,558	
12k	369	
13	791	
14	5,675	only partially cleared
15	2,001	
16	1,947	only partially cleared
17	222	
20	2,556	only partially cleared

(Nos. 10 - 12) and the round-based Marl D amphorae (Nos. 8 - 9), on the other hand, do not date later than the Nineteenth Dynasty.

The dynastic Egyptian fabrics are described with reference to the 'Vienna System.'[2] Nile B2 is characterized by a brown section, often with a faint red or black core, conspicuous

Fig. 105: Barbara Greene studying pottery from KV 5.

Fig. 106: Dr. Michael Jesudason sorting pottery from KV 5.

fine straw (< 2 mm), and fine to medium sand grains. Marl A4 is a uniform pink in section (green when highly fired), often with a light gray surface. It is characterized by fine sand and numerous fine pores from burnt-out limestone. Marl D is harder and denser with a reddish-brown section, often with a gray core. Inclusions consist of abundant fine to medium white limestone and some sand. All examples are covered in a thick cream slip. Canaanite jar fabrics are described with the Saqqara/Memphis terminology. P11[3] has a uniform orange section with abundant fine sand; P40[4] is characterized by a light brown outer zone with a gray core and fine to coarse multi-colored sand with a few red particles; while P30[5] has a white surface, thin outer zone of red, and wide inner zone of gray. Inclusions comprise abundant fine limestone and fine sand.

The Coptic Nile silt fabrics are generally coarser and more highly fired than their New Kingdom counterparts. No. 23 is made from a specialized 'cooking pot fabric' containing abundant fine sand and mica. The vessels are thin-walled and normally ribbed. No. 27 is an example of Haye's Egyptian Red Slip 'A' from Aswan[6], while 28-29 are the common brown Egyptian wine amphorae found all over Egypt.

The diameter (Di.) is measured at the lip of the vessel (the part of the rim having contact with a level plain if the pot were stood upside down).

Nineteenth Dynasty

1. Dish with inflected contour and rounded base (P-48)
   Nile B2 uncoated
   Di. 22.5 cm. Pht. 4.5 cm.
   Chamber 2, lowest meter of fill above pit

2. Rim of dish with inflected contour (P-69)
   Nile B2 red-slipped rim on uncoated interior,
   uncoated exterior
   Di. 22.0 cm. Pht. 3.2 cm.
   Chamber 2, top of fill

3. Rim of large dish with simple contour (P-85)
   Nile B2 uncoated
   Di. 38.0 cm. Pht. 4.5 cm.
   Chamber 8
   Three rows of string impressions on outside.

4. Beer jar rim (P-52)
   Nile B2 uncoated
   Base di. 9.5 cm. Pht. 5.5 cm.
   Chamber 2, lowest meter of fill above pit

5. Beer jar base (P-16)
   Nile B2 uncoated
   Base di. 6.9 cm. Pht. 8.9 cm.
   Chamber 2, pit
   Base is uneven and lumpy, indented by fingers.

6. Beer jar base (P-83)
   Nile B2 white slipped (pre-firing)
   Base di. 7.6 cm. Pht. 22.5 cm.
   Chamber 2, lowest meter of fill
   Thin ring base, roughly turned on wheel; small finger
   indents around outside of base. Slip does not extend
   completely to base.

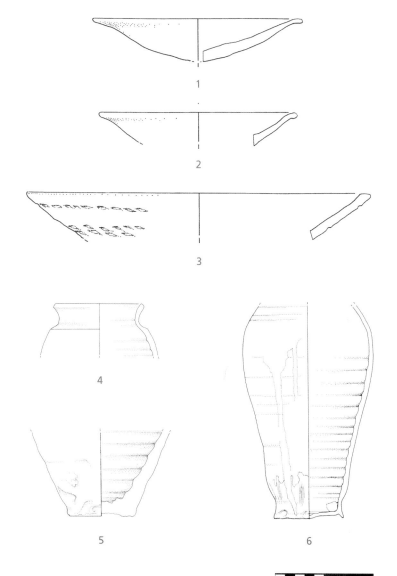

Fig. 107: Objects 1 - 6.

7. 'Meat' jar rim (P-2)
    Marl A4
    Di. 16.7 cm. Pht. 6.7 cm.
    Chamber 2, pit and Chamber 1

8. Amphora (P-24)
    Marl D cream slipped
    Di. 16.8 cm. Pht. 14.9 cm.
    Chamber 2, lowest meter of fill, and Chamber 1

9. Amphora rim/neck (P-25)
    Marl D cream slipped
    Di. 22.0 cm (approx.). Pht. 21.8 cm.
    Chamber 2, pit and fill above pit

10. Canaanite jar rim (P-72)
    P11
    Di. 9.0 cm. Pht. 5.1 m.
    Chamber 2, top meter of fill

11. Canaanite jar shoulder with handle (P-1)
    P11
    Pht. 20.8 cm.
    Chamber 2, pit and lowest meter of fill above pit

12. Canaanite jar base (P-91), rim, shoulder, handle
    P40
    Base di. 6.0 cm. Pht. 13.0 cm.
    Side-chamber 9b

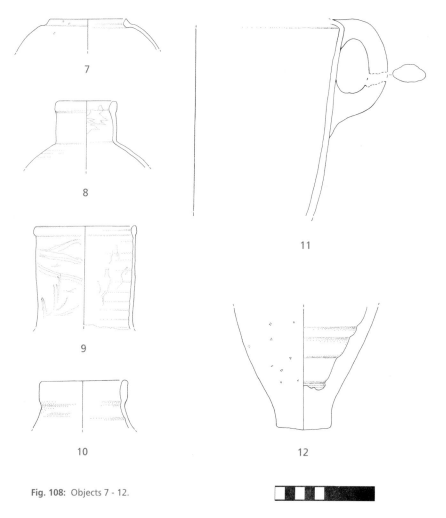

Fig. 108: Objects 7 - 12.

13. Dish with modeled rim (P-18)
    Marl A4
    Di. 16.5 - 16.9 cm. Pht. 6.1 cm.
    Chamber 2, pit and lowest meter of fill above pit

14. Carinated bowl (P-100)
    Nile B2 uncoated on the interior, cream/pink slipped
    exterior with added decoration in red. Two rows of
    string impressions at point of carination.
    Pht. 5.5 cm.
    Chambers 3 and 4

15. Carinated bowl body shard (P-102)
    Marl A4 uncoated with added decoration in black.
    Pht. 5.0 cm.
    Chamber 3.

16. Cup (P-66)
    Nile B2 uncoated
    Di. 9.7 - 10.4 cm. Ht 7.9 cm.
    Chamber 2, lowest meter of fill
    Base trimmed on wheel. Slightly warped rim.

17. Iron I Canaanite Jar base (P-92)
    P30
    Base di. 7.0 cm. Pht. 11.3 cm.
    Side-chamber 9b

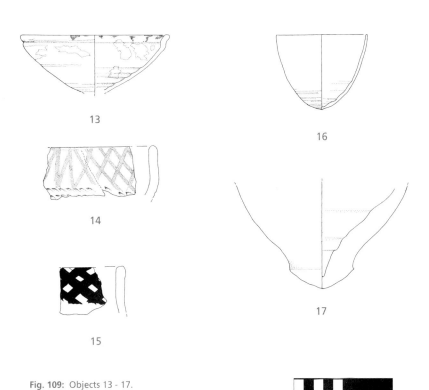

13

14

15

16

17

Fig. 109: Objects 13 - 17.

Twenty-fifth to Twenty-sixth Dynasties

18. Beaker (P-4)
     Nile B2 uncoated
     Di. 18.6 cm. Ht. 10.9 cm.
     Chamber 1
     Burned patches inside.

19. Beaker (P-5)
     Nile B2 uncoated
     Di. 16.0 cm. Ht. 11.2 cm.
     Chamber 1
     Burned patches inside.

20. Beaker (P-3)
     Nile B2 uncoated
     Di. 16.5 cm. Ht. 12.1 cm.
     Chamber 1
     Burned patches inside.

21. Beaker base (P-47)
     Nile B2 uncoated
     Base di. 10.3 cm. Pht. 7.7 cm.
     Chamber 2, lowest meter of fill above pit
     Burned patches inside. Finger indented.

22. Lid (P-42)
     Nile B2 uncoated
     Di. 6.2 cm, max. di. 10.1 cm. Ht. 5.0 cm.
     Chamber 2, fill above pit

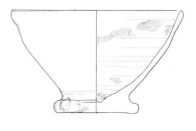

18

20

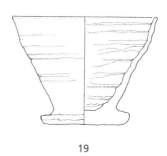

19

21

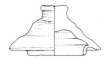

22

Fig. 110: Objects 18 - 22.

Coptic Period

23. Cooking pot (P-61)
    Nile silt, uncoated
    Di. 9.1 cm. Ht. 18.1 cm.
    Chamber 2, fill above pit

24. Cooking pot (P-49)
    Nile silt, uncoated
    Di. 15.0 cm. Pht. 11.2 cm.
    Chamber 2, fill above pit

25. Tall jar (P-51)
    Coarse Nile silt fabric, white slipped
    Di. 8.3 cm. Pht. 12.3 cm.
    Chamber 2, fill above pit

26. Saqiya-pot ("Qadus") base (P-64)
    Nile silt, uncoated
    Base di. 5.2 cm. Pht. 3.5 cm.
    Chamber 2, fill in SW quadrant

27. Bottle (P-99)
    Egyptian Red Slip A
    Di. 1.9 cm. Pht. 4.6 cm.
    Chamber 17

28. Amphora rim/neck (P-79)
    Brown Nile silt
    Di. 11.1 cm. Pht. 16.1 cm.
    Chamber 2, fill in SE quadrant

29. Amphora base (P-89)
    Brown Nile silt
    Pht. 18.7 cm.
    Chamber 9b

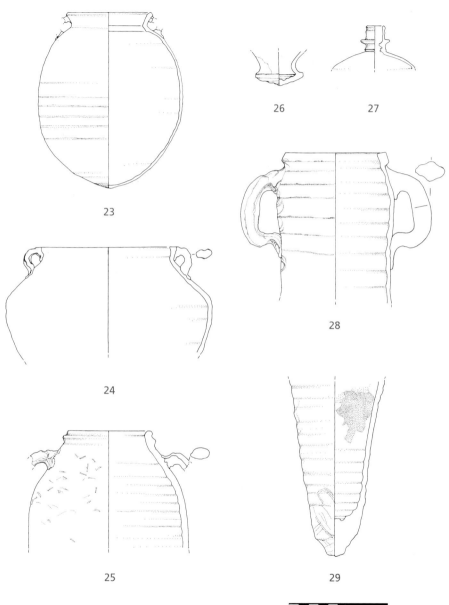

23

26   27

28

24

25   29

Fig. 111: Objects 23 - 29.

NOTES

1. Reconstruction and drawing of the pottery is being carried out by Susan Weeks and her assistants.

2. **J. Bourriau**. *Umm el-Gab: Pottery from the Nile Valley*. Cambridge, 1981. Pp. 14-15; **H.-A. Nordstrom**. Ton. *LÄ* VI: 631-4; **H.-A. Nordstrom** and **J. Bourriau**. Ceramic Technology: Clays and Fabrics. In: **Do. Arnold** and **J. Bourriau** (eds.) *An Introduction to Ancient Egyptian Pottery*. Mainz, 1993. Pp. 168-82.

3. **D. Aston**. In: **G. Martin**. *The Tomb of Tia and Tia*. London, 1997. P. 93.

4. Ibid. P. 94.

5. **D. Aston**. In: **M. Raven.** *The Tomb of Irudef*. London, 1991. P. 49.

6. **J. Hayes**. *Late Roman Pottery*. London, 1972. Pp. 387-397.

FAUNA

Salima Ikram

The faunal remains from KV 5 are extremely varied, with bones from both domestic and wild fauna forming the assemblage. This report covers most of the material excavated in the period of June 1988 to March 1999. The bones from chambers 1 - 4, chambers 7 - 13 (including some of the material found in the annexes to these rooms), Chamber 17, and Corridor 20 were examined, leaving the bones from chambers 14 - 16 still to be studied. The contents of a few of the bone bags from Chamber 14 were cursorily inspected, giving a general impression of the faunal contents of that room. When looking at final bone counts a major factor should be borne in mind: the individual rooms are of different areas and have not been equally cleared. Thus, the total number of bones found in each area (see Fig. 114) can be misleading.

The question of animal bone deposition in KV 5 is an interesting one. In addition to being placed in the tomb as part of the original funerary offerings, bones have subsequently entered the tomb in one of a variety of ways: they have been washed into the tomb by floodwaters, brought into the tomb by animals who had their dens there, or thrown into the tomb by humans. They may also be the remains of animals which lived in and/or died in the tomb. Bones bearing butchery marks would indicate humans as depositional agents; however, it is also possible that scaveng-ing animals, such as dogs (*Canis familiaris*) or foxes (*Vulpes*), brought such bones into the tomb from a nearby settlement, as many bones bear carnivore gnaw-marks. Certainly some bones, such as those of pigs (*Sus scrofa*) and other domesticates, might date

from the time when the Valley of the Kings was the site of a Coptic settlement, and the bones were either thrown or washed into the tomb or brought in by animals. However, the small number of bird bones is a curiosity, as one would expect some to have come from the settlement area. Certainly, other tombs in the Valley, such as KV 10, contain a significant number of bird bones. Similarly, donkey bones found in the tomb might date from the time when the mouth of the Valley was used as a donkey stabling area, but this is less likely as one would expect a greater number and larger variety of donkey bones than have thus far been found.

METHODOLOGY

The bones were collected by hand while excavating and by screening through a 5 millimeter by 5 millimeter wire mesh in excavation loci and lots within each room. The remains were studied in these room groupings with the idea that eventually they would be re-examined by taxa and element to see if there are any joins/relationships between bones found in different rooms. Some bones found in different areas of the same room were related. All bones were examined. Information recorded for each bone included: taxon, element, portion, side, age, butchery marks, being worked, being gnawed, burn marks, erosion, and breakage patterns. Fragments (measuring over 1.5 centimeters at least) of limb bones, ribs, and vertebrae that were identifiable only by mammal size were counted but not weighed. Mandibles and maxillae with teeth embedded were counted as one bone, although noted as being comprised of a group consisting of bones and teeth. The ageing systems for bones that were used were Silver (1969), Grant (1982), and Payne (1973). Human bones were found throughout the tomb but do not form part of this report.

RESULTS AND INTERPRETATION

Thus far 1,280 bones have been examined. Out of these only 446 bones have been identified to genus, species, and anatomical element (see Figs. 113, 114, and 115). Four bones remain unidentified, while 830 bones have been identified as belonging to limbs, vertebrae, or ribs of Large (e.g. cattle, camels), Medium to Large (younger cattle, antelope), Medium (sheep, goat), Medium to Small (fox), or Small (hare) Mammals. Out of the rooms studied the majority of bones come from Chamber 3. This, the Pillared Hall, is one of the largest rooms in the tomb. With over 50% of the room cleared, it is not surprising that it has yielded the largest number of bones. Of all the rooms, the following have been completely excavated: 1, 2, the pit in 2, 7, 8, 8a, 9, 9b, 11k, 11l, 12, 12a, 12k, 13, 15, and 17. Chambers 3, 4, 7a, 7l, 10, 11, 14, 16, and 20 have been partially cleared. All the other rooms have not been excavated. All the rooms that have been completely or partially excavated have yielded animal bones.

A cursory examination of breakage patterns shows that throughout the tomb the bones appear to be equally broken up. The weathering pattern, for the most part, is relatively uniform save for the bones that were recovered from the upper strata of each room, especially from chambers 1, 2, and 3. These bones are more eroded than those found in chambers 11 to 14. In most rooms bones appear throughout

Fig. 112: Foreleg of a cow (at center) found in the pit of Chamber 2.

the debris, generally concentrated in the areas from 250 centimeters above floor level down to the floor. As might be expected, within each layer of flood deposition the lighter and smaller bones or fragments are on the top of the layer, and the heavier ones at the bottom. Occasionally, later floods and animal activity churned up some of these layers. Bones from the whole tomb, but especially those found in the lower rooms, show a pinky-purplish discoloration. This is due to a desert fungus which is often found on bones excavated in Egypt from areas which have had brief moist spells alternating with long dry ones.

Chamber 1 contained only six bones of which one, a bird vertebra, might have blown in from outside. All bones recovered from this room were from domesticates. Chamber 2 contained 124 bones, most from different sized mammals and cows, with the largest number of bird bones recovered from any of the chambers. The pit in Chamber 2 contained one of the most interesting finds: the right articulated foreleg of a cow that was approximately three-and-a-half years old when killed (see Fig. 112). This was clearly placed on the human burial(s) found in the pit in Chamber 2 as a funerary offering. The foreleg of a cow is one of the most traditional of ancient Egyptian food offerings (Ikram 1995). When found the bones were bare, although articulated. It is possible that the joint was placed on the burial with the flesh intact and this has disintegrated over time, a phenomenon which this author has observed in other funerary offerings (e.g. at Dahshur and Saqqara). It is unlikely that a defleshed but articulated piece of meat was placed in the burial. There is a slight possibility that this joint, and the one found in Chamber 8 (see below) were once wrapped in linen, as were other funerary offerings such as those belonging to Yuya, Maiherperi, Isetemkheb D, and Tutankhmen, among others (see Ikram 1995).

Chamber 3, as mentioned above, is one of the largest chambers in KV 5. It is only 20% cleared, but the highest number of animal bones recovered from KV 5 are from here. The majority of identified bones from this room come from a cow (*Bos taurus)*, including a left foreleg, which might be a funerary offering. The foreleg belongs to an animal that was about three-and-a-half to four years old. At this point it is not clear if this leg is from the same animal as the one found in the pit in Chamber 2. The weathering on this group of leg bones is strange; it almost looks as if the joint had been

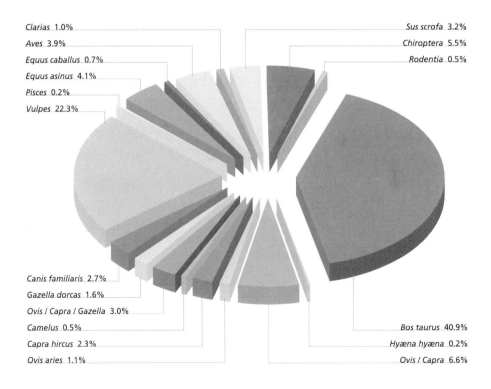

Clarias 1.0%
Aves 3.9%
Equus caballus 0.7%
Equus asinus 4.1%
Pisces 0.2%
Vulpes 22.3%

Canis familiaris 2.7%
Gazella dorcas 1.6%
Ovis / Capra / Gazella 3.0%
Camelus 0.5%
Capra hircus 2.3%
Ovis aries 1.1%

Sus scrofa 3.2%
Chiroptera 5.5%
Rodentia 0.5%

Bos taurus 40.9%
Hyæna hyæna 0.2%
Ovis / Capra 6.6%

Fig. 113: Distribution of bones found, by species.

boiled as the distal end of the humerus and the proximal articulations of the radius/ulna, the parts with the least amount of meat coverage, are more cracked and distressed than the rest of the bone. Another right radius/ulna and a left humerus bone of a mature (four year old or more) cow bone also shows a slight burn at the distal articular end. Most of the other cattle bones from this room belong to mature animals, three-and-a-half years old or more. Chamber 3 also contained a relatively high number of ovicaprine remains. One of the goat (*Capra hircus*) bones found here bore butchery marks, as did an ovicaprid tibia fragment, thus clearly identifying these as food sources. A fox (*Vulpes*) also died in this chamber, as almost its entire skeleton was recovered from Chamber 3.

Chamber 4 contains a great many *B. taurus* bone fragments, most coming from the skull of one animal. It also contains bones from at least two pigs (*Sus scrofa*), one of which was between sixteen to twenty-two months old at death. Pigs this old are quite large and are still consumed at this age in modern Egypt. One of the two camel bones found in the tomb comes from this chamber. Bones of a young fox also came from this room. Corridor 7, and side-chambers 7a, 7o, and 7l contained some domesticates as well as two definite and one possible gazelle bone. The number of donkey bones was quite high; the donkeys are mature, aged over three-and-a-half years, based on epiphysial fusion. Chambers 8 and 8c contained mainly *B. taurus* bones as well as the only rodent bone thus far recovered (Chamber 8). It is rather surprising that so few rodent bones have been found as there are numerous examples of bones gnawed by rodents. One bone, coming from Chamber 8, is of particular interest. It appears to be from some type of antelope and shows evidence of being wrapped in linen, as is the custom for funerary offerings (see above). It is currently being counted as a Medium to Large Mammal bone until its identification is secure.

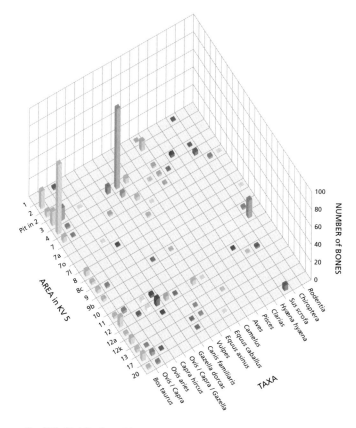

Fig. 114: Distribution of bones found, by room and species.

Chambers 9 and 9b, located opposite Chamber 8, contained many more bones than Chamber 8, with a greater diversity of fauna: *Equus asinus, Canis familiaris*, and a bat (Order *Chiroptera*, either *Rousettus, Taphozous*, or *Rhinopoma*) were found in addition to *Bos* and *Ovis/Capra*. The donkeys were quite old as shown by tooth wear and epiphysial fusion. The *Bos* bones in Side-chamber 9b and some of the Large

Mammal fragments were coloured a strange shade of orange that might be derived from ochre. Corridor 10, a partially cleared passage, contained nothing of interest, while Corridor 11 contained remains of several domestic animals as well as a *Clarias* (catfish) headbone. Catfish occur both in the Nile and in canals and are a very popular food source as they can yield quite a lot of flesh and are relatively easy to catch. *Clarias* headbones are also very robust, and survive well in the archæological record. Despite their solidity, the only other catfish bones thus far found in the tomb come from Chamber 3.

Corridor 12, a steeply sloping corridor, and its side-chambers contain the greatest diversity of animal remains. These include domesticates as well as wild animals, ranging from *Bos* to *Hyæna hyæna*. The cattle remains from this chamber show some of the youngest cattle remains found in the tomb: one individual was between five to six months old, and another was between two and two-and-a-half years old. The greatest number of gazelle bones that have been found thus far come from this area. The gazelles' ages ranged from six months to adult. Chamber 13, a small narrow space, contained far fewer and less diverse bones than Chamber 12 did, but its relatively small size might be responsible for this. Although Chamber 14's fauna has not yet been properly studied, the few bags that were cursorily examined showed a high number of hyena and fox bones, with an occasional gazelle bone fragment appearing in the assemblage as well. It is possible that at an earlier period in the tomb's history Chamber 14 was more easily accessible from the outside and used as a hyena den, and the gazelle bones are the result of the hyenas' hunts. However, the depth of this chamber makes this usage surprising as hyenas generally do not require such a deep and secret den. Examination of the remains from this room should shed some more light on its history. Chamber 17 is a very small

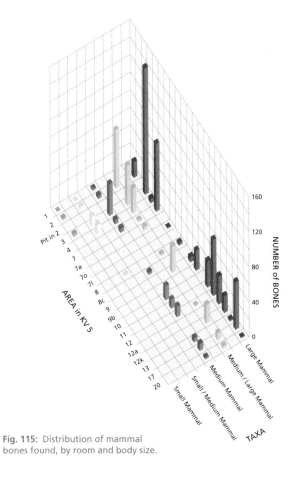

Fig. 115: Distribution of mammal bones found, by room and body size.

area which contained a few bones of cattle, sheep/goat, as well as an equid. Corridor 20 is remarkable for the (relatively) high number of pig bones that it contains. The pigs seem to be between eighteen and twenty-two months old. One of the cows found in Corridor 20, seems, based on tooth-wear, to be well over five years old: all three lower molars are extremely worn.

Out of the identified bones of domestic animals, the most commonly represented animal type is cattle, then ovicaprids, donkeys, and then pigs, with horses (*Equus caballus*) and camels (*Camelus dromedarius*) being least common. This distribution is rather surprising as throughout Egyptian history cattle have been considered higher status food animals, with ovicaprids and pigs being more commonly consumed. It is possible, given the age of many of the cattle bones, that the majority of these were not kept for food, but were used as draught animals that either died or were killed and consumed when they became old and useless. Further analysis on more material should help clarify this question. Given the proximity of a Coptic settlement, the paucity of pig bones is also interesting. Pigs, as well as goats, would flourish in a village, thus one might expect more bones from both these species to be present. The highest number of pig bones (six) comes from Corridor 20, an area deep in the tomb; the other pig concentration is in Chamber 4, which contains four pig bones. Perhaps work in chambers 5 and 6 will reveal more.

Zooarchæological analysis still remains to be done on some of the already excavated chambers, notably Chamber 14, which contains some of the most interesting and better stratified/contexted bones in the tomb, save for those found in the pit in Chamber 2. At this preliminary stage, it appears that the deeper areas of the tomb contain a higher percentage of wild animals than the more shallow parts of the tomb. At this point, due to bioturbation and the preliminary nature of this investigation, it is difficult to say which of the bones studied formed part of the original tomb deposit, and which were deposited later in the tomb's history. The pottery from each locus, one possible source of dating criteria, is fairly varied, ranging from New Kingdom to Coptic in date. Thus, the ceramics (as yet) do not provide a straightforward chronology. Even the burial in the pit in Chamber 2, with its accompanying cattle foreleg, clearly placed as a funerary offering, is a re-burial, with the same melange of pottery dates. One cannot be sure whether the other cattle forelimbs recovered from Chamber 3 are even funerary offerings, let alone be certain of their date. The mummified animal bone from Chamber 8 is definitely a funerary offering (victual mummy), but whether it comes from KV 5 or was washed in is unclear. It is even possible that it might date to the original use of KV 5: a modestly proportioned tomb of Eighteenth Dynasty date. Certainly the majority of victual mummies date to the Eighteenth Dynasty, although some are known from the Nineteenth and Twenty-first Dynasties as well (Ikram 1995: Appendix II). It is hoped that further investigation into the faunal remains of KV 5 sheds light not only onto the original burial, but also the subsequent history of the tomb.

BIBLIOGRAPHY

Brewer, D. and **R. Friedman.** *Fish and Fishing in Ancient Egypt.* Cairo: American University in Cairo Press, 1989.

Grant, A. The Use of Tooth Wear as a Guide to the Age of Domestic Ungulates. In: **B. Wilson, C. Grigson,** and **S. Payne** (eds.) *Ageing and Sexing Animal Bones from Archae-ological Sites.* Oxford: BAR British Series, 1982.

Ikram, S. *Choice Cuts: Meat Production in Ancient Egypt.* Leuven: Peeters, 1995.

Payne, S. Kill-off patterns in sheep and goats: the mandibles from Asvan Kale. *Anatolian Studies* 23 (1973): 281-303.

Silver, I. A. The Ageing of Domestic Animals. In: **D. Broth-well** and **E. S. Higgs** (eds.) *Science in Archaeology.* London: Thames and Hudson, 1969.

CONSERVATION, 1994-1999

Lotfi Khaled Hassan

INTRODUCTION

Because of its location on the floor of the Valley of the Kings, KV 5 has suffered from repeated flooding over the millennia. Water spilling over the cliffs rushed down the *wadi* and settled in the lowest levels. As a result, from the time the tomb was first cut or its entrance breached during the reign of Rameses II, both the rock and the wall paintings have been damaged through the accumulation of salts and the expansion and contraction of the stone. These factors have so affected the layer of painted plaster that much has fallen off. Even the layer of stone beneath (some carved in relief) has suffered.

When first discovered by James Burton in 1825, the tomb's entrance was blocked by debris. Clearance, beginning in 1989, has revealed a large accumulation of water-borne material, providing evidence of at least eleven flood events.

Beginning in 1994, a number of long- and short-term conservation measures have been instituted to repair the damage to the tomb and to stabilize the wall paintings. These measures have included cleaning and consolidating the wall-plaster, filling cracks, and preserving organic remains and small finds. Studies of the materials used in finishing the tomb have also been undertaken. The first part of this report is concerned with the latter, while the second describes the actual conservation procedures.

I. MATERIALS AND TECHNIQUES

Investigating the original materials and techniques used in constructing and finishing the tomb has increased our

Fig. 116: Lotfi Khaled Hassan conserving plaster relief inside KV 5.

understanding of its history and also the nature of past and present deterioration. In ancient times, plaster was also applied to give a smooth finish to walls considered unsuitable for carving. Plaster repairs were made to some of the faults in the rock walls, and ceilings were 'made good' with plaster patches.

Mortar in ancient Egypt

Two types of mortar were used in ancient Egypt before Græco-Roman times: clay for use with sun-dried bricks, and gypsum for use with stone. Clay mortar is simply ordinary Nile alluvium, consisting of clay and sand mixed with sufficient water to bring it to the required consistency. Gypsum mortar was burnt and slaked before use. It was mixed with sand to provide a compound of the proper consistency for application.

Plasters

Ancient Egyptian plaster is composed of the same materials as the two mortars, that is, clay and gypsum. Although both kinds were doubtless employed in the decoration of houses, such decoration has largely perished, and except for fragments of painted plaster found among the ruins of the palace of Amenhetep III at Malqata and the palaces and houses at el-Amarna, practically all the plaster that remains comes from tombs and temples.[1]

Clay Plaster

The use of clay plaster is known from as early as Predynastic times.[2] Its quality varies considerably, but two principal kinds may be recognized, one coarse and one fine. The coarser quality consists of ordinary Nile alluvium (essentially a mixture of clay and sand in varying proportions), with generally a small natural admixture of calcium carbonate, and occasionally a small proportion of gypsum. The latter, however, is purely accidental and has no binding property since it has not been burnt. It is generally, but not always, mixed with straw.

The finer quality is a natural mixture of clay and limestone, both in very fine particles. It is found in hollows and pockets at the foot of the hills and plateaus, washed out by the occasional rainstorm. This is still used locally, under the name of *hib*.[3] It is mixed either with or without straw and often applied as a finishing coat on top of a coarser layer. Its use may have been limited to the Theban Necropolis.

Gypsum Plaster

This is the typical wall plaster of ancient Egypt, known from Early Dynastic times. No evidence whatever can be found for the use of lime plasters before the Ptolemaic period.[4] Gypsum occurs plentifully in Egypt in two sets of locations: (1) in a rock-like formation to the west of Alexandria, in the district between Isma'ilia and Suez, in the Fayum, and near the Red Sea coast; and (2) in scattered masses of loosely-aggregated crystals, found just below the surface of the limestone desert.

It is the latter type of gypsum that was, and still is, commonly used for making plaster. At the present time, it is worked in the vicinities of Cairo and Beni Suef. There are small local deposits in other places. As found, gypsum is never pure, but contains varying proportions of calcium carbonate and quartz sand, together with small amounts of other ingredients. Ancient Egyptian plaster of the kind under consideration is crude gypsum that has been burnt, powdered and slaked, and any calcium carbonate it contains is not added artificially but is an impurity derived from the raw material in which it occurs naturally.

Gypsum, being a naturally-occurring material, varies considerably both in color and in composition. The color may be white, varying shades of gray, light brown, or even occasionally pink. This pink color, however, is merely an accidental surface discoloration due to chemical changes in the iron compounds of the plaster over thousands of years. When the color is gray, this is generally owing to the presence of small particles of unburned fuel.[5] Chemically, gypsum is calcium sulfate containing water in an inseparable combination. When brought to a temperature of about 100°C, gypsum loses about three-fourths of its water and forms a substance which has the ability to recombine with water to produce a material that sets and becomes very hard. The temperature for burning gypsum varies from about 100°C to about 200°C, but is generally kept at about 130°C, a heat readily obtained. This temperature is not sufficiently high to convert any calcium carbonate present into quicklime (to convert calcium carbonate into quicklime, a temperature of about 900°C is required).

Gypsum plaster was widely used in houses, palaces, tombs, and temples to provide a suitable surface for the application of paint. Where the wall was plastered with clay, it was generally finished with a coat of gypsum plaster. Where clay plaster was not used, gypsum plaster covered faults and irregularities in the stone and smoothed the surface for painting.

Application of Plaster

Occasionally, plaster used as a finishing coat – white, or practically white – has been found to contain a very large proportion of calcium carbonate and very little gypsum. Although this may be a poor quality gypsum containing the calcium carbonate naturally, it may also be an artificial mixture, additional calcium carbonate possibly having been added in order to produce a lighter color of plaster otherwise not white enough for the purpose required.

Sometimes the surface coating is so thin as to be merely a distemper or whitewash. In this state it consists essentially of calcium carbonate. It may contain a trace of gypsum, but this is probably simply an impurity and not the binding material. The latter may have been size, although whitewash adheres fairly well to limestone without the addition of a binder.

Plaster Studies in KV 5

Studies of plaster composition and methods of plaster application in KV 5 are currently underway.

Methodology

1) In 1996, three plaster samples (used to fill holes and cracks) taken from the side wall in Chamber 2, and two samples from the western wall of Chamber 3 were analysed by X-ray diffraction using a Philips analytical X-ray PW1710 BASED, using Cu Tube anode. The goal was to identify the compounds and proportions of their constituent materials.

2) In 1999, seven painted plaster samples were analyzed by X-ray diffraction using a Philips analytical X-ray PW1710 BASED, using Cu Tube anode. Two from the south and east wall of Chamber 1, four from the north wall of Chamber 3, and one from south side of column D of Chamber 3, were taken to identify the compounds of their constituent materials.

Results

The results indicated that all the plaster was gypsum-based $CaSo_4 \cdot 2H_2O$, calcite $CaCO_3$, and quartz SiO_2 with traces of other materials. The only exception was a small area of clay plaster on the southern wall of Chamber 2.

The plaster sample taken from the southern wall of Chamber 2 was made up of:

- Anchorite $Ca(Fe,Mg)(CO_2)_2$
- 20% sand SiO_2
- 70% Calcium carbonate $CaCo_3$
- very small percentage of other compounds such as Sepiolite $(Mg,Fe)_4Si_6O1_5(OH)_2 \cdot 6H_2O$, Despujolsite, Montmorillonite $ALSi_2O_6(OH)_2$, Sylvite KCL, Anchorite $(K,NH_4)2SO_4$, and Henouite $CaMg_5(CO_3)(PO_4)_3(OH)$.

The plaster samples (1, 2L) from Chamber 3 consisted of:

Sample No. 1
- 35% Calcium Carbonate $CaCO_3$
- 1% Calcium Sulphate(gypsum) 40% Sand SiO_2
- 7% Caminite $Mg_3 (SO_4)2(OH)_2$ 4%, Anchorite $Ca(Fe,Mg)(CO_3)_2$ and others.

Sample No. 2L
- 17% Gypsum $CaSO_4 2H_2O$
- 16% Calcite $CaCO_3$
- 9% Sand SiO_2
- 17% Brushite $CaPO_3(OH).2H_2O$, 2% Anchorite $Ca(Fe,Mg)(CO_3)_2$, and others.

Examination of the Wall-Paintings

The extant scenes in KV 5 have been carved in relief and/or painted. In some cases the stone surface was carved and the plaster applied over it also carved. In other parts of the tomb only carving of the plaster was undertaken. The walls of chambers 1 and 2 were covered with carved plaster from ceiling to floor level. The columns of Chamber 3 were covered with painted plaster from ground level up.

Pigments

Many different colored pigments were used – black, blue, green, red, yellow, and white.

Black

The black pigment was almost always carbon, obtained as soot probably scraped from the bottom of cooking vessels. Spurrell identified black pigment of the Twelfth Dynasty at Beni Hassan as charcoal and pyrolusite.

Three samples of the black color extracted from Chamber 3 (north wall) and Side-chamber 7l were analyzed by X-ray diffraction. The material identified in the pattern is carbon.

Blue

The Egyptian blues are very beautiful and range from a light sky blue to a dark ultramarine. The principal blue pigment of ancient Egypt was an artificial frit consisting of a crystalline compound of silica, copper, and calcium (calcium-copper silicate). This was made by heating together silica and a copper compound (generally malachite). The nature of Egyptian blue was uncovered only very recently through the thorough studies of Noll and laboratory investigation by Bayer and Weidem (1976) and Ulrich (1979). Egyptian blue was found almost without interruption in wall decorations from the Fifth Dynasty until the time when monuments were erected during the reign of Cæsar Tiberius.

The major component of the pigment is Cuprorivaite $Ca Cu Si_4 O$. Cuprorivaite could be synthesized below 1,050°C by heating a mixture of malachite, calcium carbonate, and silica according to the equation:

$$Cu_2 ((OH)_2 / CO_3) + 8 SiO_2 + 2 Ca CO_3 \longrightarrow \ddagger 2Ca Cu Si_4O_{10} + 3 CO_2 = H_2O$$

Two samples of blue (blue and dark blue) extracted from painted plaster on the north wall and south side of column D in Chamber 3 were analyzed by X-ray diffraction. The results indicated that the blue is Cuprorivaite, syn. $Ca Cu Si_4O_{10}$ (Egyptian blue).

Green

Noll and Hangst first identified copper-bearing Wollastonite (green frit). There are two types of fiollastonite: Type 1 with Wollastonite as a minor phase, and Type 2, a

Wollastonite-rich pigment with glass and silica as minor phases. Both types may be present in the sample due to a lack of thorough mixing during manufacture. Technologically the second type is superior because of the minor amount of hue. During the Old and Middle Kingdoms the glass-rich pigment appears more frequently. Starting with the reign of Thutmes III (material examined in TT 86, the tomb of Menkheperraseneb in Thebes), the Wollastonite-rich pigment appears more often. Its use seems to culminate in the Nineteenth Dynasty. The Wollastonite-bearing pigment was prepared by heating the same starting mixture for Egyptian blue under reducing conditions, whereupon Cuporoivaite breaks down to Cuprite, Silica, and Wollastonite according to the following equation:

$$2 Ca\, Cu\, Si_4 O_{10} \longrightarrow Cu_2 O + 6\, SiO_2 + 2\, Ca\, SiO_3 + 1/2\, O_2$$

Some samples of green color were examined from Twelfth and Eighteenth Dynasty tombs by Spurrell, who concluded that the Egyptian green was a mixture of yellow ochre and blue frit.

One green color sample extracted from painted plaster on the south wall of Chamber 2 in KV 5 was analyzed by X-ray diffraction. The results indicated that the green pigment is a mixture of Egyptian Blue (Calcium Copper tetrasilicate) and Orpiment (Arsenic Sulphide).

Red

Red can be seen more than any other color in this tomb. A popular belief is that the red pigment used by the Egyptians was red ochre, but this is incorrect. Ochre is yellow naturally and only turns red when burned or calcined. Ochre normally contains between ten percent to twenty percent iron oxide. The reds of the Egyptians contain more than fifty percent iron oxide, and from the orange/red hue it is certainly Hematite. This is never a very bright red, and is always associated with a brick color[6].

One sample of red color extracted from painted plaster from the north wall of Chamber 3 was analyzed by X-ray diffraction. The results indicated it is iron oxide (Hematite $Fe_2 O_3$).

Yellow

All of the yellows used in ancient Egypt were made of the native ochre, a clay stained with iron rust. The royal tombs of the Eighteenth Dynasty exhibit a fine selection and variety of various yellow pigments: yellow ochre Gethite $FeO\,(OH)$, Jarosite $(Na\, Fe_3)(SO_4)_2\,(OH)$, pure orpiment $As_2 S_3$, and ochre blended with orpiment. Noll (1977)[7] verified the presence of Dimorphite, $As_4 S_3$, in a mixture of ochre and other mineral components in paintings in the tomb of Horemheb (TT 78, ca. Thutmes III - Amenhetep II). This was the first evidence of blending ochre with a high-quality pigment to enhance the glaze and brightness.

Orpiment is not only used generously to decorate the hieroglyphs but also to inlay the deities carved on the sarcophagus of Thutmes III. A thin layer of brown resin identified by Jaksch (1985) as mastic covers the paint.[8] Orpiment was found in a pure form without the mastic cover on the sarcophagi of Amenhetep II and Thutmes IV. The pigment was never used in its pure form on wall decorations.

One yellow color sample from KV 5 is under study.

White

White pigments are among the earliest painting materials in use since the Predynastic period. Calcium carbonate and calcium sulfate (gypsum) were the only two white pigments known.

Spurrell found gypsum present from the Fourth Dynasty onward, but only calcium carbonate from the Twelfth Dynasty at el-Bersha. Russell found gypsum from the Greco-Roman period at Hawara. Lucas identified calcium carbonate from the Fifth Dynasty; calcium sulfate from the Sixth Dynasty; calcium carbonate and calcium sulfate from the Eighteenth Dynasty.

Prior to the New Kingdom, calcium sulfate and the carbonates were the dominant materials. The Hunitite $Mg_3 Ca (Co_3)_4$ was also used by the ancient Egyptians. This mineral is pure white and much brighter than calcium sulphates and carbonates. It also has good adhesion and suspension qualities. The pigment appeared for the first time in the New Kingdom, especially during the reigns of Hatshepsut and Thutmes III.

Two samples of white color extracted from chambers 2 and 3 were analyzed by X-ray diffraction. The patterns were obtained by means of a Philips analytical X-ray PW1710 BASED, using Cu Tube anode:

Sample 1: White color, Chamber 2 South Wall
The material seems to be a mixture of two phases, Calcium Carbonate $CaCO_3$ and Silica SiO_2.

Sample 2: White color, Chamber 3 North Wall
This sample is composed of Quartz SiO_2, Calcite $CaCO_3$, Bassanite $CaSO_4 ! 0.5H_2O$, and trace of Dolomite Ferroan $Ca(Mg,Fe)_9 (CO_3)_2$.

Binding Materials

The principal adhesives employed as cementing materials in ancient Egypt were albumin (white of egg), beeswax, clay, glue, gum, gypsum, natron, resin, salt, and starch.

One color sample from KV 5 was analyzed by infrared spectrometry to identify the binding material used in wall paintings. The results indicated that the bond material is a small portion of samg (gum).

Infrared report:

1. Qualitative inorganic
0.86   Silver perchlorate
0.85   Lithium tetrafluoroborate

2. Inorganic groups
Phosphates
Cyanides and Cyanates
Ammonium

3. Bond material
Small portion of samg (gum)

II. CONSERVATION PROCEDURES

Introduction

Conservation work in KV 5 began in 1994 with the cleaning and fixing of wall surfaces. Calcified salt was found to be heavily imbeded in the inscriptions. In 1996, the conservation and restoration of the wall paintings recommenced. Conservation of small finds and organic remains continued in tandem with the excavation.

1994: Conservation of Wall Surfaces
Quick Intervention

Mechanical cleaning of the entrance wall involved removal of a heavy cover of calcified salts occluding the inscriptions. Chamber 1 had some inscriptions on the plaster layer. There was a layer of plaster on most walls although the walls of the north and the northeast had not yet been discovered. The walls were treated on the west, north, and south sides only.

Consolidation by acrylic resin (Paraloid B72 in acetone) was used to strengthen the inscriptions. This was done when the chambers were dry (after cleaning). As a quick intervention, the edges of the plaster were fixed to the walls with mortar to prevent more fragments from falling off. This enabled conservation work of these walls to continue over the coming seasons.[9]

June 1996: Conservation of Wall Paintings Immediate Intervention[10]

Conservation intervention was carried out on:

1) The western wall of Chamber 3, along the doorway between Chamber 2 and Chamber 3

The western wall of Chamber 3 was covered with debris and surface dirt. Mechanical cleaning using scalpels, soft brushes, and special sponges, removed the dust, debris, and salt deposition.

Chemical cleaning was done in some areas using solvents (acetone) and a 2:1 solution of alcohol and distilled water.

Consolidation was done using acrylic emulsion Primal AC33 1:1 in distilled water to consolidate the cracks along the wall. Some traces of paint were also treated with Paraloid B72 in 3% acetone. Detached pieces of rock were fixed to the wall using both Araldite 106 (an epoxy resin) and mortar.

On the eastern side of the wall Primal AC33 was used to consolidate the ancient mortar. In some areas, cracks in the wall were filled with a mortar similar in consistency to the original compound. The mixture was made up of tomb dust, limestone powder, and gypsum, in the proportion of 1:1:2, as formulated respectively.

After application and prior to drying, the mortar was retouched with a wooden needle to give it a tough and more authentic look.

2) The walls on either side of Corridor 7, between doorways to side-chambers 7a and 7b

Mechanical cleaning was done on the side walls of Corridor 7 using scalpels and brushes. The plaster layers were consolidated with Primal AC33 mixed 1:1 with distilled water.

Additional Intervention

Endangered areas of plaster in chambers 1 and 2 were fixed with Japanese paper and Paraloid B72 15% as an interim measure.

November 1996: Conservation Intervention

During this time intervention was carried out on:

1) The paintings on the pit side wall of Chamber 2

The paintings were covered with debris and surface dirt. Because of the weakness of the plaster, all debris and dust up to a depth of one centimeter was taken off before conservation intervention. It was carefully removed using a scalpel and soft brushes, with some consolidation done during the removal process. The plaster was in bad condition. The higher areas of the walls were lost due to the presence of salt crystals (on and behind the plaster) and the fragile nature of the stone.

2) Eastern wall of Chamber 2 (pit side)

Mechanical cleaning using a scalpel and soft brushes was carried out. During this process some consolidation with mortar was effected to permit the continuation of the cleaning process.

Consolidation involved two materials, mortar and acrylic resin (Primal AC33 1:1) to consolidate the painted layer and the plaster, and Paraloid B 72 in 2% acetone to fix the colors. Filling was done using hydrolic mortar composed of tomb dust and gypsum in a 3:1 ratio with distilled water. The same material was used to consolidate the edges of the plaster and to fill in the missing parts.

3) Northern wall of Chamber 2

Mechanical cleaning was accomplished with a scalpel and soft brushes. During this process some consolidation with mortar was carried out to permit continuation of the cleaning process. Consolidation to secure the painting and plaster involved two materials, mortar and acrylic resin (Primal AC33 1:1). Paraloid B 72 in 2% acetone was used for fixing the colors.

To consolidate the edges of the plaster and to fill in the missing parts, hydrolic mortar composed of tomb dust and gypsum 3:1 with distilled water was used. Stacco, a method of detatching and reattaching plaster, was done on one piece of completely-detached painted plaster. The surface was covered with Japanese paper and strengthened with Paraloid B72 in a 12% acetone solution before the fragment was replaced.

4) Western wall of Chamber 2 (pit side)

Mechanical cleaning was effected with a scalpel and soft brushes. During this process some consolidation with mortar permitted continuation of the cleaning process. Some areas of relief were subjected to chemical cleaning, using alcohol in distilled water and acetone. Consolidation employed two materials, mortar and acrylic resin (Primal AC33 1:1) to consolidate the painted and plastered layers. Paraloid B 72 in 2% acetone was used for fixing the colors. To consolidate the edges of the plaster and to fill in the missing parts, hydrolic mortar composed of tomb dust

and Gypsum 3:1 with distilled water was used.

Stacco was done on one piece of painted plaster. The surface was covered with Japanese paper and strengthened with Paraloid B 72 in a 12% acetone solution before the fragment was replaced.

Consolidation Test

One consolidation test was conducted on the painted plaster covering the southern wall of Chamber 2 using Ethyl Silicate RC 70. Applied prior to cleaning, this chemical penetrates the plaster and the rock, entering its pores and consolidating from within. This enables mechanical cleaning to be carried out on the surface of the painted layers, which otherwise would have been damaged when touched.

Additional Intervention

Conservation and restoration of some objects (alabaster canopic jar fragments) from the excavations was carried out. Mechanical and chemical cleaning and consolidation employed the scalpel, applying alcohol in distilled water (0.5:12) and Paraloid B72 to fix the colored inlays.

April 1997: Conservation Intervention

Intervention was carried out on the wall paintings located on:

1) The wall paintings of the northern side of Chamber 2

Conservation and restoration of the northern wall of Chamber 2 continued during this season. Mechanical cleaning was carried out using scalpel and soft brushes. During this activity some consolidation with mortar permitted continuation of the cleaning process. Two materials, mortar and acrylic resin (Primal AC33 1:1), were injected to consolidate the painted and plastered layers. Paraloid B 72 in 2% acetone was used for fixing the colors. Filling was done using hydrolic mortar composed of tomb dust and gypsum in a 3:1 ratio with distilled water to consolidate the edges of the plaster and to restore the missing parts.

2) Eastern and western walls of Chamber 2, either side of the pit

Hydrolic mortar composed of lime and sand was used to fill deep holes and to prepare the area for application of the the final mortar.

3) Side wall of the entrance to Chamber 3

Consolidation and filling of the cracks and the hollow of the stone wall on both sides of the entrance to Chamber 3 was done using mortar (lime and sand) and epoxy resin (Araldite 456, Hardener 956) mixed with linen fibers.

4) Southern wall of Chamber 2

Conservation and restoration of wall paintings started from the southwest side of this room. Mechanical cleaning was done using scalpel and soft brushes. During this process some consolidation with mortar permitted the continuation of the cleaning process.

Consolidation was done by injecting two materials, mortar and acrylic resin (Primal AC33 1:1) to consolidate the painted and plastered layers. Paraloid B 72 in 2% acetone was used for fixing the colors.

Hydrolic mortar consisting of grey tomb dust from Chamber 3, red dust, white dust, and hydrolic lime (Lafarge) as 3.1:1:4 (inert: lime 2:1) was mixed with distilled water to consolidate the edges of the plaster and fill in the missing parts.

Additional Intervention

Conservation and restoration of some more fragments of alabaster canopic jars from the excavations was carried out. Mecanical and chemical cleaning and consolidation was effected using a scalpel, alcohol in distilled water and Paraloid B72 to fix the colored inlays.

In the bottom of the pit in Chamber 2, three human skulls, a complete skeleton, fragments of mummy wrapping, wooden objects, and a cooked leg of beef (a food offering for the deceased) were found. The identity of the individuals is unknown. Cleaning was carried out using soft brushes.

Graphic documentation, using drawings of the walls and colored symbols, was completed. This recorded (1) the state of conservation of the areas of intervention, and (2) treatment after intervention.

November 1997 - January 1998:
Conservation Intervention

Conservation of wall paintings on the southern wall of Chamber 2 continued during this season.

Mechanical cleaning was carried out using a scalpel and soft brushes. Some consolidation with mortar was carried out at the same time to permit the continuation of the cleaning process. Consolidation involved injecting two materials, mortar and acrylic resin (Primal AC33 1:1) to consolidate the painted and the plaster layers. Paraloid B 72 in 2% acetone was used to fix the colors. To consolidate the edges of the plaster and to fill in the missing parts, hydrolic mortar made of grey tomb dust from Chamber 3, red dust, white dust, and hydrolic lime (Lafarge) 3.1:1:4 (1:2 inert:lime) mixed with distilled water was used.

Conservation intervention was carried out on wall paintings on the northern wall of Chamber 1. Work started on half of the wall before any debris was removed. On the other half of the wall it was necessary to consolidate the first section of the wall before removing the debris from the northeast side. The plaster was in poor condition – weak, fragile, and hollow. The painted plaster was covered with an encrustation of dust and other residue.

Conservation Processes

Mechanical cleaning was carried out using a scalpel and soft brushes. During this process some consolidation with mortar permitted continuation. Consolidation was done by injecting two materials, mortar and acrylic resin (Primal AC33) 1:1 to consolidate the painted and the plaster layers. Paraloid B 72 in 2% acetone was used to fix the colors.

Consolidation of the edges of the plaster and the filling in of missing parts employed hydrolic mortar. This consisted of grey tomb dust from Chamber 3, red dust, white dust, and Hydrolic lime (Lafarge) 3.1:1:4 (1:2 inert : lime) mixed with distilled water.

Additional Intervention

Conservation and restoration of some more fragments of alabaster canopic jars and shabtis from the excavations were carried out. Mechanical and chemical cleaning and consolidation were effected using a scalpel, alcohol in distilled water, and Paraloid B72 to fix the colored inlays.

January - March 1999: Conservation Intervention

The conservation and restoration of wall paintings in KV 5 continued from November 1998 to March 1999 in tandem with the excavations. This began with the cleaning of the relief on the wall of Corridor 7, and the filling of the deep holes in chambers 1 and 2 with hydrolic mortar. The second step was conservation of the wall paintings on the western wall of Chamber 2 and the southern wall of Chamber 1.

Intervention was carried out on:

1) The relief on the northern wall of Corridor 7
   Mechanical Cleaning of the relief of the sides of the entrance to Chamber 9 employed scalpels and brushes. Consolidation was done by injecting two materials, mortar and acrylic resin (Primal AC33 1:1) into the plaster. Hollow parts were filled with hydrolic mortar. This process is as yet incomplete.

2) The deep holes in Chamber 1 and Chamber 2
   Filling, using two kinds of hydrolic mortar, was done to consolidate the deep holes and for aesthetic reasons. One mortar consisted of lime, sand and small pieces of stone for consistency; the other, of lime and tomb dust, (2:1 inert: lime) was used to produce a very fine, thin layer to match the current wall surface.

3) The northern wall in Chamber 2
   Mechanical cleaning was done using scalpel and soft brushes. During this process some consolidation with mortar was carried out to permit continuation. Consolidation of the painted and plastered layers by injection involved two materials, mortar and acrylic resin (Primal AC33 1:1). Paraloid B 72 in 2% acetone was used to fix the colors.

Filling was done using hydrolic mortar consisting of grey tomb dust from Chamber 3, red dust, white dust, and hydrolic lime (Lafarge) 3.1:1:4 (1:2 inert:lime) mixed with distilled water to consolidate the edges of the plaster and to fill in the missing parts.

Fig. 117: Northern wall of Room 2, before (left) and after (right) conservation.

4) The northern wall of Chamber 1

Conservation of the wall paintings on the other section of the wall (northwest) continued after careful removal of the debris.

Mechanical cleaning was carried out using a scalpel and soft brushes. During this process some consolidation with mortar permitted continuation of the cleaning process.

Consolidation was done by injecting two materials, mortar and acrylic resin (Primal AC33 1:1) to consolidate the painted layer and the plaster. Paraloid B 72 in 2% acetone was used to fix the colors.

Filling was done using hydrolic mortar consisting of grey tomb dust from Chamber 3, red dust, white dust, and Hydrolic lime (Lafarge) 3.1:1:4 (1:2 inert:lime) mixed with distilled water to consolidate the edges of the plaster and to fill in missing parts.

Additional Intervention

Conservation and restoration of fragments of alabaster canopic jars, shabtis and pottery jars from the excavation was effected. This involved mechanical and chemical cleaning and consolidation using a scalpel, alcohol in distilled water, and paraloid B72 to fix the color.

NOTES

1. **A. Lucas** and **J.R. Harris.** *Ancient Egyptian Materials and Industries,* fourth edition. London, 1962. P. 77.
2. **Lucas** and **Harris**, 1962. P. 77.
3. **Lucas** and **Harris**, 1962. P. 76.
4. **Lucas** and **Harris**, 1962. Pp. 76-77.
5. **Lucas** and **Harris**, 1962. Pp. 76-78.
6. **Maximillian Toch.** *The Pigment of the Tomb of Perneb.* New York, 1918. Reprinted from the *Journal of Industrial and Engineering Chemistry*, 10, 2: 1-4.
7. *ibid.*
8. *ibid.*
9. **Lamia El Hadidi.** Report on the Remedy and Restoration of KV 5, 1994. Unpublished.
10. **Lotfi Khaled Hassan.** Report on the Conservation and Restoration of Wall Paintings and Objects from KV 5, June 1996. Unpublished.

Appendix I:
ROCK MECHANICS INDEX TESTS
Advanced Terra Testing, Inc.

Irregular Lump Point Load Test

Client:	Theban Mapping Project
Date:	7-10-95
Job No.:	2218-01
Comments:	Egypt
Tested by:	DSR Date: 6-5-95
Checked by:	WEB Date: 7-10-95

Sample ID	L (in)	D (in)	L/D	Gauge Failure Load (psig)	p (lb$_f$)
Chamber 1	4.81	1.87	2.57	432	894.0
Chamber 1	3.35	1.78	1.88	1360	2815.0
Chamber 1	2.90	1.45	2.00	1140	2360.0
Chamber 1	2.20	1.70	1.29	555	1149.0
Esna Shale Tombs	2.70	1.10	2.45	245	507.2
Esna Shale Tombs	1.55	1.10	1.41	210	434.7
Esna Shale Tombs	1.60	0.80	2.00	405	838.4
Esna Shale KV 20	1.85	0.92	2.01	194	401.6
Esna Shale KV 20	2.20	1.23	1.79	350	724.5
Esna Shale KV 20	2.95	1.10	2.66	385	797.0

Notes:
L   Longest dimension perpendicular to platens
D   Platen separation
P   Gauge failure load * 2.07 in^2 piston area

Compressive Strength in psi not calculated due to uncertainities with correction factors.

Slake Durability Test - ASTM D 4644

Client:	Theban Mapping Project
Date:	7-10-95
Job No.:	2218-01
Comments:	Egypt
Tested by:	DSR Date: 6-5-95
Checked by:	WEB Date: 7-10-95

Rock Type	Chamber I UK Limestone	Esna Shale Tombs Shale	Esna Shale UK - KV 20 Shale
Initial Weight (wet) Pan + Sample (A)	1619.9	1714.5	1750.8
Initial Weight (dry) Pan + Sample (B)	1612.6	1682.0	1730.8
Ist Cycle Weight Pan + Sample (C)	1544.5	1274.2	1407.8
2nd Cycle Weight Pan + Sample (D)	1465.0	1221.0	1264.9
Pan No.	1	2	4
Pan Weight (E)	1131.8	1190.3	1258.4
B-E	480.8	491.7	472.4
C-E	412.7	83.9	149.4
D-E	333.2	30.7	6.5
Ist Cycle Durability (C-E)/(B-E)* 100%	85.84	17.06	31.63
2nd Cycle Durability (D-E)/(B-E)* 100%	69.30	6.24	1.38
Moisture Content (A-B)/(B-E)* 100%	1.5	6.6	4.2
Type	11	111	111

Consolidation/Swell Test - ASTM D 4546

Client	Theban Mapping Project
Job No.	2218-01
Boring No.	UK Limestone
Sampled	7-2-94 DMR
Depth	
Test Started	7-3-95 DSR
Test Finished	7-7-95 DSR
Sample No.	
Soil Descr.	
Setup No.	Att-3

Moisture/Density Data	Before Test	After Test	Load (Psf)	Consol. (in)
Wt. Soil & Ring(s) (g)	189.8	199.2	100	0.0000
Wt. Ring(s) (g)	39.5	39.5	400	-0.0036
Wt. Soil (g)	150.4	159.8	400	-0.0229
Wet Density PCF	125.1	133.1	800	-0.0222
			1600	-0.0166
Wt. Wet Soil & Pan (g)	153.9	163.4	3200	-0.0085
Wt. Dry Soil & Pan (g)	139.9	139.9	6400	-0.0022
Wt. Lost moisture (g)	14.0	23.4	12800	0.0057
Wt. of Pan Only (g)	3.6	3.6	136.3	136.3

Moisture Content %	10.3	17.2
Dry Density PCF	113.4	113.6
Max. Dry Density PCF		
Percent Compaction		

	Load(Psf)	Log Load	Consol. (in)	Defl. (in)
	100	2.000	0.0000	0.0000
	400	2.602	-0.0036	0.0036
Saturate	400	2.602	-0.0229	0.0229
	800	2.903	-0.0222	0.0222
	1600	3.204	-0.0166	0.0166
	3200	3.505	-0.0085	0.0085
	6400	3.806	-0.0022	0.0022
	12800	4.107	0.0057	-0.0057

Data entered by: NAA	Date: 7-11-95	
Data checked by:	Date: 7-11-95	
File name:	DACOUKL	

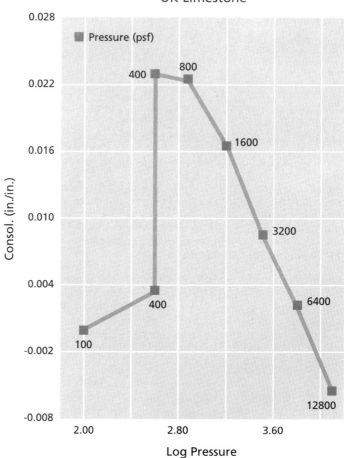

Consolidation Test Data
UK Limestone

Consolidation/Swell Test - ASTM D 4546

Client	Theban Mapping Project
Job No.	2218-01
Boring No.	UK Limestone
Sampled	7-2-94 DM
Depth	
Test Started	7-3-95 DS
Test Finished	7-7-95 DS
Sample No.	
Soil Descr.	
Setup No.	Att-3

Time Reading Data
400 psf load

Elapsed Time (min)	SQRT Time (min)	Dial Reading (in)	Deflection (in)
0.0	0.00	0.0945	0.0000
0.1	0.32	0.0945	0.0000
0.3	0.50	0.0945	0.0000
0.5	0.71	0.0945	0.0000
1.0	1.00	0.0945	0.0000
2.0	1.41	0.0945	0.0000
4.0	2.00	0.0945	0.0000
9.0	3.00	0.0945	0.0000
16.0	4.00	0.0946	-0.0001
30.0	5.48	0.0947	-0.0002
60.0	7.75	0.1057	-0.0112
120.0	10.95	0.1104	-0.0159
240.0	15.49	0.1123	-0.0178
480.0	21.91	0.1132	-0.0187

Data entered by: NAA	Date: 7-11-95
Data checked by:	Date: 7-13-95
File name:	DACOUKL

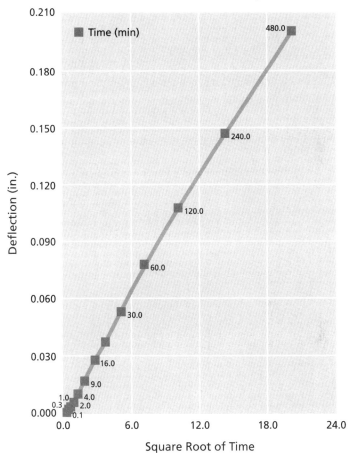

Time Reading Data
Esna Shale, UK, KV 20, 400 psf load

Atterberg Limits Test - ASTM D 4318

Client	Theban Mapping Project
Boring No.	4K
Job No.	2218-01
Test Started	6-26-95 Web
Test Finished	6-27-95 Web
Sample No.	Chamber I
Soil Descr.	Limestone
Test Type	Atterberg

Plastic Limit Determination

	1	2	3
Dish	2003	B39	30C
Wt Dish & Wet Soil	7.62	8.72	9.03
Wt Dish & Dry Soil	6.14	6.97	7.20
Wt of Moisture	1.48	1.75	1.83
Wt of Dish	1.03	1.04	1.06
Wt of Dry Soil	5.11	5.93	6.14
Moisture Content	28.96	29.51	29.80

Liquid Limit Determination
Device Number 258

	1	2	3	4	5
Dish	B61	2059	2027	48C	B20
Number of Blows	31	24	26	22	16
Wt Dish & Wet Soil	16.15	18.41	18.80	20.07	22.48
Wt Dish & Dry Soil	12.01	13.56	13.69	14.50	15.19
Wt of Moisture	4.14	4.85	5.11	5.57	7.29
Wt of Dish	1.05	1.06	1.05	1.04	1.05
Wt of Dry Soil	10.96	12.50	12.64	13.46	14.14
Moisture Content	37.77	38.80	40.43	41.38	51.56

Liquid Limit	40.5
Plastic Limit	29.4
Plasticity Index	11.0

Atterberg Classification   ML

Data entered by: NAA	Date: 6-28-95
Data checked by:	Date: 6-29-95
File name:	DAG04KI

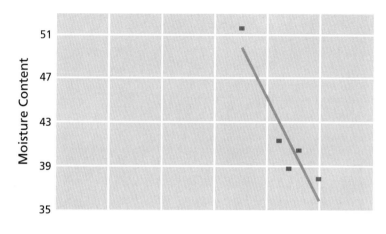

Atterberg Limits, Flow Curve
4K, KV 5, Chamber 1

Moisture Content

—— Number of Blows

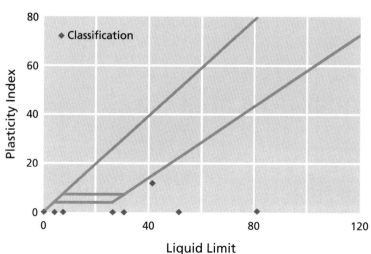

Plasticity Chart
4K, KV 5, Chamber 1

Plasticity Index

◆ Classification

Liquid Limit

Consolidation/Swell Test - ASTM D 4546

Client	Theban Mapping Project
Job No.	2218-01
Boring No.	Esna Shale
Sampled	7-2-95 DMR
Depth	
Test Started	7-3-95 DSR
Test Finished	7-11-95 DSR
Sample No.	Roadway & Tombs
Soil Descr.	Shale
Setup No.	Att-9

Moisture/Density Data	Before Test	After Test	Load (Psf)	Consol. (in)
Wt. Soil & Ring(s) (g)	194.3	192.1	100	0.0000
Wt. Ring(s) (g)	46.3	46.3	400	0.0233
Wt. Soil (g)	148.0	145.8	400	-0.0661
Wet Density PCF	123.1	129.3	800	-0.0641
			1600	-0.0568
Wt. Wet Soil & Pan (g)	151.9	149.7	3200	-0.0425
Wt. Dry Soil & Pan (g)	120.2	120.2	6400	-0.0259
Wt. Lost Moisture (g)	31.7	29.5	12800	-0.0032
Wt. of Pan Only (g)	3.9	3.9	25600	0.0234
Wt. of Dry Soil (g)	116.3	116.3	51200	0.0587
Moisture content %	27.2	25.3		
Dry Density PCF	96.8	103.2		
Max. Dry Density PCF				
Percent Compaction				

	Load(Psf)	Log Load	Consol. (in)	Defl. (in)
	100	2.000	0.0000	0.0000
	400	2.602	0.0233	-0.0233
Saturate	400	2.602	-0.0661	0.0661
	800	2.903	-0.0641	0.0641
	1600	3.204	-0.0568	0.0568
	3200	3.505	-0.0425	0.0425
	6400	3.806	-0.0259	0.0259
	12800	4.107	-0.0032	0.0032
	25600	4.408	0.0234	-0.0234
	51200	4.709	0.0587	-0.0587

Data entered by:	NAA	Date:	7-12-95
Data checked by:		Date:	7-13-95
File name:	DASOESRT		

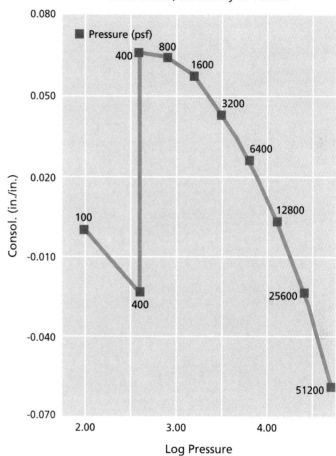

Consolidation Test Data
Esna Shale, Roadway & Tombs

Consolidation/Swell Test - ASTM D 4546

Client	Theban Mapping Project
Job No.	2218-01
Boring No.	Esna Shale
Sampled	7-2-95 Dm
Depth	
Test Started	7-3-95 Ds
Test Finished	7-11-95 Ds
Sample No.	Roadway & Tombs
Soil Descr.	Shale
Setup No.	Att-9

TIME READING DATA
400 psf load

Elapsed Time (min)	SQRT Time (min)	Dial Reading (in)	Deflection (in)
0.0	0.00	0.0245	0.0000
0.1	0.32	0.0245	0.0000
0.3	0.50	0.0245	0.0000
0.5	0.71	0.0241	0.0004
1.0	1.00	0.0234	0.0011
2.0	1.41	0.0223	0.0022
4.0	2.00	0.0205	0.0040
9.0	3.00	0.0170	0.0075
16.0	4.00	0.0133	0.0112
30.0	5.48	0.0080	0.0165
60.0	7.75	0.0007	0.0238
120.0	10.95	-0.0082	0.0327
260.0	16.12	-0.0205	0.0450
480.0	21.91	-0.0353	0.0598

Data entered by:	NAA	Date:	7-12-95
Data checked by:		Date:	7-13-95
File name:	DASOESRT		

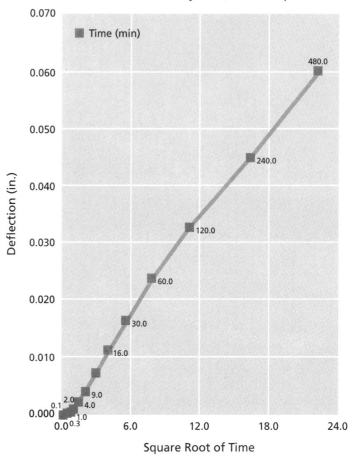

Time Reading Data
Esna Shale, Roadway & Tombs, 400 psf load

Atterberg Limits Test - ASTM D 4318

Client	Theban Mapping Project		
Job No.	2218-01		
Roadway Between Rest House and Tomb			
Test Started	6-29-95 JB		
Test Finished	6-30-95		
Test Type	Atterberg		

Plastic Limit Determination

	1	2	3
Dish	36C	12C	4100
Wt Dish & Wet Soil	3.79	3.59	4.08
Wt Dish & Dry Soil	3.13	3.02	3.36
Wt of Moisture	0.66	0.57	0.72
Wt of Dish	1.06	1.07	1.05
Wt of Dry Soil	2.07	1.95	2.31
Moisture Content	31.88	29.23	31.17

Liquid Limit Determination
Device Number 258

	1	2	3	4	5
Dish	B26	24	34CX	B72	B11
Number of Blows	34	20	16	14	12
Wt Dish & Wet Soil	8.92	8.29	7.03	6.81	8.29
Wt Dish & Dry Soil	5.93	5.50	4.67	4.50	5.34
Wt of Moisture	2.99	2.79	2.36	2.31	2.95
Wt of Dish	1.06	1.04	1.06	1.04	1.07
Wt of Dry Soil	4.87	4.46	3.61	3.46	4.27
Moisture Content	61.40	62.56	65.37	66.76	69.09

Liquid Limit	62.6
Plastic Limit	30.8
Plasticity Index	31.9

Atterberg Classification   CH

Data entered by: SR	Date: 7-3-95	
Data checked by:	Date: 7-5-95	
File name:	DAGODOA	

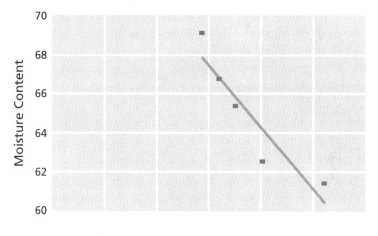

Atterberg Limits, Flow Curve
Roadway between Resthouse and KV 5

——— Number of Blows

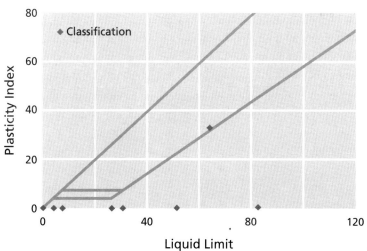

Plasticity Chart
Roadway between Resthouse and KV 5

◆ Classification

Consolidation/Swell Test - ASTM D 4546

Client	Theban Mapping Project
Job No.	2218-01
Boring No.	Esna Shale
Sampled	7-2-94 DMR
Depth	UK
Test Started	7-3-95 DSR
Test Finished	7-14-95 DSR
Sample No.	KV20
Soil Descr.	
Setup No.	Att-4

Moisture/Density Data	Before Test	After Test	Load (Psf)	Consol. (in)
Wt. Soil & Ring(s) (g)	198.1	213.7	100	0.0000
Wt. Ring(s) (g)	46.2	46.2	400	0.0103
Wt. Soil (g)	151.9	167.5	400	-0.2620
Wet Density PCF	126.4	137.4	800	-0.2550
			600	-0.2322
Wt. Wet Soil & Pan (g)	155.7	171.3	3200	-0.1963
Wt. Dry Soil & Pan (g)	138.8	138.8	6400	-0.1547
Wt. Lost Moisture (g)	16.9	32.6	12800	-0.1054
Wt. of Pan Only (g)	3.8	3.8	25600	-0.0598
Wt. of Dry Soil (g)	135.0	135.0	51200	-0.0183
Moisture Content %	12.5	24.1		
Dry Density PCF	112.3	110.7		
Max. Dry Density				
PCF Percent				
Compaction				

	Load (Psf)	Log Load	Consol. (in)	Defl. (in)
	100	2.000	0.0000	0.0000
	400	2.602	0.0103	-0.0103
Saturate	400	2.602	-0.2620	0.2620
	800	2.903	-0.2550	0.2550
	1600	3.204	-0.2322	0.2322
	3200	3.505	-0.1963	0.1963
	6400	3.806	-0.1547	0.1547
	12800	4.107	-0.1054	0.1054
	25600	4.408	-0.0598	0.0598
	51200	4.709	-0.0183	0.0183

Data entered by: NAA   Date: 7-17-95
Data checked by: Date: 7-18-95
File name: DASOKV20

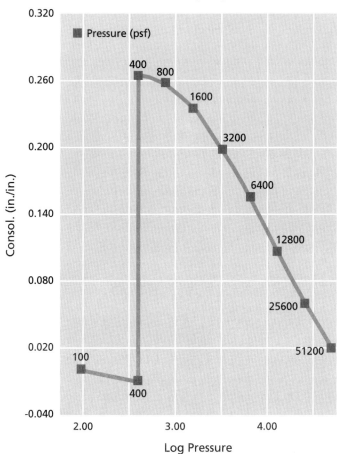

Consolidation Test Data
Esna Shale, UK, KV 20

Consolidation/Swell Test - ASTM D 4546

Client	Theban Mapping Project
Sampled	7-2-94 DMR
Job No.	2218-010
Test Started	7-3-95 DSR
Test Finished	7-14-95 DSR
Boring No.	Esna Shale
Depth	UK
Setup No.	Att-4
Sample No.	KV20

Time Reading Data
400 psf load

Elapsed Time (min)	SQRT Time (min)	Dial Reading (in)	Deflection (in)
0.0	0.00	0.0810	0.0000
0.1	0.32	0.0811	0.0001
0.3	0.50	0.0820	0.0010
0.5	0.71	0.0836	0.0026
1.0	1.00	0.0860	0.0050
2.0	1.41	0.0906	0.0096
4.0	2.00	0.0976	0.0166
9.0	3.00	0.1084	0.0274
16.0	4.00	0.1178	0.0368
30.0	5.48	0.1339	0.0529
60.0	7.75	0.1585	0.0775
120.0	10.95	0.1878	0.1068
240.0	15.49	0.2270	0.1460
480.0	21.91	0.2805	0.1995

Data entered by: NAA	Date: 7-17-95	
Data checked by:	Date: 7-17-95	
File name:	DASOKV20	

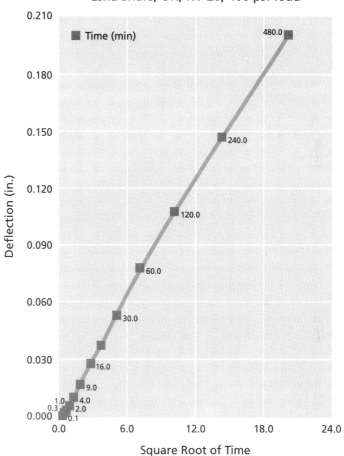

Time Reading Data
Esna Shale, UK, KV 20, 400 psf load

Atterberg Limits Test - ASTM D 4318

Client	Theban Mapping Project
Job No.	2218-01
Boring No.	KV 20
Sampled	7-2-94 Depth
Test Started	6-23-95 Web
Test Finished	6-24-95 Web
Soil Descr.	Esna Shale
Test Type	Atterberg

Plastic Limit Determination

	1	2	3
Dish	B4	20CB	16C
Wt Dish & Wet Soil	6.89	7.37	5.92
Wt Dish & Dry Soil	5.55	5.83	4.79
Wt of Moisture	1.34	1.54	1.13
Wt of Dish	1.05	1.03	1.07
Wt of Dry Soil	4.50	4.80	3.72
Moisture Content	29.78	32.08	30.38

Liquid Limit Determination
Device Number 258

	1	2	3	4	5
Dish	B29	B24	B42	4108	B67
Number of Blows	14	37	31	8	10
Wt Dish & Wet Soil	22.46	22.13	22.10	20.75	16.66
Wt Dish & Dry Soil	13.34	13.58	13.46	11.44	9.36
Wt of Moisture	9.12	8.55	8.64	9.31	7.30
Wt of Dish	1.06	1.03	1.04	1.07	1.05
Wt of Dry Soil	12.28	12.55	12.42	10.37	8.31
Moisture Content	74.27	68.13	69.57	89.78	87.85

Liquid Limit	72.2
Plastic Limit	30.7
Plasticity Index	41.4

Atterberg classification   CH

Data entered by: NAA	Date:	6-26-95
Data checked by:	Date:	7-5-95
File name:	DAGOKV20	

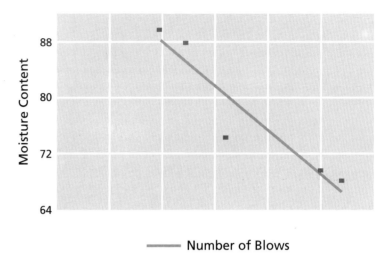

**Atterberg Limits, Flow Curve
KV 20, Esna Shale**

Moisture Content

—— Number of Blows

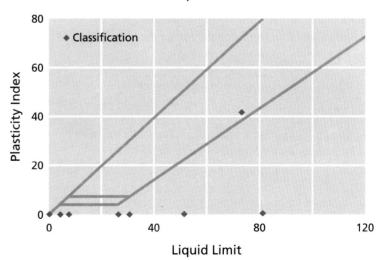

**Plasticity Chart
KV 20, Esna Shale**

◆ Classification

Plasticity Index

Liquid Limit

Appendix IIa:
MINERALOGY OF THE ESNA SHALE SAMPLE: KV 20

Hamza Associates, Consultants & Engineers
Civil, Structural, Geotechnical, Electrical, Mechanical Engineering,
& Environmental Studies

1. INTRODUCTION

One rock sample (KV 20) has been received for detailed lithologic and mineralogic investigations. It is an 'Esna Shale' sample.

Geologic Setting of the Esna Shale

The term 'Esna Shale' was used by Ball as early as 1900 when he compared the shales above the chalk deposits in Kharga Oasis to those exposed in the Nile Valley in the neighborhood of Esna to which the designation 'Esna Shale' has been applied in the reports of the geological survey. However, the credit of coining the term is given to Beadnell who apparently introduced this term in the geological survey reports and who described this formation fully in 1905. The type locality by designation is Gebel Aweina, opposite Esna, lying about 8.5 km northeast of Sebaiya railway station.

The term 'Esna Shale' is used only for the succession of the laminated green and grey shale clays that overlie the chalk rocks of the Upper Cretaceous age and underlie the Lower Eocene Thebes formations. It is sometimes referred to as upper Esna Shale (Hume, 1911, 1912).

Esna Shale is rich in foraminferal fauna, including several planktonic species, and it dates from the upper Paleocene (Landenian) period.

2. AIM OF THE STUDY

Detailed examinations of the following aspects should be carried out:

a. Lithologic characterization with regard to their textural and bedding habitat using binocular microscope. Macroscopic description of the sample to be given.
b. Mineralogic identification of both coarse and fine components using X-ray diffraction (XRD) analysis for bulk sample and clay mineral fraction.
c. Detailed petrographic examination using polarizing microscope especially for the coarse sand fraction greater than 63 microns in diameter.

3. MACROSCOPIC DESCRIPTIONS

Using the naked eye, hand lens and binocular microscope the received sample looks thin, very delicate, and crumbles easily between the fingers. The sample is slightly gypsiferous and exhibits a high degree of fissility and is yellowish green in color. Biological remains are represented by macrofossils such as thin, delicate shells, as well as microfossils such as planktonic foraminifers (e.g. Operculina Sp).

4. ANALYTICAL TECHNIQUES

The main methods applied in the present report include the following:

4.1 Grain Size Analysis

This was performed using wet and dry sieving techniques by mechanical shaker and 0.5 phi set of sieves following the conventional time as recommended by Folk and Ward (1957) and Folk (1966).

4.2 Heavy Mineral Separation

Such separation is applied in the present sample using bromoform as a heavy liquid (specific gravity 2.85). The separated fraction (light and heavy mineral fractions) were mounted separately in Canada Balsam for microscopic examination, identification, and grain counting.

4.3 X-ray Diffraction (XRD) Technique

Clay and silt fractions (less than 63 microns in diameter) have been separated and prepared for detailed clay mineral analysis using the XRD technique. To achieve this, three oriented slides were prepared for the clay and silt fraction. These three slides were treated as follows:

i. One slide was analyzed without treatment (i.e. bulk sample).
ii. The second slide was analyzed after exposure to glycerol vapor in a vacuum desiccator at 6,000°C for two hours.
iii. The third one was analyzed after heating up to 5,000°C for two hours.

The reflection peaks between 20=2° and 35° were obtained. The corresponding d (in Angstroms, A°) and relative intensities (I/I°) were obtained and compared with the standard data (A.S.T.M. cards).

The Pierce and Siegel (1969) method for semi-quantitative estimation of clay minerals was used, as outlined below:

i. The integrated intensity of the 14 A° glycolate peak is equal to the relative amount of montmorillonite.
ii. The area of 10 A° glycolate peak multiplied by four is equivalent to the relative amount of illite.
iii. The 7 A° glycolate peak area is multiplied by two for the relative amount of the kaolinite.

Philips XRD equipment was used: model PW/17 10, with nickel filter, copper radiation (X_λ=1.542 A°), at 40 kV, 30 mA, and a scanning speed of 0.2°/s. The reflection peak between 20=20° and 60° was obtained and compared with standard data (A.S.T.M. cards).

5. RESULTS

5.1 Results of Mechanical Analysis

The desegregated sample was subjected to wet sieving, in order to separate the silt and clay size fraction from the sand size fraction, and the data obtained are tabulated

(Table 1). The sand size fraction was subjected to dry sieving, and the majority of this fraction was composed of fine to very fine sand fractions (63-250) microns in diameter).

5.2 Results of the Heavy Liquid Separation

Sand size fraction (4.65% by weight of the total sample) has been subjected to heavy liquid separation. The obtained results are tabulated in Table 2.

5.3 Results of X-ray Diffraction (XRD) Analysis

5.3.1 Bulk Sample

XRD analysis for the bulk sample indicated the presence of the following minerals in decreasing order:

Calcite, dolomite, montmorillonite. quartz, kaolinite, minor amounts of anorthite (a-plagiociase) and traces of gypsum

5.3.2 Oriented Sample (Clay and Silt Size)

Semi-quantitative analysis of clay minerals gave the following mineral assemblage:

| Montmorillonite | 60 % |
| Kaolinite | 40 % |

X-ray analysis results for the sample can be written collectively as follows:

X-RAY DIFFRACTION ANALYSIS

ROCK SAMPLE: Esna shale (KV20)

LITHOLOGY: Highly fissile, very soft, yellowish green in color, slightly gypsiferous shale containing thin, delicate shells and foraminiferal tests.

XRD RESULTS: XRD analysis revealed that the sample is composed of the following mineral association in a decreasing order of abundance:

Carbonate minerals:	calcite and dolomite
Caly minerals:	montmorillonite and kaolinite
Oxide minerals:	quartz
Silicate minerals:	anorthite (feldspar)
Sulfate minerals:	gypsum

Table 1: Results of the Wet Sieving Analysis

Size	Silt and Clay Size < 63 µm	Sand Size > 63 µm
Weight percentage	95.35%	4.65 %

Table 2: The mineral composition of sample KV 20 (sand size fraction) expressed in percentages

Light Minerals (sp.gr. < 2.85)		Heavy Minerals (sp. gr. > 2. 85)	
Quartz	50.67[1]	Tourmaline	1.35%
Feldspar	1.69	Zircon	1.69
Shell Fossil	33.78[2]	Garnet	0.34
Opaques	10.14[3]	Rutile	0.34

1. The given figures are count percentages.
2. Shell fragments, represented by tests of *Operculina sp.*, are composed mainly of calcite.
3. Opaque minerals are represented mainly by iron oxides (magnetite and limonite) which replaced the fossils and coat many quartz grains.

Appendix IIb:
LITHOLOGIC, PETROGRAPHIC, AND MINERALOGIC IDENTIFICATION OF TWO SURFACE SAMPLES (INDURATED ROCKS)

Hamza Associates, Consultants & Engineers

1. INTRODUCTION

Two rock samples were received for detailed lithologic, petrograhic, and mineralogic examination and identification. The two samples represent two main rock categories of muddy texture as follows:

Sample 1:   Limestone.
Sample 2:   Shale (of two varieties, compact and laminated).

Detailed examinations for the following aspects should be carried out:

(a) Lithologic characterization with regard to their textural and bedding habitat, using normal light microscope.
(b) Mineralogic identification of both coarse and fine components using chemical as well as XRD analysis for bulk and clay mineral fraction.
(c) Detailed petrographic examination using the Polarizing microscope, especially for the limestone sample.

2. LITHOLOGIC ASSIGNMENTS

Detailed lithologic examination by the naked eye and normal light microscope, microchemical tests, and staining techniques were applied on the two samples. In the following, a description of both types will be presented.

2.1 Limestone

The received sample was massive, partly thin laminated, yellowish white, almost homogenous texturally, and of lime-mudstone type. Staining with Alizarin Red S was applied and the sample was found to be calcite dominated.

The I.R. (Insoluble Residue) ratio for the two experiments is less than 3% of the total components.

This rock type will be examined petrographically using the polarizing microscope for thin section examination.

2.2 Shale

The samples are categorized under two sub-types:

2.a Partly blocky, compact, indurated, of equi-sized partings due to fracturing, mottled with iron oxides, especially along fracture surfaces.

2.b Thin laminated, very well indurated, flaky, partly fissile, ferruginated with iron and manganese oxides on fracture and lamination surfaces. Fissility

surfaces are mottled with manganese dendrites. Grayish yellow original color is masked due to ferrugination into reddish brown and violet stainings.

Both types are scarcely calcareous. These rock types will be treated by XRD techniques for detailed mineralogic identification with special emphasis on clay-mineral associations.

3. PETROGRAPHIC ASPECTS

Two thin sections were prepared from the limestone sample in two perpendicular orientations, one of them is parallel to the lamination. Microchemical stainings using the dilute HCl (2%) and Alizarin Red S methods were applied on a part of the thin section for accurate carbonate mineral differentiation.

Description

Fossiliferous limestone (of mud-to-wackestone texture), or Foraminiferal biomicrite.
Bioclasts are entirely of small-sized foraminiferal tests (uniserial and globular calcareous forms). The biogenic remains are distributed in an almost parallel manner that coincides with the microlamination pattern of the rock mass. Fossils do not exceed 7% of the total contents. Scattered equi-sized fecal pellets are also seen but in a random distribution and some of them form micro-pockets within the muddy matrix. The skeletal remains are floating in the lime-mud matrix that is entirely formed of micro-crystalline calcite.

Diagenetic features

The examined rock sample revealed the presence of the following main Digenetic features:

(a) Agcrading recrystallization of the lime-mud matrix into fine and meso-crystalline calcite spar.
(b) Neomorphism of the skeletal remains.
(c) Biomoldic cavity filling by secondary calcite.
(d) Microfracturing and refilling by fine crystalline calcite spar.

4. X-RAY DIFFRACTION ANALYSIS

This part of the report deals with the X-ray diffraction analysis of a limestone sample (designated as KV 5) and shale sample (designated as shale outcrop).

Analytical Techniques

1. For limestone sample (KV 5):
One diffractogram was done for the bulk sample to investigate its mineral constituents.

2. For clay mineral fraction:
The shale sample from the outcrop was subdivided to two samples according to lithological characters to the following:

2a Compact shale.
2b Laminated shale.

For each sample three oriented slides were prepared for the clay and silt fraction (less than 63 microns in diameter). These three slides were treated as follows:

1. One slide was analyzed without treatment.
2. The second slide was analyzed after exposure to glycerol vapor in a vacuum desiccator at 60°C for two hours.
3. The third one was analyzed after heating up to 500°C for two hours.

The reflection peaks between 2=2° and 35° were obtained. The corresponding spacing d (in Angstroms, A°) and relative intensities (I/I°) were obtained and compared with the standard data (A.S.T.M. Cards).

The Pierce and Siegel (1969) method for semi-quantitative estimation of clay minerals was used, as outlined below:

1. The integrated intensity of the 14 A° glycolate peak is equal to the relative amount of montmorillonite.
2. The area of 10 A° (glycolate peak) multiplied by four is equivalent to the relative amount of illite.
3. The 7 A° glycolate peak area is multiplied by two for the relative amount of Kaolinite.

Philips XRD equipment was used: model PW/17 10, with nickel filter, copper radiation (X_λ=1.542 A°) at 40 kV, 30 mA, and a scanning speed of 0.02°/s. The reflection peaks between 20=2° and 60° were obtained. The corresponding spacings (d in Angstrom) and relative intensities (I/I°) were obtained and compared with standard data (A.S.T.M. Cards).

Semi-quantitative estimation of clay minerals in shale samples 2a and 2b:

The following table shows a semi-quantitative estimation of clay minerals in the two shale samples, 2a and 2b (compact shale and laminated shale), that were investigated:

Sample No.	Illite (%)	Montmorillonite	Kaolinite
Compact Shale 2a	95	3	2
Laminated Shale 2b	96	4	-

Results of X-ray Diffraction Analysis
Sample 1: KV 5 (Compact Limestone)

Rock Sample:	1 (KV 5).
Lithology:	Hard, compact, finely crystalline, creamy white limestone.
XRD Experimental Conditions:	Cu Ka radiation, X_{lambda} = 1.5420A°, Nickel filter and scanning speed of 0.02°/s.
0 range:	2° - 60°

Results
XRD revealed that the sample is composed of the following minerals in decreasing abundance as follows:

Carbonate minerals:	Calcite, dolomite, or magnesian calcite.
Clay minerals:	Montmorillonite
Halide minerals:	Halite
Oxide minerals:	Quartz

Results of X-ray Diffraction Analysis
Sample 2a: Shale Outcrop (Moderately Compact Shale)

Rock Sample:	Shale from outcrop (2a).
Lithology:	Moderately compact, creamy, buff-colored shale.
XRD Experimental Conditions:	Cu Ka radiation, X_{lambda} = 1.5420A°, Nickel filter and scanning speed of 0.02°/s.
0 range:	2° - 60°

Results
XRD revealed that the sample is composed of the following minerals in a decreasing abundance as follows: (see Fig 16 - 17).

Carbonate minerals:	Calcite, dolomite, or magnesian calcite.
Clay minerals:	Illite, montmorillonite
Halide minerals:	Halite

Appendix III:
HYDRAULIC RESPONSE OF
THE VALLEY OF THE KINGS IN LUXOR

Dr. Sherif M. A. El-Didy
Associate Professor, Irrigation and Hydraulic Dept.
Faculty of Engineering, Cairo University, Giza, Egypt

1. INTRODUCTION

While rainfall in the Valley of the Kings is normally quite low, heavy storms do occur from time to time, causing severe flash floods. In this study, the hydraulic response of the Valley of the Kings to such flooding was determined at different sections on its main trunk, as a result of combining its meteorological, geological, and morphological characteristics.

The output of the study is in the form of the rate and volume of water flow and the associated sediment load. The study was performed for storms of return periods of 500, 300, 200, 100, 50, 30, 10, 5, and 2 years. A one-hour storm duration was considered according to the meteorological records.

The Valley of the Kings is located on the west bank of the River Nile in Luxor in Upper Egypt. The average length of the Valley is about 900 meters with the average width about 550 meters, covering an area of almost half a square kilometer.

The highest altitude in the Valley of the Kings is on the watershed divide, changing from 420.0 meters to 220.0 meters. The level of the valley bed, along its main trunk, changes approximately from 220.0 meters to 155.0 meters. The average slope of the main trunk is about 252.0 m/km.

The geological formation and the type of surface rocks control water infiltration and drainage rates and quantities. In general, the ground surface formation in the Valley of the Kings consists of igneous rocks that cover most of the highlands, with sedimentary soil and gravel boulders on the surface along the paths of basins, carried there by flash floods.

The catchment of the Valley has low infiltration rates due to the rock formation of the ground surface. As a result, a high percentage of the rainfall becomes surface runoff, causing flash floods. Infiltration occurs only through the fissures of the hard rocks or through the sedimentary formation in the valley bed.

2. METEOROLOGICAL STUDY

Despite the arid nature of the Luxor region, it has been exposed to dense thunderstorms of various return periods. The rain that comes with these storms is accumulated in the watershed causing flash floods that become a source of danger for the existing communities.

Rainfall records for sixty-one years have been collected from the meteorological station in Luxor. Out of the statistical analysis of the data, the maximum daily rainfall in millimeters has been plotted versus the probability of its being equal or greater than the corresponding return periods (Figure III.2).

From this plot, the maximum daily rainfall for return periods of 500, 300, 100, 50, 30, 10, 5, and 2 years has been determined (Table III.1). It is clear that storms of shorter return periods have lesser rainfall density. Storms of longer return periods that come every few decades are dangerous, causing flash floods.

3. MORPHOLOGICAL CHARACTERISTICS

The morphological characteristics of watersheds control their hydraulic behavior during storms in terms of the peak discharge and the runoff duration. In this study, the morphological characteristics are represented in terms of topographic features, the number and length of branches of different orders, and the area of their collection basins. A map of the Valley at 1:2,000 was employed for this study.

The catchment of the Valley of the Kings has been divided into fifteen basins: A, B, C, D, E1, E2, F, G, H, I, J1, J2, K, L, and M (Figure III.1). The hydraulic response of the Valley was determined at five different sections on the main trunk at I, II, III, IV, and V.

Basins E1, E2, and F share the flow at section I. Basins E1, E2, F, and G contribute to the runoff at section II. Basins E1, E2, F, G, I, and C contribute to the runoff at section III. Basins E1, E2, F, G, C, and B contribute to the runoff at section IV. Section V represents the main outlet of the Valley where all the basins contribute to the runoff at that section.

Strahler's approach was used for ranking the order of the different branches in each basin. Only first-, second-, and third-order branches were identified. For each rank, the number, the average length of branches, and their collection area were calculated. The total area of each basin, the length of the main trunk, and the average slope (m/km) were also calculated, in addition to the average velocity for each basin.

Because the average water velocities inside the different branches of the basins are crucial for the hydro-morphological model, special care has been given to this parameter as it could considerably affect the hydrograph shape. During flash floods, the water velocities could change with time. The velocity values depend on the rainfall density and duration, the basin slope in its different branches, the width of the sections of interest, and the surface roughness coefficient.

The roughness coefficient is a function of the surface, i.e. a function of the size and the shape of soil particles forming the wetted perimeter. It also depends on vegetation, channel irregularity, channel alignment, silting, and scouring. In this preliminary and general study, a rough estimate of the velocity was adopted using the table from the U. S. Navy's Technical Publication Navdocks TP-PW-5 for similar basins.

Using the average velocity in the main trunk of each basin and the distance between the outlet of each basin and the main outlet of the Valley, the lag time of each basin was estimated. While the minimum velocity is 7.3 km/hr in basin J2, the maximum is 9.2 km/hr in basins F and G. The minimum lag time is 0.082 hours in basin E2 for a distance of 0.689 kilometers between the basin outlet and section V at the Valley's main outlet.

Table III.1: Maximum Daily Rainfall for Various Return Periods

Return Period (Years)	500	300	100	50	30	10	5	3
Max. Daily Rainfall (mm)	46.0	39.0	23.5	14.5	10.0	4.5	4.0	0.05

161

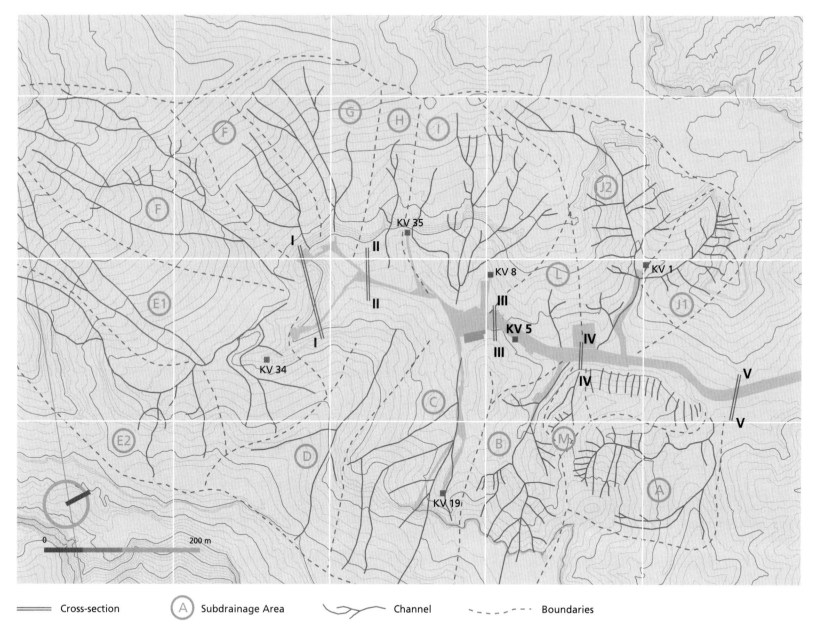

Fig. III.1: Morphological Characteristics of the Valley of the Kings Watershed.

Cross-section (A) Subdrainage Area Channel Boundaries

4. HYDRAULIC RESPONSE OF THE VALLEY

A study of the hydraulic response of the Valley of the Kings was performed using a hydro-morphological model that combines the meteorological, geological, and morphological characteristics of the Valley. The model was developed by the Massachusetts Institute of Technology, USA. It was verified for different valleys in Egypt by the Development Research and Technological Planning Center at Cairo University. It was also modified by S. El-Didy to calculate the volume of water infiltration and surface detention, in addition to sediment load in terms of rate and volume.

Three sets of data are required by the model:

- meteorological data, in the form of the maximum daily rainfall of different periods.

- surface geological information concerning soil infiltration. The method of the US Soil Conservation Department was employed to estimate a curve number depending on soil cover, land use, and moisture content.

- morphological data, including the number of branches of each order. The average length and the corresponding catchment area for each order are required as well.

The model gives the hydraulic response of the Valley at a particular section in the form of :

- runoff hydrograph
- runoff volume
- infiltration volume
- surface detention

The computer model was used to determine the hydraulic response of the Valley for storms of return periods of 500, 300, 100, 50, and 30 years. A storm duration of one hour was considered. An average curve number of 95 was used.

Because of the steep slope of the different basins of the Valley, the corresponding hydrographs are almost uniform, reaching peak discharge in a short period (Figures III.3 and III.4). The peak discharge decreases for storms of short return periods. However, it increases from section I through section V because more basins are contributing to the flow going down the main trunk of the Valley. Tables III.3 through III.7 give the peak discharge at sections I through V.

The corresponding volume of runoff and infiltration, using the same hydromorphological model, are presented in the tables. The calculated volume of the water interception changes from 447.0 m^3 in section I to 620.0, 941.0, 1061.0, and 1310.0 m^3 in sections II, III, IV, and V respectively.

4. SEDIMENT LOAD

Strobe's Equation was used to determine the rate and volume of the moving sediment as a bed load. The calculations were performed at sections I, II, III, IV, and V on the main trunk. The results are dependent on the average bed slope, the cross-sectional width, and the empirical value Ψ which is a function of the soil grain size. The sediment particles were assumed to be fine to medium sand. More accurate results could be obtained when the sieve analysis for soil samples is available. The rate and volume of the sediment load are given in Tables III.3 to III.7 for the sections of study for the storms considered.

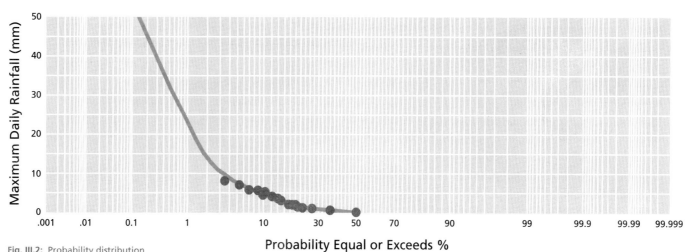

Fig. III.2: Probability distribution of Maximum Daily Rainfall.

	Number of Branches			Average Length of Branches (km)			Collection Area (km²)			
Basin	First Order	Second Order	Third Order	First Order	Second Order	Third Order	First Order	Second Order	Third Order	Average Slope (m/km)
E1	46	20	7	0.530	0.110	0.125	0.1010	0.0295	0.0155	252
E2	11	5	3	0.042	0.092	0.063	0.0297	0.0210	0.0069	284
F	16	12	2	0.0569	0.0444	0.0075	0.0246	0.0176	0.0064	454
G	06	3	1	0.0771	0.0870	0.0320	0.0183	0.0067	0.0233	456
I	16	11	3	0.0520	0.0325	0.0436	0.0289	0.0085	0.0025	315
C	7	4	1	0.1120	0.0653	0.0503	0.0252	0.0118	0.0052	400
B	21	7	8	0.0399	0.0307	0.0289	0.0218	0.0046	0.0052	303
A	21	9	8	0.0310	0.0200	0.0220	0.0168	0.0033	0.0046	239
J1	16	4	5	0.0270	0.0180	0.0220	0.0090	0.0013	0.0028	278
J2	19	9	7	0.0450	0.0270	0.0300	0.0224	0.0096	0.0073	185
K	3	2	-	0.1200	0.0300	-	0.0151	0.0021	-	400
D	3	1	-	0.1010	0.1410	-	0.0184	0.0078	-	392
H	4	3	-	0.0330	0.0470	-	0.0067	0.0051	-	583
M	6	6	-	0.0214	0.0157	-	0.0020	0.0019	-	454
L	2	1	-	0.0150	0.0250	-	0.0049	0.0048	-	280

Table III.2: Morphological Characteristics of the Valley

Table III.3: Calculated Sediment Load at Section I for One-hour Storm Duration

Return Period (Years)	Runoff Peak Discharge (m³/sec)	Runoff Volume (m³)	Infiltration Volume (m³)	Sediment Rate (m³/sec)	Sediment Volume (m³)
500	1.25	5,529.0	1,706.0	1.16	4,173.0
300	1.00	4,434.0	1,632.0	0.89	3,202.0
100	0.48	2,118.0	1,360.0	0.37	1,319.0
50	0.21	927.0	1,048.0	0.14	489.0
30	0.11	482.0	824.0	0.06	223.0

* Interception volume is 447.0 m³

Table III.4: Calculated Sediment Load at Section II for One-hour Storm Duration

Return Period (Years)	Runoff Peak Discharge (m³/sec)	Runoff Volume (m³)	Infiltration Volume (m³)	Sediment Rate (m³/sec)	Sediment Volume (m³)
500	2.20	7,681.0	2,370.0	1.87	6,715.0
300	1.78	6,160.0	2,267.0	1.43	5,153.0
100	0.85	2,942.0	1,889.0	0.59	2,122.0
50	0.37	1,287.0	1,456.0	0.22	787.0
30	0.19	670.0	1,145.0	0.10	359.0

* Interception volume is 620.0 m³

Table III.5: Calculated Sediment Load at Section III for One-hour Storm Duration

Return Period (Years)	Runoff Peak Discharge (m³/sec)	Runoff Volume (m³)	Infiltration Volume (m³)	Sediment Rate (m³/sec)	Sediment Volume (m³)
500	3.41	11,654.0	3,596.0	2.57	10,159.0
300	2.73	9,347.0	3,440.0	1.97	7,796.0
100	1.31	4,464.0	2,866.0	0.81	3,211.0
50	0.57	19,54.0	2,209.0	0.30	1,191.0
30	0.30	1,017.0	1,738.0	0.14	544.0

* Interception volume is 941.0 m³

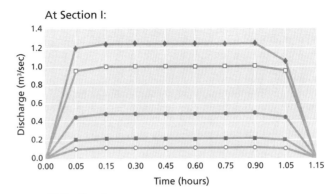

At Section I:

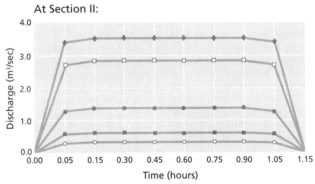

At Section II:

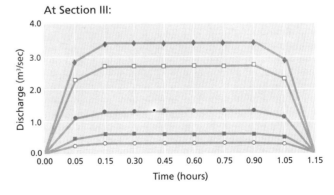

At Section III:

♦ 500 years storm   □ 300 years storm
● 100 years storm   ■ 50 years storm
○ 30 years storm

Fig. III.3: Discharge Rates at Sections I, II, and III.

Table III.6: Calculated Sediment Load at Section IV for One-hour Storm Duration

Return Period (Years)	Runoff Peak Discharge (m³/sec)	Runoff Volume (m³)	Infiltration Volume (m³)	Sediment Rate (m³/sec)	Sediment Volume (m³)
500	3.65	13,144.0	4,056.0	3.19	11,488.0
300	2.90	10,542.0	3,880.0	2.45	8,816.0
100	1.40	5,035.0	3,232.0	1.10	3,632.0
50	0.60	2,203.0	2,491.0	0.37	1,347.0
30	0.32	1,147.0	1,960.0	0.17	615.0

* Interception volume is 1061.0 m³

Table III.7: Calculated Sediment Load at Section V for One-hour Storm Duration

Return Period (Years)	Runoff Peak Discharge (m³/sec)	Runoff Volume (m³)	Infiltration Volume (m³)	Sediment Rate (m³/sec)	Sediment Volume (m³)
500	3.85	16,224.0	5,006.0	3.58	12,891.0
300	3.10	13,011.0	4,788.0	2.75	9,891.0
100	1.48	6,215.0	3,990.0	1.13	4,075.0
50	0.64	2,684.0	3,075.0	0.41	1,488.0
30	0.34	1,416.0	2,419.0	0.19	690.0

* Interception volume is 1310. m³

At Section IV:

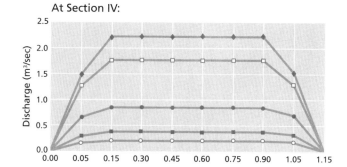

At Section V:

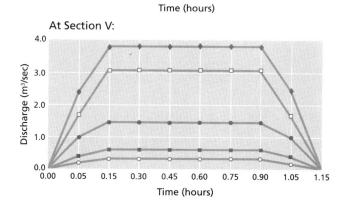

Fig. III.4: Discharge Rates at Sections IV and V.

♦ 500 years storm   □ 300 years storm
● 100 years storm   ■ 50 years storm
○ 30 years storm

Appendix IV:
SLOPE DEFORMATIONS IN
THE VALLEY OF THE KINGS

Michael Bukovansky, Bukovansky Associates Ltd., Lakewood, Colorado, U.S.A
Donald P. Richards, Parsons Brinckerhoff Intl., Cairo, Egypt

1. INTRODUCTION

Professionals involved in archæological, geological, or other work in the Valley of the Kings have often noted the presence of certain geologic features that could not be readily explained and that have evidently influenced the conditions of several tombs. Specifically, the current excavations of KV 5 revealed the presence of large, open, vertical fractures in the rock mass. These fractures contributed to often severe damage of the walls of many rooms in the tomb and to the damage of the rock pillars supporting larger rooms in the tomb.

Large, open vertical fractures have also been observed on the surface, on slopes adjoining both sides of the Valley of the Kings (Curtis, 1979, Curtis and Rutherford, 1981, Romer, 1979, Rutherford, 1990).

Structural damage to the tombs have been attributed by the same authors to the presence of certain clay minerals in the rocks underlying the valley bottom. These clay minerals (specifically montmorillonite) are sensitive to increased moisture content – their volume increases with increasing moisture. This feature, called swelling, is quite common in rocks or soils at numerous locations around the world. It has caused often severe damage to structures built in or founded on such materials.

During the recent excavation of the KV 5, limited engineering geological studies were performed to explain the reasons for the occurrence of the vertical fractures both at the surface and in the tombs in a more detail. Correct understanding of these features is evidently important if individual tombs are to be mitigated, their current conditions improved, and their safety and satisfactory performance for future generations accomplished.

Based on the results of the engineering geological studies performed during the excavations of the KV 5 in 1995 - 1996, it is believed that the presence of the vertical fractures, both on the surface and in the KV 5 tomb, is the result of ancient slope deformations (spreading of large blocks of rock). The slope deformations are very probably related to the presence of montmorillonite in the rock formations underlying the valley (Bukovansky, Richards, and Weeks, 1997).

2. MORPHOLOGY AND GEOLOGY OF THE AREA

The Valley of the Kings is located several kilometers west of the River Nile, in a geographic unit of the Western Desert. The area is typical of a high plateau, underlain by relatively soft, horizontally bedded, sedimentary rock. The valley is deeply incised, northeast-southwest trending, drainage flowing generally east to the Nile. The valley is bounded on both sides by hills that are typically sixty meters high above the valley bottom. Further to west, maximum elevations reach nearly 300 meters above the valley bottom (el Gurn, elevation 455 meters). The morphology of the valley indicates two types of slopes: steep-to-vertical cliffs and flat valley slopes. Steep-to-vertical slopes have typically developed at higher elevations, in the upper valley parts, while the lower parts of the valley are formed by much flatter hills, with slopes typically of

25 - 30 degrees. It is probable that the remarkable difference between these two morphological types has been caused by different types of rock: steep slopes and cliffs have developed in harder rocks (cliff-forming rocks) while flat slopes are underlain by much softer rocks, less resistant to erosion and weathering (slope-forming rocks).

Geology of the area has been described in general by Said (1962) and in detail by Curtis (1979). The rocks underlying the area are of sedimentary origin, of Lower Eocene (Tertiary) age. Two formations outcrop in the area: The upper Theban (sometimes also called Thebes) Limestone formation and the lower Esna Shale formation. They are both flat lying (practically horizontal). The contact between both formations is below the bottom of the Valley of the Kings; for this reason, Esna Shale does not outcrop in the valley. The contact can be found in the West Valley, close to the Davis house, at an elevation of approximately 150 meters.

The Theban Limestone is a moderately hard, tan limestone, with several beds of dark gray shaley limestone in the lower part, close to the contact with the Esna Shale. The lower beds of the limestone are known to contain montmorillonite. The Esna Shale is a dark gray, softer rock containing significant quantities of montmorillonite and probably anhydrite ($CaSO_4$).

A fault, approximately parallel with the valley, with a displacement of about thirty meters was identified by Curtis (1979). The fault is visible in several side valleys, on the west side of the main Valley.

With the exception of the alluvial soils, there are no important soil types developed in the area. The cover of colluvial or residual soils on the slopes is negligible and of no technical importance. The accumulations of the alluvial soils in the main valley and in larger side valleys are, however, very important. The alluvial soils are mostly formed by a coarse (gravel) fraction, mixed with sand and silt. The gravel and boulders are angular, formed by local limestone and sandstone. The angular character of the limestone fragments indicates a limited length of transport and a flood-event origin of these sediments.

Important accumulations of the alluvial sediments in the area indicate the occurrence of infrequent flash-floods in the area. Such floods are a result of infrequent but important precipitation events. Alluvial sediments deposited during such events carry significant amounts of rock debris and loose soils. They have been deposited not only in the valleys but also in the tombs which have unprotected entries located at or close to the valley bottom and downward-inclined entry corridors. KV 5 has been filled to a large extent by such alluvial deposits.

Most of the tombs in the Valley of the Kings have been excavated in the limestone of the Theban formation. The rock containing important sets of vertical or subvertical joints is of a relatively soft material which facilitated the construction of the tombs. As discussed in Appendix V, the rock strength is not always high enough to always support the walls and the pillars of some larger rooms, such as in KV 5.

Because the Esna Shale is located relatively deep below the valley bottom, only a few tombs penetrated into this formation. The Esna Shale is not a material suitable for underground excavation and support methods available to the ancient tomb builders, and it was not used for tomb construction.

3. ROCK STRUCTURE - BEDDING PLANES AND JOINTS IN THEBES LIMESTONE

Because of the limited extent of the soil deposits in the Valley of the Kings area, the properties of the underlying rock are of a major importance for the behavior of the tombs and for the slope deformations that have been currently studied. The contemporary methods of engineering geology and rock mechanics usually separate the properties of the rock itself and of the rock mass. The rock is characterized by the

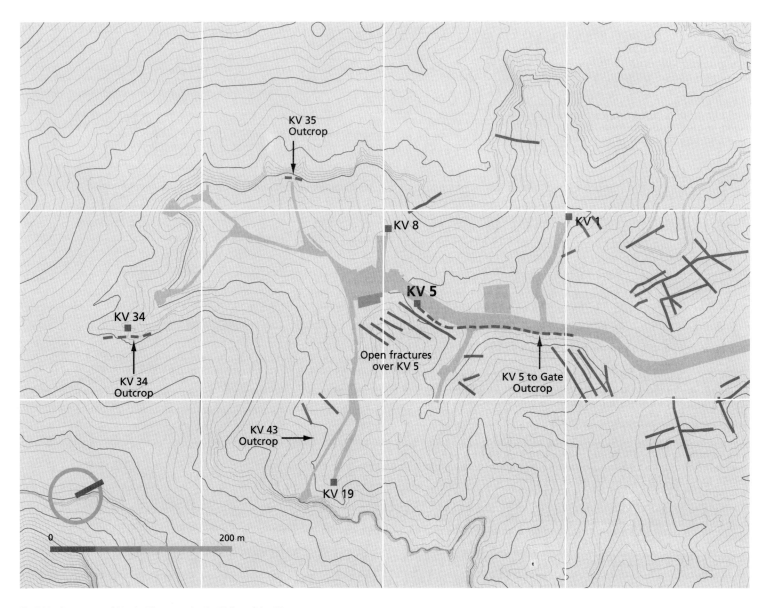

Fig. IV.1: Outcrops and Vertical Fractures in the Valley of the Kings.

properties of a small sample (such as the fragment of the rock, or as the core sample obtained from a boring). The rock mass is a larger mass that contains not only the rock but also all dividing planes, or the planes of mechanical discontinuity, such as the faults, the bedding planes, and the joints. Such dividing planes often are of a greater importance for the behavior of the rock mass than the properties of the rock itself.

The orientation and properties of such dividing planes often influence the behavior of the rock mass, the stability of the underground openings excavated in the mass, or any slope deformations that may have occurred in the rock mass. The orientation of the rock mass dividing planes is often called the rock structure.

In the absence of any systematic data on the rock structure identified by previous studies, measurements of the orientation of the rock mass dividing planes have been taken in the KV 5 tomb and on several additional outcrops in the valley recently. All these measurements were taken in the limestone of the Theban formation.

There are two dominant sets of rock mass dividing planes in the limestone:

- Bedding planes. Bedding planes are horizontal or subhorizontal rock mass dividing planes, the origin of which is related to the original sedimentation of the formation. Their orientation cannot be accurately measured and it would have to be evaluated with the help of exploratory drilling in the area. For practical purposes, and in absence of any other data, bedding has been considered to be horizontal.

- Joints. Joints comprise a complementary set of the rock mass dividing planes. As is typical in sedimentary rock formations, most joints are roughly perpendicular to the bedding planes, i.e., they are vertical or subvertical. The presence of vertical joints is visible at most cliff-forming rock outcrops in the valley. Vertical joints are the only system of joints considered for the slope deformations evaluation (although joints other than vertical have also been documented).

Several hundred of joint orientation measurements have been taken in the valley. Most joint measurements were taken in KV 5 but additional measurements were made on several rock outcrops in the valley. Approximate locations of these outcrops are shown in Figure IV.1.

A detailed evaluation of the joint measurements is presented in Appendix V. Methods of stereographic projection and statistics have been used for this evaluation. For the purpose of slope deformations, only one rosette diagram showing a radial histogram of the strike density (frequency) of all vertical and subvertical joints measured on surface outcrops is shown in Figure IV.2. Figure IV.2 indicates the prevailing presence of vertical joints striking in a northeast-southwest direction. The same joint system has been identified in KV 5 (see Figure V.14) and it can be observed in numerous outcrops and cliffs in the valley. Based on all measurements in the valley, the mean strike of this primary joint system is N62°E, with the mean dip close to ninety degrees (vertical).

The remaining joints are oriented in various directions, but the majority are close to perpendicular to the primary joint system, oriented in a northwest-southeast direction. Based on all measurements, the mean strike of this secondary joint system is N48°W, again with a mean dip close to vertical.

These two joint systems comprise two sets of dividing planes in the Theban Limestone in the Valley of the Kings area. As they are almost perpendicular to each other, they have caused the rock mass to separate into blocks limited by these joint sets and by the horizontal bedding planes.

4. INDICATIONS AND ORIGIN OF SLOPE DEFORMATIONS

Vertical open fractures that can be observed both at the surface and in some underground tombs are an indication of the slope deformations that have influenced the slopes on both sides of the Valley of the Kings.

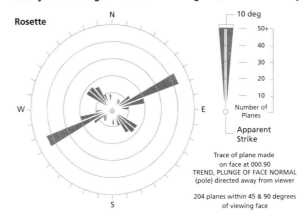

Valley of the Kings - Cumulative Diagram, Surface Outcrops

Fig. IV.2: Strike Density of Vertical and Subvertical Joints.

Large open fractures at the valley sides are probably the most frequently noted feature. They disturb the slopes where the tombs have been constructed but they are also present on slopes where no known tombs exist. They are present in the Valley of the Kings but they extend beyond the valley, specifically to the north. They can be found at numerous other locations, often at a distance from the main valley. The most significant accumulation of open vertical fractures occurs at the west valley side, north of the gate to the valley.

Some of the more important vertical fractures are shown on the map in Figure IV.1. The map is approximate only and does not show all the fractures existing in the area. The map indicates that the majority of the fractures are close to parallel with the major valleys. The strike of the fractures does not always coincide with the strike of the earlier defined joint sets. The majority of the fractures strike north-south (similar to the general Valley of the Kings direction). There are notable exceptions such as a series of open fractures on the south side of the West Valley, close to its confluence with the Valley of the Kings. These fractures are parallel with the West Valley and strike approximately east-west. Similar, east-west-striking open fractures are present east of the Valley of the Kings, at its confluence with the Valley of the Wells.

The only location where the strike of the open fractures coincides with the strike of the dominant, primary joint set (N62°E) is the immediate vicinity of KV 5. At this location, open vertical fractures that have developed along this joint system are visible at the surface. More importantly, numerous open vertical fractures that follow the same joint set have been found at numerous locations inside KV 5. It should be noted that at this location, the valley axis closely coincides with the primary joints strike.

The vertical surface fractures are often open to 1 meter or more (Figure IV.3). In all cases, they seem to be filled with rock debris and soil. The fractures above KV 5 are open only ten to twenty centimeters and they do not appear to be filled. The fractures inside KV 5 are open only several centimeters and do not have any significant infilling material.

The character and orientation of the open vertical fractures are typical of the processes that are usually related to slope deformations. Unlike landslides or other slope failures, such slope deformations are usually slow and of a limited magnitude. They may be of recent origin but very often they are ancient. They may have developed under the different climatic conditions, when the precipitation was significantly higher than that at present. The deformations may not be continuing at present. Such slope deformations would typically be classified as an ancient feature.

Modern geologic classifications (Turner and Schuster, 1996) use a number of names for such slope deformations. They may be called slope creep, gravitational, or lateral spreading. They were first described by Zischinsky (1966), who used the German word *Sackungen* for large slope deformations found in the Alps.

The gravity action is usually the primary reason for slope deformations. They have been identified and described mostly in high mountains in areas of steep slopes and large differences in altitude (Zischinsky, 1966, Varnes, 1989). In such cases, slope deformations are usually manifested by large, vertical fractures that may penetrate deep below the surface. In other cases where the topographic relief is limited, slope deformations are often found when local, unfavorable geologic conditions contribute to slope deformation development. A layer of a soft, less resistant rock in sedimentary formations may cause deformations, or limited sliding of large rock blocks along such a weak layer. Unfavorable groundwater conditions may often contribute to the development of important slope deformations.

The large open vertical fractures in the Valley of the Kings are considered to be the result of such slope deformations. Based on the available evidence, they are large and open at the surface (although they are evidently filled with rock and soil debris), and they also have been found in the recently excavated tomb KV 5. They are open to some ten centimeters in this tomb, indicating that the magnitude of the fracture openings decreases with the depth below the topographic surface.

Because the geographic unit where the Valley of the Kings is located does not re-present the high mountains where the slope deformations are most typical, there is a high probability that there are additional geologic factors contributing to the slope deformations development. It is probable that the presence of montmorillonite (and possibly anhydrite) in the underlying Esna Shale is the most important factor contributing to slope deformation development. All previous studies performed in the valley and our own studies confirmed the presence of montmorillonite and anhydrite in the Esna Shale (see Appendix II, and Skala and Bukovanska, 1966), but also in few shaley layers that occur at the base of the Theban Limestone formation.

As both montmorillonite and anhydrite are the minerals sensitive to changes in moisture levels, the occurrence of the documented slope deformations can be explained. Events of exceptionally high precipitation and flood events in the valley have been well documented (Romer, 1979, Appendix B). Alluvial debris filling individual tombs confirm such precipitation events. The documented rock structure, with important sets of vertical joints in the Theban Limestone, is another factor contributing to slope deformation development. During periods of high precipitation, water can seep through these joints until it reaches the less permeable rock mass - the underlying Esna Shale. It is most probable that after any larger precipitation event, the Esna Shale was saturated for an extended period of time. As the moisture content of the shale increased, the rock swelled and lifted up the overlying overburden. Rock testing performed during our studies evaluated the magnitude of the swelling pressures of the montmorillonite-bearing rocks (see Appendix I). The magnitude of these pressures exceeds the pressure caused by the weight of the overburden rocks, confirming that uplifting of the overburden rocks did occur at the time of the underlying rock saturation.

In addition of the overburden uplifting, gravity action contributed to the non-uniform slope deformations. The area is dissected by a series of valleys, which include the Valley of the Kings and a number of its tributaries. Along all these valleys, the horizontal stresses in the rock mass have been reduced during the time of the valleys' erosion. The reduction in horizontal stresses may cause deformations of large rock blocks; such deformations may be just an inclination of individual blocks or small deformations of the blocks along the layer of a softened Esna Shale. Figure IV.4 shows the interpretation of the slope deformations identified in the Valley of the Kings.

There is not enough data or information available at present to evaluate whether the existing slope deformations comprise merely an inclination of large rock blocks or whether the deformations also include lateral spreading of the individual blocks along a layer of a softened shale at the base of a large rock block. There is, however, little doubt about the slope deformations in the Valley and about their influence on the Valley slopes and the tombs.

The presence of slope deformations in the Western Desert, in an area of relatively flat topography, with no permanent groundwater and very little average precipitation, is rather unique, and it can be mostly attributed to the presence of the minerals with swelling properties in the Esna Shale and in lower sections of the Theban Limestone, and to the occurrence of the significant precipitation events. The presence of these minerals and their important influence on slope stability is evident at a different location, where the outcrops of the Theban Limestone and the underlying Esna Shale rim the Nile valley, such as in the nearby Valley of the Queens. At that location, the combined influence of the underlying rock mineralogy and the influence of water have contributed to the development of very large landslides. Occurrence of such large landslides is seemingly improbable given the arid conditions of this area and the relatively favorable rock structure of the Tertiary sediments. It is most probable that these landslides occurred during climatic conditions different from those at present.

5. INFLUENCE OF SLOPE DEFORMATIONS ON THE TOMBS

Although no accurate data are available to us on the location of all individual tombs, it is highly probable that nearly all of them were constructed in the limestone of the Theban formation, and it cannot be ruled out that some of them penetrated into

Fig. IV.3: Vertical joints in the hillside above KV 5 (left), being filled by workmen with cement (right).

the underlying Esna Shale. As the rocks of the Esna Shale have much less favorable physical properties, it is probable that any excavations in them were abandoned.

Based on the interpretation of the slope deformations as shown in Figure IV.4, it is evident that most, if not all the tombs in the Valley of the Kings were constructed in rocks that may have been influenced by the slope deformations. The documentation of the surface, open vertical fractures (Figure IV.1) shows that the fractures occur only in certain areas of the valley and that at numerous locations, the indications of the slope deformations are absent.

As shown in the example of the recently excavated KV 5, the vertical fractures indicating slope deformations are present both on the surface and inside the tomb. In this particular case, both the surface and underground fractures coincide with the most important vertical joint set, striking in a northeast-southwest direction. The influence of the slope deformations on this tomb is evident.

The available data do not enable an evaluation of the age of the identified slope deformations. The slope deformations may be much older than the existing tombs, but it cannot be ruled out that they developed after the tomb construction. We believe that the slope deformations are older than the tombs and that they developed probably during the period after the last continental glaciation when climatic conditions (specifically precipitation) were more severe than those at present. In other words, the large, open fractures were already present in the area when the tombs were constructed. It is also possible that the construction of the tombs tried to avoid the areas with the highest concentration of surface cracks.

It is not possible to evaluate whether the identified slope deformations are continuing at present or whether they only developed during the post-glacial period and are inactive at present. In our opinion, further studies are needed to clarify some of these factors.

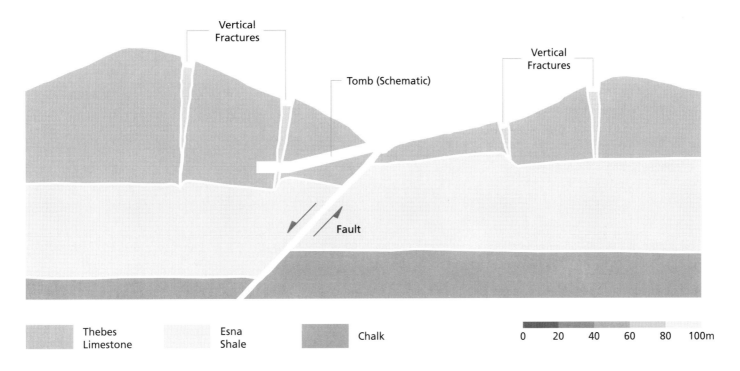

Fig. IV.4: Diagrammatic view of slope deformations in the Valley of the Kings and their effect on the tombs.

6. DATA NEEDED FOR SLOPE DEFORMATIONS MITIGATION

The location of certain tombs within the large rock blocks that either have experienced slope deformations in the past, or may be experiencing the deformations at present and in the future is an important factor to be taken into account in planning the preservation of the tombs for the future generations. Specific mitigation at KV 5 is discussed in the Appendix VI.

To mitigate the stability problems effectively, further data should be collected. They should include:

- Evaluation of the geological conditions of the area; specifically, the position of the Thebes limestone and of the underlying Esna shale. The contact between both these formations is known only from the outcrop of the Esna shale in the West Valley but is largely unknown in the parts of the valley where the tombs were constructed. Drilling of vertical core-holes at selected locations is required for this purpose.

- Mineralogical analyses of the rocks of the Thebes limestone and of the Esna shale, paying specific attention to montmorillonite and anhydrite.

- Collection of data on physical properties of the limestone and shale. Tests should be performed on the rock cores obtained by drilling the recommended borings.

- Accurate evaluation of the Valley of the Kings fault identified by Curtis (1979). The contact between the Thebes limestone and Esna shale will be at different elevations at both sides of the fault. In addition to geological mapping, drilling would also be required for this purpose.

- Collecting data on slope deformations. Such data should provide information on whether the identified deformations are continuing at present, or whether they occur following important precipitation events. Such data are essential for any plans for the tombs' mitigation, prevention of water inflows into the tombs, etc.

7. REFERENCES

Bukovansky, M., D.P. Richards, and **K.R. Weeks.** Influence of Slope Deformations on the Tombs in the Valley of the Kings, Egypt. *Proceedings, International Symposium, Engineering Geology and the Environment, Athens, Greece.* Rotterdam: A.A. Balkema, 1997.

Curtis, G.H. The Geology of the Valley of the Kings, Thebes, Egypt, Theban Royal Tomb Project, The Brooklyn Museum Theban Expedition. Report to Egyptian Antiquities Organization (unpublished), 1979.

Curtis, G.H. and **J.B. Rutherford.** Expansive Shale Damage, Theban Royal Tombs, Egypt. *Proceedings, Conf. ISSMFE.* 1981.

Rutherford, J.B. Geotechnical Causes of Ancient Tomb Damage, Valley of the Kings, Egypt. *Proceedings, IAEG Symposium on Geotechnical Aspects of Restoration Works on Infrastructures and Monuments.* Rotterdam: A.A. Balkema, 1990.

Said, Rushdi. *The Geology of Egypt.* Amsterdam and New York: Elsevier Publishing Company, 1962.

Skala, R. and **M. Bukovanska.** Petrology and Mineralogy of the Esna Shale (unpublished), 1996.

Turner, A.K. and **R.L. Schuster.** *Landslides, Investigation and Mitigation, Special Report 247.* Washington D.C.: Transportation Research Board, 1996.

Varnes, D.J., D.H. Radbruch-Hall, and **W.Z. Savage.** Topographic and Structural Conditions in Areas of Gravitational Spreading of Ridges in the Western United States. U.S. Geological Survey Professional Paper 1496. Washington D.C., 1989.

Zischinsky, U. On the Deformation of High Slopes. *Proceedings of the First Congress of the International Society of Rock Mechanics, Lisbon, Portugal.* 1966.

Appendix V:
GEOTECHNICAL STUDIES FOR KV-5

Donald P. Richards, Parsons Brinckerhoff Intl., Cairo, Egypt
Michael Bukovansky, Bukovansky Assoc., Lakewood, CO, USA
John F. Abel, Jr., Mining Consultant, Golden, CO, USA

1. INTRODUCTION

The rock-cut tombs of the Pharaonic era in Egypt represent some of the oldest underground excavations in the world. The New Kingdom tombs in the Valley of the Kings of ancient Thebes represent some of the largest rock cut tombs in Egypt. The currently known layout of KV 5 in the Valley of the Kings makes it the most extensive and elaborate of these rock-cut tombs. It represents one of the most extensive underground excavations of ancient times that is still accessible today (see Fig. V.1).

Over the last 250 years, numerous travelers and researchers have investigated the rock cut tombs in the Valley of the Kings (see Reeves and Wilkinson, 1996 for relevant references), but only very recently (1980s to 1990s) have any of these researchers extended their studies beyond archæology to other aspects of the Valley, such as the geologic and geotechnical conditions contributing to tomb conditions and stability.

Although Curtis (1979, 1995), Curtis and Rutherford (1981), Romer and Romer (1981), Rutherford (1990), and Rutherford and Ryan (1995) have discussed both the general geology of the Valley of the Kings and the geologic influences upon tomb stability, they have concentrated primarily upon stratigraphic studies of rock type versus elevation within the Valley, and the possibility of swelling shale affecting tomb stability.

To the authors' knowledge, none of the geologic studies to date except those of the Theban Mapping Project (see Bukovansky 1997) have addressed rock structure (naturally occurring discontinuities in the rock mass) and its influence upon tomb stability, i.e. a conventional rock mechanics analysis of tomb condition and stability. This Appendix reports upon the initial studies by the Theban Mapping Project to evaluate the geotechnical aspects of KV 5, with comparisons, where relevant, to the rest of the Valley of the Kings.

2. SITE DESCRIPTION

2.1 General

The Valley of the Kings is located in an incised valley (wadi) on the northeast side of el Gurn, a pyramid-shaped peak of the Theban Massif on the west side of the River Nile near present-day Luxor at approximate latitude 25° 52′ N, and longitude 32° 35′ E. The majority of the tombs there, including KV 5, lie in the main or eastern valley, with KV 5 located at the lower (northeastern) end near the entrance to the Valley, as shown in Figure IV.1.

2.2 Geology

The Theban Massif is composed of a layered, generally flat-lying sedimentary rock sequence known as the Theban (Thebes) Limestone (Tel) of Tertiary age. Said (1962) has reported on the general geology of the Luxor (Thebes) area, but has concentrated mainly on the stratigraphy (rock types, ages, and sequences) with very little inform-

ation on rock structure (discontinuity type, orientation, extent, and location in three dimensional space). The geology of the area has also been documented in various maps, but these do not include rock structure data (see Survey of Egypt, 1946; GOGRMGS, 1968; MIMR, 1978; MPWWR, 1992).

In the Valley of the Kings, all the tombs are located within the lowest member (Member I) of the Theban Limestone (see Figure V.2). Generally, Eighteenth Dynasty tombs are at the highest elevation within this member, Twentieth Dynasty tombs are at the lowest elevations, and Nineteenth Dynasty tombs are in between, as shown in Figure V.3. KV 5 of the Nineteenth Dynasty is approximately mid-range in elevation for the Nineteenth Dynasty. This lowest member has been generally described by Curtis (1977) as a massive buff marly limestone with lenses of flint and shale interbeds in the lower layers of the member above its contact with the underlying Esna Shale.

Mineralogy evaluations by thin section examination, microchemical, and X-ray diffraction analysis of the rock samples from KV 5 conducted during this study characterize the lower limestone member as a hard, compact, finely crystalline, creamy white, massive, almost homogeneous lime-mudstone composed mostly of carbonate minerals, calcite, and dolomite, and traces of montmorillonite clay, halite, and quartz (Appendix II). Further X-ray powder diffraction studies (Skala and Bukovanska, 1996) describe this lower limestone member as primarily calcite and dolomite, with traces of quartz and montmorillonite, confirming the earlier analysis. Although these data were not used in any engineering analysis, it serves to help characterize the material in terms of anticipated engineering behavior when considered in conjunction with other rock mechanics index tests to be discussed later in Section 3.

For comparison purposes, and considering the potential for the lowest level chambers in KV 5 to penetrate down to near the Theban Limestone contact with the underlying Esna Shale, mineralogical tests were also conducted on the shaly layers at the bottom of the Theban Limestone, and on Esna Shale samples. At present, however, there is no evidence of either the shaly portion of the lower Theban Limestone or the Esna Shale being present in any of the KV 5 chambers, even at the lowest elevations. The shale layer of the Theban Limestone was characterized (Appendix II) as moderately compact, creamy, buff-colored shale composed (in decreasing abundance) of carbonate minerals (calcite, dolomite, or magnesian calcite), clay minerals (illite and montmorillonite) and halide minerals. The sample of suspected Esna Shale from the debris pile near the entrance to KV 20 was described as finely laminated grayish colored shale composed (in decreasing abundance) of calcite, illite, montmorillonite and quartz.

3. ROCK CHARACTERIZATION TESTS

3.1 General

In support of the rock mechanics studies for KV 5, a small testing program was undertaken to characterize the KV 5 Theban Limestone from a rock mechanics perspective, and to supplement the mineralogical characterization as noted above. Due to the close proximity of the Esna Shale beneath the lower member of the Theban limestone, and the shaly zone in the lower portion of the limestone near the contact zone, these two materials were also tested for comparison purposes and for geotechnical reference. These tests are described in the following paragraphs.

3.2 Point Load Strength

This test (a recommended procedure by the International Society of Rock Mechanics) provides an estimate of the uniaxial compressive strength of the rock, by splitting irregular pieces of rock between two conical platens and measuring the load required

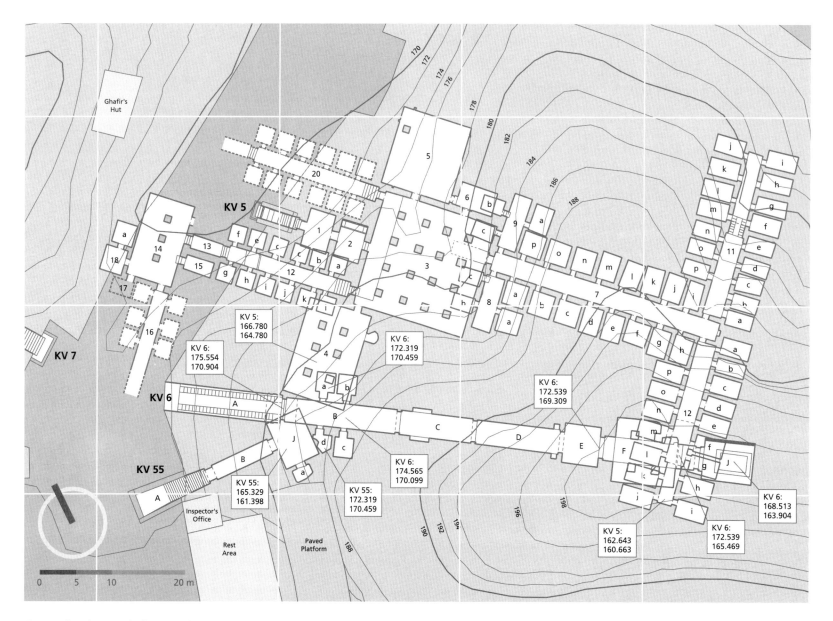

Fig. V.1: Plan of KV 5 and adjacent tombs.

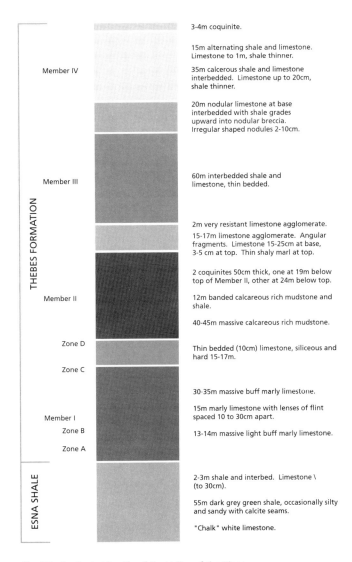

	3-4m coquinite.
Member IV	15m alternating shale and limestone. Limestone to 1m, shale thinner.
	35m calcerous shale and limestone interbedded. Limestone up to 20cm, shale thinner.
	20m nodular limestone at base interbedded with shale grades upward into nodular breccia. Irregular shaped nodules 2-10cm.
Member III	60m interbedded shale and limestone, thin bedded.
	2m very resistant limestone agglomerate.
	15-17m limestone agglomerate. Angular fragments. Limestone 15-25cm at base, 3-5 cm at top. Thin shaly marl at top.
Member II	2 coquinites 50cm thick, one at 19m below top of Member II, other at 24m below top.
	12m banded calcareous rich mudstone and shale.
	40-45m massive calcareous rich mudstone.
Zone D	Thin bedded (10cm) limestone, siliceous and hard 15-17m.
Zone C	
	30-35m massive buff marly limestone.
	15m marly limestone with lenses of flint spaced 10 to 30cm apart.
Member I	
Zone B	13-14m massive light buff marly limestone.
Zone A	
	2-3m shale and interbed. Limestone \ (to 30cm).
	55m dark grey green shale, occasionally silty and sandy with calcite seams.
	"Chalk" white limestone.

(Left margin labels: THEBES FORMATION, ESNA SHALE)

Fig. V.2: Geological Profile of the Valley of the Kings. Drawn after **G. Curtis.** *The Geology of the Valley of the Kings, Thebes, Egypt,* 1979.

to initiate failure. Although this test is not a direct measurement, it provides a relative strength index for various rock materials, and the results may be used to estimate the actual strength in the absence of better test data. Test results are shown below in Table V.1. These values should be reduced for rock mass strength due to the presence of natural discontinuities. A reduction factor of four or more may be appropriate, and is discussed in more detail in Section 6.2.

3.3 Slake Durability

This test (as recommended by the International Society of Rock Mechanics) provides an accelerated weathering index on rock samples by subjecting them to alternating cycles of wetting and drying while simultaneously subjecting them to mechanical abrasion. At both intermediate and final stages of the test, the 'durability' is measured by measuring the amount of weight loss from the test samples due to degradation during the test. The test produced a durability class II with 30.7% weight loss during the test for the limestone, and class III with more than 90% weight loss for the shale samples (both the shaly layer of the lower Theban Limestone and the suspected Esna Shale). The limestone results indicate fairly good performance which would suggest little rock deterioration due to alternating cycles of wetting and drying due to infiltrating rainwater or changes in humidity of the air in the tomb. However, the shales exhibited significantly worse behavior, and would indicate the potential for deterioration and swell/heave problems if exposed in the floor of any tomb chambers.

3.4 Atterberg Limits

The Atterberg Limits test (a modification for applications to rock samples of the procedure by the American Society for Testing and Materials) represents a determination of the relative plasticity of geological materials. The test was originally developed for testing clayey soils as a method to determine the 'relative cohesiveness.' It is equally beneficial for testing disaggregated rocks that contain clay materials, since it provides a measure of the behavior of the clay minerals present by quantifying their behavior on a relative basis. The test results can be compared to the results of the mineralogical analysis and the slake durability test to obtain a more complete visualization of the engineering behavior of the rock types being tested.

The test results on the pulverized limestone from KV 5 indicate a liquid limit of 40.5%, plastic limit of 29.4%, and plasticity index of 11.0%. These results classify the pulverized material as ML (low plasticity silt according to the ASTM Unified Soil Classification System), indicating a negligible plasticity or tendency for swelling and shrinking when subjected to moisture changes. The shale samples (both shaly layer of Theban Limestone and suspected Esna Shale), classified as CH (high plasticity silt according to the ASTM Unified Soil Classification System), with a liquid limit of about 60 - 70% and plasticity index of 30 - 40%, and could be expected to exhibit significant volume change if exposed to moisture. This confirms the behavior as indicated by the slake durability and Atterberg Limits tests and would be expected based on the mineralogical analysis.

3.5 Swell Potential

The swell test is also performed on disaggregated rock samples as with the Atterberg Limits Test. The pulverized sample is re-compacted into a mold at a predetermined density. Two types of tests were done. The first was to load the sample with a nominal surcharge (0.2 MPa for this test program) and then saturate the sample and monitor the swell amount as the sample increases in volume when any clay minerals absorbed water. The second test technique was to load the sample as above and saturate it, but to allow it to swell to its maximum potential, then to continue to add sufficient load to reduce the volume increase to zero. This technique measured the potential swell pressures. The higher the content of swelling clay minerals present, the higher the swell volume or pressure.

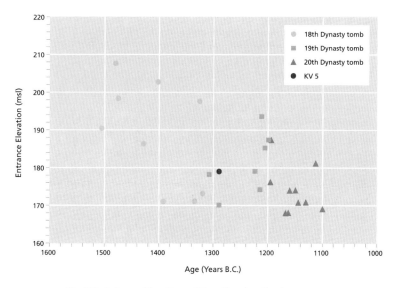

Fig. V.3: Entrance Elevations of New Kingdom Tombs.

As expected, the limestone samples exhibited only minimal swell potential, with a swell pressure of approximately 0.3 MPa and a swell volume of 2.3%. These results indicate that volume changes due to changes in moisture content would be negligible, especially since the test is performed on a pulverized sample with a high specific surface area not encountered in the intact rock in the tomb. The shale samples (both the shaly layer of the lower Theban Limestone and the suspected Esna Shale) however, exhibited much more severe swell potential, with 'free' swell as high as 26% and swell pressures as high as 2.45 MPa for the suspected Esna Shale. These results are consistent with the other index test results for shales noted above, and reflect the montmorillonite clay constituent.

3.6 Summary

All rock mechanics test data are summarized in Table V.2. All tests for each rock type were consistent within that rock type, with the limestone exhibiting generally 'good' performance and the shale indicating 'poor' performance as a host rock to tomb excavations.

4. ROCK STRUCTURE MAPPING

4.1 General

The naturally occurring rock discontinuities, normally characterized as 'joints' and 'bedding planes' in geologic literature, were mapped in three dimensional space using a special compass, and the results presented using a geological engineering technique known as stereographic projection. The three dimensional orientation of individual joints exposed in either excavation faces or natural rock outcrops was measured. In order to document the geological rock structure (joint orientation) of KV 5, detailed mapping was done in chambers 1, 2, 3, and 4, and corridors 7, 10, and 11 (see Figure V.1 for room identifications). In addition, similar mapping was done in the entrance road outcrops, north of KV 5, and near the entrances of tombs KV 35, KV 34, and KV 43 in an attempt to relate the KV 5 joint patterns to those in other parts of the Valley of the Kings. Details of the mapping carried out to date are included in Figure V.4 for KV 5, Figures V.5 to V.8 for surface outcrops for comparison purposes, Figure V.9 for all surface outcrops measured, and Figure V.10 for summarizing all joint orientations mapped in the Valley (see Appendix IV).

4.2 Field Measurements

It can be seen in the data plots of the above-noted figures that the rock discontinuities generally are near vertical, with dips measured from the horizontal of 80° to 90°. The discontinuity orientations are also relatively consistent in the north end of the Valley with the strike of the primary joint (azimuth of an imaginary level horizontal line drawn on the joint surface) oriented at approximately N50°E to N70°E. This orientation appears to represent only a secondary joint in the upper, south end of the Valley, where the primary joint set is oriented approximately N40°W to N60°W.

It should also be noted that the primary joint orientations at the north end of the Valley in and around KV 5 are also consistent with the orientation of the open vertical fractures exposed on the surface as noted in Appendix IV. These fractures are prominent features in KV 5, as noted in Figure V.14, where major, continuous, partially open joints are mapped on a plan of KV 5.

4.3 Stability Implications for KV 5

It can be seen from the data plots in Figure V.4 that the large majority of the joints mapped in KV 5 are near vertical. It can also be seen that there are other minor joints which represent a random pattern, with dips ranging from about 10° to 80°. Although no joints parallel to bedding were measured in the roof of the tomb – i.e., parallel to the roof – there are also undoubtedly joints which are parallel with the near horizontal bedding of the sedimentary formation.

Table V.1: Summary Point Load Strength Tests			
Rock Type	Sample No.	Est. Uniaxial Compressive Strength (MPa)	ISRM Strength Class
Lower Theban Limestone	1	39	R3 = Med. Strong
	2	134	R5 = Very Strong
	3	106	R5 = Very Strong
	4	59	R4 = Strong
	Avg.	85	R4 = Strong
Shaly Layer of Lower Theban Limestone	1	55	R4 = Strong
	2	47	R3 = Med. Strong
	3	158	R5 = Very Strong
	Avg.	87	R4 = Strong
Esna Shale (?) From KV-20	1	59	R4 = Strong
	2	64	R4 = Strong
	3	86	R4 = Strong
	Avg.	70	R4 = Strong

Nearly all of the non-horizontal joints would tend to weaken the rock mass, as discussed further in Section 6.2. However, isolated joint planes could also produce preferential weaknesses, where present in critical parts of the excavation and dipping at critical angles, i.e. greater than approximately 30° or 40°. If such a plane crosses a roof or wall pillar and is fairly continuous, slippage along the plane could occur under load from above, regardless of the strength of the intact rock forming the pillar.

Also, in the roof and wall pillars, strength/stress relationships address only failure by compression. Where vertical or near vertical joints are continuous through a roof or wall pillar, the pillar is effectively divided into two independent structural members each with a slenderness ratio (height/width ratio) greater than the single structure as originally excavated. Depending on the height of the original excavation, size of the pillar, and the location and continuity of the vertical joint, this could lead to the potential for pillar failure by buckling rather than uniaxial compression. The absence of obvious buckling failure in tomb walls indicates that the joint bond strength exceeds the buckling stress.

The flat-lying, near-horizontal joints parallel to the bedding have the potential, if overlying the roof, to allow the roof block below the joint to loosen from the overlying rock mass. Within this 'loose' block, the orthogonal vertical joints combined with bedding plane weaknesses can define blocks that can easily fall into the excavation if left unsupported either naturally (by roof or wall pillars) or artificially with supplemental structural support. This failure mechanism is evident in KV 5 where large blocks have already fallen or are intact but detached from the rest of the rock mass above the roof. It should be noted that these major roof falls are relatively recent when compared to the age of the tomb, since they are usually present on top of the alluvial fill in the tomb rather than embedded within or below the fill. This type of roof fall is commonly encountered in mining, with the flat roof stabilized with rock bolts or structural steel supports. Conceptual excavation failure modes are shown in Figure V.11.

5. TOMB STABILITY IMPLICATIONS

5.1 General

A number of factors influence the overall stability of the tomb, including the overburden depth, rock strength (both intact and rock mass), rock discontinuities (spacing, orientation, condition, and extent), humidity, alluvial fill, and excavation geometry (i.e., pillar sizes, room widths, and wall pillar widths). Due to the large number of variables it has not been possible to do detailed analysis that would include the influence of all variables. Consequently, the results presented herein should be considered preliminary, with more detailed evaluations to follow as time and funding are available.

In conventional contemporary underground excavations in rock, the length of time an excavation roof can be expected to be stable without supplemental support is known as the 'stand-up time'. Normally, an unsupported roof span of three to four meters, similar to those in KV 5, is considered excellent if stand-up time exceeds a hundred years, and the normal graphical empirical relationships do not extend beyond about sixty or seventy years (see figure V.12). The fact that the roof in KV 5 has been essentially stable (with only isolated relatively recent roof falls and complete collapse only in Chamber 5) indicates exceptionally good performance when extending the stand-up time relationships from 70 to 3500 years as shown in Figure V.12.

5.2 Existing Conditions - Roof

The current condition of the KV 5 tomb is fair at best. In most rooms, the roof has failed locally, with blocks bounded by horizontal and vertical joints having fallen out of the roof (see Figure V.11). In most cases, the roof fall, although appearing serious, has probably contributed to overall roof stability since the roof shape in the failed areas is arched shaped rather than flat, which is inherently a more stable shape. The loose blocks represent the material between the flat and arched roof profiles. In various locations, there are still loose blocks in the roof that represent safety hazards to workmen, but do not necessarily threaten overall roof stability. In about half of the smaller rooms, and along most of the long corridors, the original flat roof profile as excavated is still intact.

An exception to the overall generally 'stable' condition of the roof in KV 5 is Chamber 5, which is in a state of almost total collapse. Due to the extremely poor condition of this room, very little exploration activity has taken place, and no geological mapping has been done.

5.3 Existing Conditions - Pillars

In chambers 3, 4, 5, and 14, the roof is supported by unmined limestone pillars, left in place during the excavation process. Chamber 3, the largest, contains 16 pillars in various states of distress. In Chamber 4, the pillars all appear to be in a relatively good condition compared to those in Chamber 3. In Chamber 5, access is very limited, and no specific evaluations have been made, although only one of the original pillars appears to be left, with all the others having collapsed. In Chamber 14, which has three pillars, no detailed evaluation has yet been made.

Since the loads applied to roof pillars (individual columns supporting the roof in larger rooms) and wall pillars (dividing walls between individual rooms, and other rooms, or between the room and the main corridor) are critical to stability, the overburden depth above the tomb is of prime importance. The surface topography above the tomb is shown in Figure V.1. Figure V.13 shows representative cross-sections taken longitudinally and transversely along KV 5 corridors. Figure V.15 shows a preliminary

Table V.2: Rock Mechanics Test Results

Rock Test	Units	Sample Location: Theban Limestone KV-5	Shaly Layer of Lower Theban Limestone	Esna Shale (?) from Portal of KV-20
Point Load Strength (average)	MPa	85 (4 tests)	87 (3 tests)	70 (3 tests)
Slake Durability Classification	% loss	30.7 II	93.8 III	98.6 III
Atterberg Limits				
Liquid Limit	%	40.5	62.6	72.2
Plastic Limit	%	29.4	30.8	30.7
Plasticity Index	%	11.1	31.8	41.5
Classification		ML	CH	CH
Swell Test				
Free Swell*	%	2.3	6.5	26.0
Swell Pressure	MPa	0.31	1.22	2.45

*One-Dimensional swell under nominal surcharge of 0.2 MPa

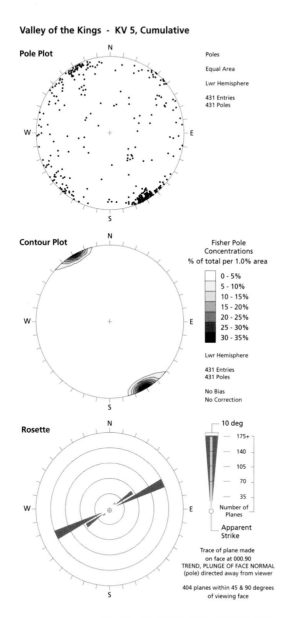

Fig. V.4: All Joint Data Measured in KV 5.

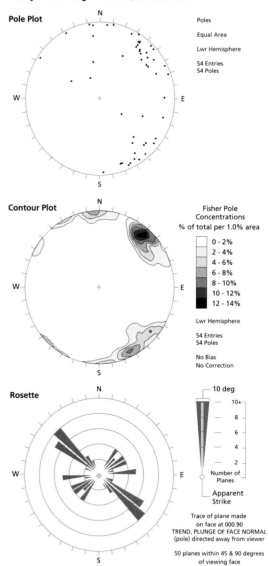

Fig. V.5: Joint Data near KV 34 - South End of the Valley.

178

Valley of the Kings - KV 35, Entrance Area

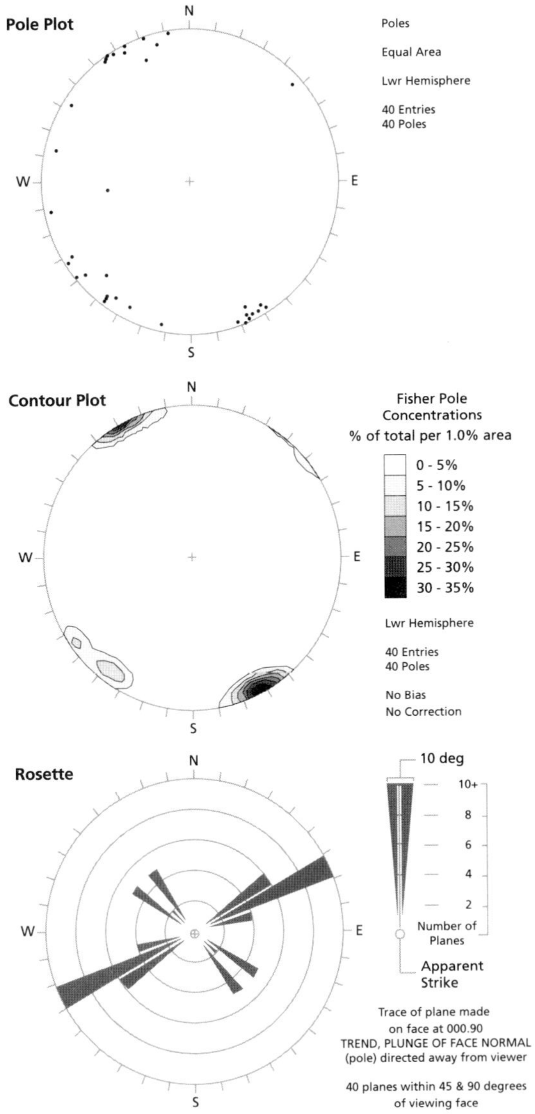

Pole Plot

Poles

Equal Area

Lwr Hemisphere

40 Entries
40 Poles

Contour Plot

Fisher Pole
Concentrations
% of total per 1.0% area

0 - 5%
5 - 10%
10 - 15%
15 - 20%
20 - 25%
25 - 30%
30 - 35%

Lwr Hemisphere

40 Entries
40 Poles

No Bias
No Correction

Rosette

10 deg

10+
8
6
4
2

Number of
Planes

Apparent
Strike

Trace of plane made
on face at 000.90
TREND, PLUNGE OF FACE NORMAL
(pole) directed away from viewer

40 planes within 45 & 90 degrees
of viewing face

Fig. V.6: Joint Data near KV 35 - West End of the Valley.

Valley of the Kings - KV 43, Entrance Area

Pole Plot

Poles

Equal Area

Lwr Hemisphere

57 Entries
57 Poles

Contour Plot

Fisher Pole
Concentrations
% of total per 1.0% area

0 - 4.5%
4.5 - 9%
9 - 13.5%
13.5 - 18%
18 - 22.5%
22.5 - 27%
27 - 31.5%

Lwr Hemisphere

57 Entries
57 Poles

No Bias
No Correction

Rosette

10 deg

20+
16
12
8
4

Number of
Planes

Apparent
Strike

Trace of plane made
on face at 000.90
TREND, PLUNGE OF FACE NORMAL
(pole) directed away from viewer

55 planes within 45 & 90 degrees
of viewing face

Fig. V.7: Joint Data near KV 43 - East End of the Valley.

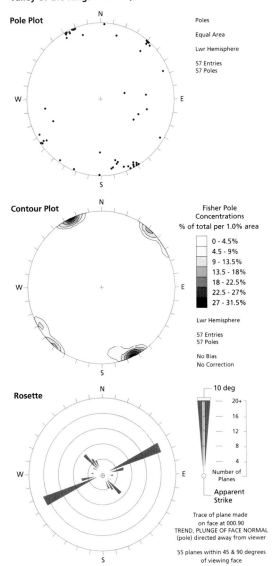

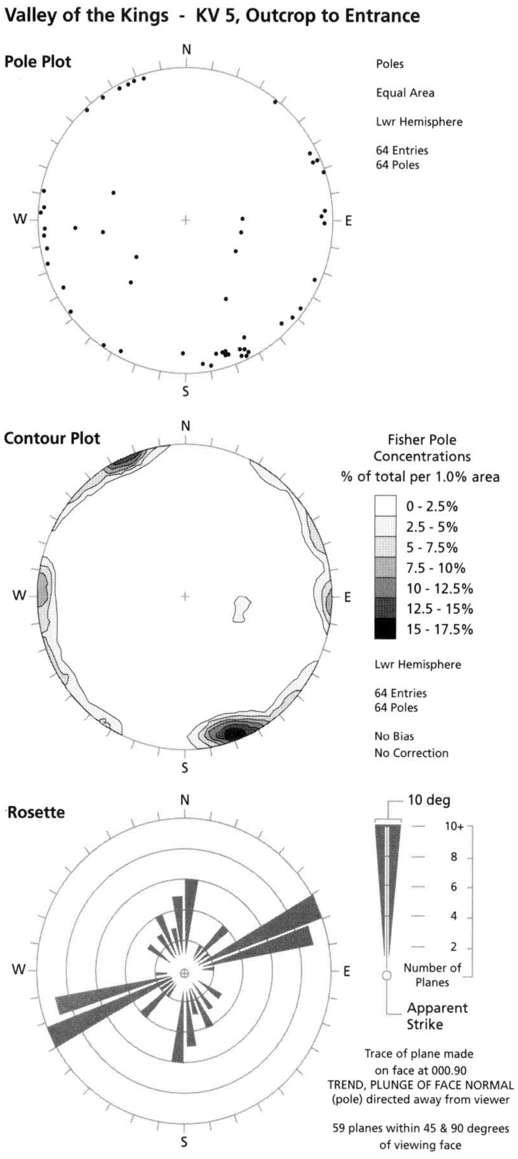

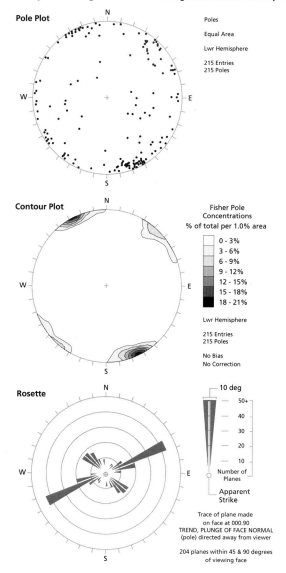

Valley of the Kings - KV 5, Outcrop to Entrance

Pole Plot

Poles

Equal Area

Lwr Hemisphere

64 Entries
64 Poles

Contour Plot

Fisher Pole
Concentrations
% of total per 1.0% area

0 - 2.5%
2.5 - 5%
5 - 7.5%
7.5 - 10%
10 - 12.5%
12.5 - 15%
15 - 17.5%

Lwr Hemisphere

64 Entries
64 Poles

No Bias
No Correction

Rosette

10 deg

10+
8
6
4
2
Number of
Planes

Apparent
Strike

Trace of plane made
on face at 000.90
TREND, PLUNGE OF FACE NORMAL
(pole) directed away from viewer

59 planes within 45 & 90 degrees
of viewing face

Fig. V.8: Joint Data near KV 5 - North End of the Valley.

Valley of the Kings - Cumulative Diagram, Surface Outcrops

Pole Plot

Poles

Equal Area

Lwr Hemisphere

215 Entries
215 Poles

Contour Plot

Fisher Pole
Concentrations
% of total per 1.0% area

0 - 3%
3 - 6%
6 - 9%
9 - 12%
12 - 15%
15 - 18%
18 - 21%

Lwr Hemisphere

215 Entries
215 Poles

No Bias
No Correction

Rosette

10 deg

50+
40
30
20
10
Number of
Planes

Apparent
Strike

Trace of plane made
on face at 000.90
TREND, PLUNGE OF FACE NORMAL
(pole) directed away from viewer

204 planes within 45 & 90 degrees
of viewing face

Fig. V.9: Joint Data for all Surface Outcrops Measured.

Valley of the Kings - Cumulative Diagram, All Measurements

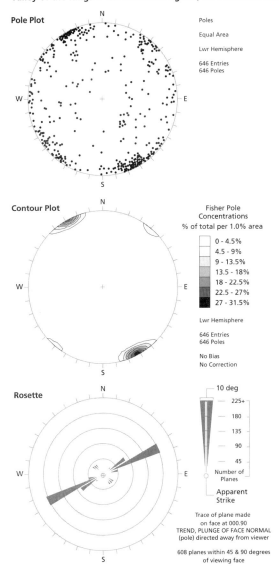

Pole Plot

Poles

Equal Area

Lwr Hemisphere

646 Entries
646 Poles

Contour Plot

Fisher Pole
Concentrations
% of total per 1.0% area

	0 - 4.5%
	4.5 - 9%
	9 - 13.5%
	13.5 - 18%
	18 - 22.5%
	22.5 - 27%
	27 - 31.5%

Lwr Hemisphere

646 Entries
646 Poles

No Bias
No Correction

Rosette

10 deg

225+
180
135
90
45

Number of
Planes

Apparent
Strike

Trace of plane made
on face at 000.90
TREND, PLUNGE OF FACE NORMAL
(pole) directed away from viewer

608 planes within 45 & 90 degrees
of viewing face

Fig. V.10: All Joint Data Measured in the Valley.

assessment of overburden depth contours above the tomb, superimposed on the tomb layout. It can be seen in these figures that the overburden depth above the excavation roof varies from about 6 to 36 meters.

In addition, Figure V.16 shows the condition of both the roof and wall pillars. In examining these last four figures together, it can be seen that the highest overburden in Chamber 3 is at the back (east) end of the room (approximately 17 meters, which coincides with the pillars that are either missing or severely damaged. Pillars near the room entrance on the west side, coinciding with the lowest overburden conditions, are in the best condition.

Similarly, it can be seen that the deepest overburden is above the transverse corridor, Corridor 10. This also coincides with the worst condition of wall pillars as shown in Figure V.16.

It is therefore evident that the existing tomb conditions appear to be directly related to the overburden depth, indicating a relationship between the applied load and the pillar rock strength (to be discussed further in Section 6).

a) Roof Failure

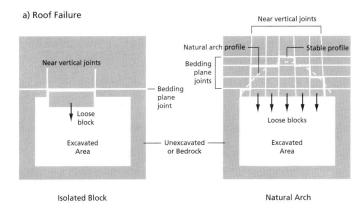

Isolated Block   Natural Arch

b) Roof Pillar and Wall Pillar Failure

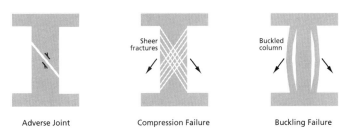

Adverse Joint   Compression Failure   Buckling Failure

Fig. V.11: Conceptual Excavation Failure Modes.

181

5.4 Effect of Rock Defects

The rock discontinuities evident in the exposed rock surfaces in KV 5 introduce weaknesses in the rock mass, resulting in the rock mass strength (discussed in Section 6) being somewhat less than the intact rock strength (as discussed in Section 3.2). As an example, along the thirty-meter length of Corridor 7, 124 individual joint orientation measurements were made, along both sides of the corridor. Assuming that half of the measurements were made on each wall, and assuming linear distribution along the full length of the wall, this would result in a joint 'density' of about two joints per linear meter, or a spacing of 0.5 meters. Since not all joints were measured, the spacing locally could be substantially less than this, contributing to a decrease in rock mass strength compared to intact rock strength, for both roof pillars and wall pillars.

5.5 Humidity

The infrequent historic 'catastrophic' floods in the Valley of the Kings have resulted in flooding of KV 5 periodically over the years, often leaving in place a new layer of water-saturated alluvial debris. As noted by Weeks (1992 and 1995) and in Appendix III, these flood cycles vary as a function of time, precipitation amount, and storm duration. These cyclic floods were followed by alternate cycles of drying out, periodically interrupted by the infiltration of surface water runoff (even though the tomb did not actually flood) through the open fractures exposed at the surface as described in Appendix IV. These alternate cycles of wetting and drying result in similar cycles of increasing and decreasing humidity conditions in the tomb, which could result in further rock mass deterioration. However, as noted in Section 3.3, laboratory test results on the Theban Limestone exposed in KV 5 indicate a fairly good performance,

with only negligible to moderate deterioration and no significant reduction in rock strength due to 'weathering' since the tomb was excavated. The shale samples (either in the Theban or Esna formations) exhibited poor behavior, but these are not yet known to be exposed in the accessible chambers of KV 5.

5.6 Alluvial Infill

As noted in Section 5.5 above, historic floods have left the KV 5 chambers and corridors substantially filled with sedimentary debris varying from grapefruit-sized angular rock fragments down to silts.

In the pillared halls where pillar stability is the key to overall chamber stability, the pillars are surrounded on all sides with this alluvial fill to a depth of 1.0 to 1.5 meters. For the pillars that are in poor condition with substantially reduced *in situ* strength (or even possibly having failed in the past), the alluvium provides confinement to the pillar, increasing its strength and resistance to further deformation. This confinement appears to be a key factor in maintaining the stability of Chamber 3, even though many of the pillars are in poor to extremely poor condition. Further excavation of Chamber 3 down to floor level will have to be done very carefully so that no pillars are allowed to fail, which could lead to catastrophic failure of the roof.

5.7 Influence of Lower Level Rooms

It can be seen in the KV 5 tomb layout in Figure V.1 that there are several documented small chambers, 8b, 8c, 9b, and 9c that are beneath the large 16-pillared hall (Chamber 3). Since these lower rooms have not yet been exposed and examined, their condition is unknown. Also, their influence upon the stability of the pillars in the overlying Chamber 3 has not yet been evaluated since their presence introduces a more complex three-dimensional problem. However, a concentrated pillar load on the floor of Chamber 3, which is underlain by discontinuous rock could cause more extensive yielding of the floor, especially on the far (east) side of Chamber 3 where the overburden is the highest.

These same conditions also occur with partial overlap of Chamber 4 with the side-chambers of Corridor 12, and possibly at other locations where a multiple level excavation is unknown. Depending upon the extent of the tomb areas yet to be excavated, there could conceivably be influences from or upon adjacent tombs as noted below.

In addition, any lower level rooms will lie closer to the shaly zone at the bottom of the Theban Limestone and the underlying Esna Shale. In the future, if any of the rooms are determined to lie very close to or within these shales, this introduces additional potential problems of rock mass deterioration, and of swelling and heave due to moisture changes from humidity and/or floodwater infiltration. However, until these lower level rooms are fully exposed, the nature and extent of any new rock mechanics stability problems can only be speculated at best.

5.8 Influence of Overlapping Tombs

Figure V.1 shows the plan view of KV 5 superimposed with adjacent tombs KV 6 and KV 55. It can be seen that KV 6 has some overlap with KV 5, and KV 6 has in turn some overlap with KV 55. It is evident that KV 6 could effect the performance of KV 5, but it is unlikely that KV 55 would have any significant effects upon KV 5. KV 6 overlaps KV 5 in both Chamber 4 and in Corridor 10, and in side-chambers 10f to 10m.

At the Chamber 4 overlap, the main corridor and two side-chambers of KV 6 overlay the south end of Chamber 4 of KV 5. Although the overlap is small, there could be minor influences. There is approximately 3.7 meters of rock in between the roof of KV 5's Chamber 4 and the floor of the KV 6 side-chambers. The side-chamber excavations would shed the overburden load to the surrounding rock and the central pillar in between. The central pillar, carrying a load slightly higher than overburden, would therefore transmit a concentrated load to the roof of KV 5 Chamber 4, although the 3.7 meters of rock in between would have a tendency to redistribute this load such that the effects upon KV 5 Chamber 4 would be minimal if any.

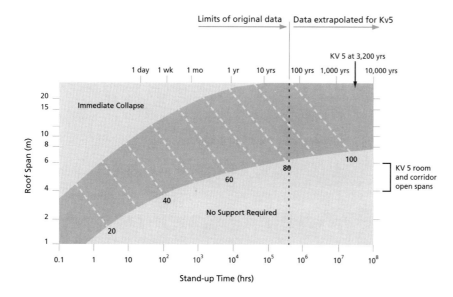

Fig. V.12: Stand-up Time vs. Roof Span and Age.

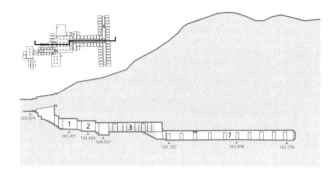

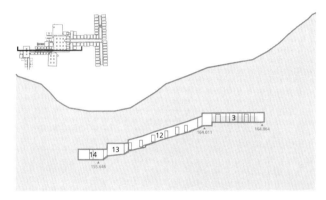

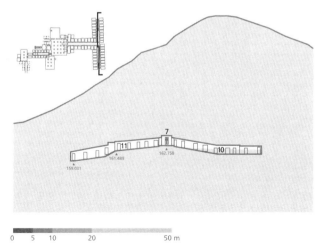

0   5   10   20   50 m

Fig. V.13: KV 5 Sections.

At the overlap of KV 5 Corridor 10 with the lower end of KV 6, the interaction would be more complicated, due to the complex arrangement of the excavation of both tombs. In the overlap zone, the apparent clearance between the roof of KV 5 and the floor of KV 6 is approximately 1.3 to 2.8 meters, depending upon which particular room of the tombs is being evaluated. Generally, the relatively simple layout of KV 6 would not create complicated stress patterns distributed to KV 5 below. The corridor excavation of KV 6 would, however, shed the overburden load to the walls beside the corridor, increasing the stress in the rock to one somewhat greater than that due to overburden. This effect however, would tend to redistribute with depth. The deepest part of KV 6 appears to be slightly beyond side-chambers 10g and 10f of KV 5, reducing the effects of the overlying excavation. The excavation of KV 6 above KV 5 would reduce the overlying rock load to be carried by KV 5 excavation walls and pillars, but the relatively close proximity and the three dimensional effects could affect the performance of KV 5 locally. Near the lower end of KV 6, a small chamber with two roof pillars lies directly over KV 5 side-chambers 10k, 10l, and 10m, with one roof pillar located directly over the wall pillar between 10l and 10m, and the other one over the roof of chamber 10k. The concentrated load carried by the KV 6 roof pillars would provide an additional 'surcharge' to the underlying chambers of KV 5. It can be seen, however, in Figure V.16, that the wall pillars in this area of Corridor 10 of KV 5 have less evidence of distress than other parts of Corridor 10, even in the zone of relatively high overburden compared to other parts of KV 5 as shown in Figure V.15.

It can therefore be concluded, that the presence of KV 6 overlying parts of KV 5 have not had any particularly detrimental effects upon the performance of the KV 5 excavations due to the interaction between the two tombs in close proximity.

5.9 Seismicity

A preliminary study was made to evaluate the seismic risk in the Valley of the Kings/Luxor area. Although the archæological literature occasionally refers to historic earthquake effects in ancient Thebes, this appears to be poorly documented. A study of historic earthquakes was made based upon studies by Maamoun et al (1985). Earthquakes listed in that study that are close enough to Luxor to have had any effects are shown in Figure V.17. These earthquakes date as far back as 600 B.C. and as recently as 1972 A.D. It can be seen in Figure V.17 that most of the seismic events of any potential risk in Luxor are about 200 kilometers or more away. At this distance, even considering estimated Richter Magnitude 6+ earthquakes, the local accelerations in Luxor would be expected to be less than 4 or 5% of the acceleration of gravity, consistent with the recommendations of the Egyptian Society for Earthquake Engineering (1988).

6. STRESS ANALYSIS

6.1 General

In order to estimate the influence of stress (applied load per unit of area) conditions in the KV 5 tomb for both the roof and wall pillars, several steps were necessary. These included extrapolation of intact rock strength to rock mass strength, evaluation of overburden conditions in the different parts of the tomb, evaluation of stress conditions in different parts of the tomb, and lastly, a comparison of the predicted stress to the estimated strength as a measure of pillar stability. These issues are discussed in the following paragraphs.

6.2 Rock Mass Strength Implications

The intact rock strengths estimated by the point load test discussed in Section 3.2 were used to estimate rock mass strength in the tomb. It should be noted that since only a few samples were tested, and since no actual uniaxial tests were performed by conventional laboratory procedures, these 'estimates' should be considered only 'estimates' for assessing the stability of rock structures in the tomb.

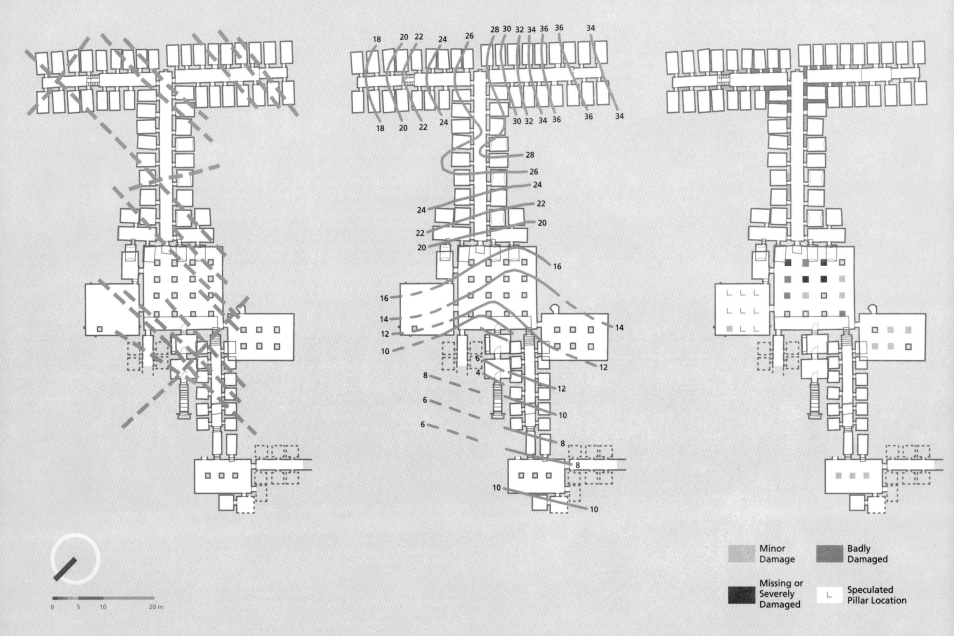

Fig. V.14: KV 5 and Prevailing Rock Fractures.

Fig. V.15: KV 5 Overburden Contours.

Fig. V.16: KV 5 Wall and Pillar Conditions.

Minor Damage

Badly Damaged

Missing or Severely Damaged

Speculated Pillar Location

0   5   10   20 m

For extrapolating the intact rock strength estimate to the rock mass strength estimate, the Hoek-Brown criteria was used (see Hoek, 1995). In making this evaluation, several parameters were varied, such that the results served as a parametric evaluation of rock strength upon rock structure stability. For this study, only the roof pillars in Chamber 3 were evaluated, since this is the critical room for stability, as discussed previously. In making the evaluation, the following parameters were varied:

- Intact uniaxial compressive strength: The strength values used were 40MPa (lower bound value, representing ISRM class R3-medium-strong), and 85MPa (average of the four-test values representing ISRM class R4-strong).

- Overburden depth: In Chamber 3, the overburden above the roof varies from about 10 to 17 meters as shown previously in Figure V.15. These values were used as the lower and upper bounds respectively.

- Estimated pillar stress: Using the lower and upper bound values of overburden, an average pillar size in Chamber 3 of 1.2 m² (1.1 m x 1.1 m) and a tributary area for each pillar of 9 m² (3 m x 3 m), corresponding lower and upper bound values of pillar stress were developed.

- Rock mass conditions: For each value of the estimated intact rock strength, two different conditions were assumed for estimating the rock strength decrease due to the presence of rock mass discontinuities as discussed in Sections 4 and 5. These were 'blocky' rock – very well interlocked undisturbed rock mass consisting of cubical blocks formed by three orthogonal joint sets as the upper bound, and 'very blocky' rock – interlocked partially disturbed rock mass with multifaceted angular blocks formed by four or more discontinuity sets. These conditions were intended as an approximate representation of initial conditions shortly after tomb excavation, and after initiation of instability due to pillar deformations under load and possible fracturing and/or deterioration with time, respectively.

Results of this preliminary parametric study are shown in Table V.3. It can be seen in this table that for the assumptions of highest overburden and lowest strength, the safety factor (strength ÷ stress) is only somewhat greater than 1. Considering the

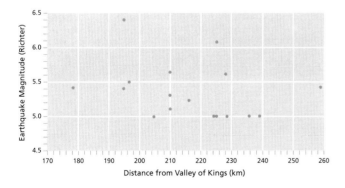

Fig. V.17: Seismic Activity near the Valley of the Kings.

accuracy of the input parameters, and the validity of the assumptions made, it is possible, if not probable, that the highest loaded pillars at the back of Chamber 3 failed in compression, consistent with the observations noted in Section 5.3.

The required pillar size must also consider the rock type (strength), extraction ratio (volume of rock removed compared to that left in place), and the roof and floor conditions. Recognizing that these variations influence the required pillar size, it is probable that the Chamber 3 pillars would be in the lower bounds of the required size estimates regardless of the assumptions. This also is consistent with the observation of possible overstress and failure of the pillars at the back of Chamber 3.

6.3 Numerical Evaluation

Due to the complex arrangement of KV 5 with its many chambers and corridors, a simple evaluation of stress conditions at locations other than Chamber 3 is almost impossible. Consequently, a numerical model was used to produce a 'first estimate' of stress conditions in other parts of the tomb. Due to the model limitations, the complexity of the grid required to prepare the model, the variable overburden depth above the tomb, the variable roof elevations, and the interaction with KV 6 as described in Section 5.8, it was necessary to make this 'first estimate' a very simplified evaluation. To do this, various overburden depths were assumed between 5 and 30 meters and a separate stress analysis done for each. These were then integrated together in a final 'composite' plot to approximate the actual range of overburden depths.

The numerical model used was a boundary element model called MULSIM/NL developed by the U.S. Bureau of Mines (Zipf, 1992). It was originally developed for calculating stresses and displacements in coal mines, or thin tabular metalliferous mines. The size of the fine grid used for the analysis was varied to approximate actual excavation geometry, which is well suited to the complex layout of KV 5.

The results of this stress analysis are shown in Figure V.18. It can be seen in this figure that within the restrictions and assumptions noted above for this simplified analysis, the stresses appear to be the highest in Corridor 10, and moderately high at the intersection of corridors 7, 10, and 11, also consistent with the observations noted previously in Section 5.3. The pillars in Chamber 3 appear to have relatively low stress, consistent with the moderate overburden depth, and given the deteriorated condition of the Chamber 3 pillars, it is possible that the overlying Theban Limestone could be transferring at least some of the overburden load to the unmined adjacent rock.

6.4 Arching Effects

As noted in Section 5.2, in some areas of the long corridors, the roof has partially collapsed to form a natural arch shape. Associated with this arching is a stress redistribution in which the vertical stress over the opening is redistributed to the rock adjacent to the opening, resulting in a higher than normal stress in the adjacent rock. This phenomenon occurs whether or not the roof rock within the arch has dropped out. However, it is not typical if the rooms are wide, or if the overburden is shallow relative to the room size. The overlying rock must be massive and competent to accomplish this load transfer.

In Chamber 3, approximately 15 meters in width, the overburden varies from about ten to seventeen meters as noted in Section 6.2. In this case, the room size exceeds the overburden depth except at the back of the room. Under these conditions, it is doubtful that the required arching would take place. Without significant load transfer, the stone pillars must carry the full overburden loads. However, for the long corridors, corridors 7, 10, 11, and 12, the corridor width is small compared to the overburden depth, and it is likely that arching will take place, with the vertical stress redistributed to the rock mass adjacent to the opening.

In these long corridors, the physical situation is much more complex than this simplified evaluation due to the side chambers excavated adjacent to the long corridor. In this case, the wall pillars between the corridor and side-chamber and between side-chambers will carry part of the load, with the balance of the load distributed to the rock mass behind the side chambers. At the intersection of corridors 7, 10, and 11,

Table V.3: Pillar Stress Parametric Study

Uniaxial Strength (MPa)	Overburden Depth (m)	Pillar Stress (MPa)	Rock Mass Strength (MPa)	Estimated Factor of Safety Strength/Stress
40^1	10^3	1.98^5	5.80^7	2.9
	10	1.98	9.96^8	5.0
	17^4	3.37^6	5.80	1.7
	17	3.37	9.96	2.9
85^2	10	1.98	12.3^7	6.2
	10	1.98	21.1^8	10.6
	17	3.37	12.3	3.6
	17	3.37	21.1	6.3

Notes:
1. Lower bound of intact strength estimated by point load test
2. Average intact strength estimated by point load test
3. Minimum overburden in Room 3
4. Maximum overburden in Room 3
5. Lower bound pillar stress for 9m² tributary area
6. Upper bound pillar stress for 9m² tributary area
7. Estimated rock mass strength for very blocky rock conditions
8. Estimated rock mass strength for blocky rock conditions

the load redistributed to produce three dimensional effects, with stress in the wall pillars near side-chambers 7g, 7h, 7i, 7j, 10p, and 11p higher than the adjacent wall pillars with only two dimensional effects. This is further complicated by the variable vertical stress due to the variable overburden in this area. The net result is evident in Figure V.18 in which it may be seen that despite the higher overburden at the back of the tomb, the stresses are lower than at the Chamber 3 - Corridor 7 intersection, and the stresses near the ends of chambers 10 and 11 are lower than those near their intersection with Corridor 7.

As noted previously in Section 6.3, the composite overburden depth assumed in the stress analysis is a simplifying assumption that complicates the interpretation of Figure V.18, but the stress redistribution tendencies noted above would still be valid but perhaps more prominent if a more accurate stress analysis assuming non-uniform overburden depth were performed.

7. SUMMARY

7.1 Existing Conditions

KV 5, the largest tomb known in Egypt, has numerous corridors and rooms in a complicated arrangement. Historic flooding of the tomb has left it filled with alluvial debris, requiring removal to fully expose the tomb. The tomb chambers are in various states of distress from relatively good to very poor condition. The poor condition of

186

USBM Mulplt of KV 5 Mar. 15. FMD
KV 5, 0.6m Elements, 5-35m Depth
Total Normal Stress - Z Direction

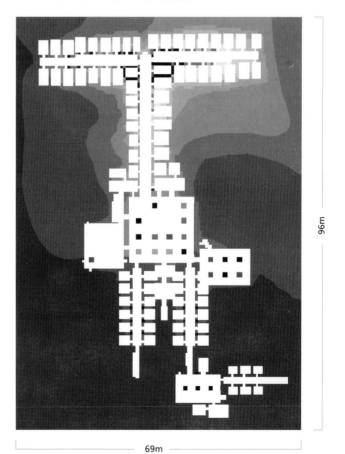

96m

69m

Normal Stress (Mpa)

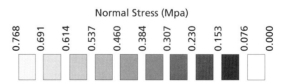

0.768   0.691   0.614   0.537   0.460   0.384   0.307   0.230   0.153   0.076   0.000

Fig. V.18: Stress Plot for KV 5.

the roof and pillars in parts of the tomb has resulted in localized failure, creating unsafe working conditions, although total collapse has not yet happened, with the exception of Chamber 5. It is the intention of the geotechnical studies summarized herein to provide the background information to develop stabilization measures necessary to improve the stability where required, and prevent total collapse in the other rooms from occurring.

7.2 Rock Mechanics Implications

The geotechnical studies indicate that the currently known layout of the tomb has been excavated in the lower member of the Theban Limestone, which is a relatively massive formation, but which contains a systematic orthogonal jointing system which is common to sedimentary formations.

The mineralogy of the limestone is of a nature that weathering and swelling is not a serious problem, although the shaly portion of the formation near its contact with the underlying Esna Shale could exhibit these undesirable characteristics (although it has not yet been seen to be exposed in any of the KV 5 chambers). The studies indicate that the most serious risk to tomb stability is the systematic jointing, which has several implications. Firstly, the jointing weakens the rock mass, making the roof and wall pillars weaker than if they were unjointed, substantially reducing the load-carrying capacity. Secondly, the secondary joints parallel to the bedding planes, although not as frequent as the vertical joints, combine with the vertical joints to produce loose blocks in the roof, some of which have already fallen over time. Some of these blocks still pose a serious safety risk but do not necessarily represent a risk of total collapse of the openings.

Lastly, many of the joints in the primary joint sets have opened with gravity, spreading as discussed in Appendix IV. These open joints extend to the ground surface and provide a conduit for surface water runoff to infiltrate the tomb from the infrequent but occasional intense rainfall as discussed in Appendix III. It cannot be ruled out that further slope deformations are possible in the future, if future floods again introduce water to the lower level shales from tomb flooding or infiltration through the existing open fractures.

7.3 Future Works

As noted above, geotechnical studies reported herein form the preliminary database from which to conduct further engineering studies to develop appropriate stabilization measures for both the short-term safety for archæological excavation purposes and for long-term stabilization for permanent preservation.

Although these studies have not yet reached the development stage for detailed designs to be implemented, initial concepts include those commonly used in underground structures in the civil and mining engineering fields. These include scaling down loose blocks in the roof and supporting the roof where required with either tensioned rock bolts or untensioned rock dowels, rebuilding or reinforcing the roof pillars with high strength mortar and/or encapsulating them in a shell of reinforced concrete, and rebuilding the deteriorated wall pillars in a similar fashion.

Although the limestone is not severely vulnerable to humidity changes in the tomb, humidity and temperature sensors have been installed to monitor these changes in the future. Additionally, when the roof and wall pillars have been restored, they will be instrumented with strain meters to monitor deformations under load as a check on the adequacy of the repairs. During the remaining archæological work in the tomb, a series of benchmarks will be set up in the roof of the main corridors chambers in order to monitor periodically any further movements of the rock blocks in the roof and to detect any further signs of instability.

As archæological excavation work continues, and more chambers and corridors are exposed, more signs of distress and deterioration may become evident and further studies conducted. Thus the stability plan must be flexible to account for new developments, especially since deeper chambers will be nearer the shaly formations which could present a different and potentially more serious stability problem than currently experienced in the excavations in limestone.

Lastly, as noted herein and in Appendices III and IV, diversion works must be developed to prevent precipitation from entering the tomb both through the overlying open rock joints and through the entrance as flood water. This activity is urgent not only for KV 5, but for all the tombs in the Valley of the Kings. In addition, it is hoped that the geotechnical data presented here will be used beneficially by other investigators in restoration works in the Valley of the Kings.

8. Acknowledgments

The authors would like to thank their respective organizations and other supporting organizations for their contribution, in time and material, to this study, as follows:

- Parsons Brinckerhoff International, Cairo, Egypt.
- Bukovansky Associates, Lakewood, Colorado, U.S.A.
- Sabbour Associates, Cairo, Egypt.
- Hamza Associates, Cairo, Egypt.
- Advanced Terra Testing, Lakewood, Colorado, U.S.A.
- Skala and Bukovanska, Prague, Czech Republic.
- Karen Richards, for her preparation of the text, and support of project activities while they were in progress.
- Dr. Kent Weeks, for his support during the studies, and for his invitation to participate in and contribute to this most interesting aspect of the Theban Mapping Project.

9. REFERENCES

Bukovansky, M., D. Richards, and **K. Weeks**. Influence of Slope Deformations on the Tombs in the Valley of the Kings, Egypt. *Proceedings, International Symposium, Engineering Geology and the Environment, Athens, Greece*. Rotterdam: A.A. Balkema, 1997.

Curtis, G. *The Geology of the Valley of the Kings, Thebes, Egypt*. Unpublished Report, Brooklyn Museum Theban Expedition, 1979.

Curtis, G. Deterioration of the Royal Tombs. In: **Richard H. Wilkinson** (ed.) *Valley of the Sun Kings: New Explorations in the Tombs of the Pharaohs*. Tuscon: University of Arizona Press, 1995.

Curtis, G. and **J. Rutherford**. Expansive Shale Damage, Theban Royal Tombs, Egypt. *Proceedings, 10th Conference International Society of Soil Mechanics and Foundations Engineering, Stockholm*. 1981.

Egyptian Society for Earthquake Engineering. *Regulations for Earthquake Resistant Design of Buildings in Egypt*. 1988.

General Organization for Geological Researches and Mining Geological Survey. Geological Map, Idfu-Qena Area. USSR Techno Export Contract 1247, 1968.

Hoek, E. Strength of Rock and Rock Masses. *International Society for Rock Mechanics News Journal*, Vol.2, No.2 (1994).

Maamoun, M., A. Megahed, and **A. Allam**. Seismicity of Egypt. *Bulletin of the National Research Institute of Astronomy and Geophysics*, Volume IV, Series B, Helwan, Egypt (1984): 109-160.

Ministry of Industry and Mineral Resources, Egyptian Geological Survey and Mining Authority. Geologic Map of the Aswan Quadrangle, Egypt. (Published in association with U.S. Geological Survey), 1978.

Ministry of Public Works and Water Resources. Geologic Map - Luxor. Water Research Center, Research Institute for Groundwater, 1992.

Reeves, N. and **R. H. Wilkinson**. *The Complete Valley of the Kings*. American University in Cairo Press, Cairo, 1996.

Romer, J. *Valley of the Kings*. London: Michael O'Mara, 1981.

Rutherford, J. Causes of Ancient Tomb Damage - Valley of the Kings, Egypt. *Proceedings, Symposium on Geotechnical Aspects of Restoration Works on Infrastructure and Monuments*. Rotterdam: A.A. Balkema, 1990.

Rutherford, J. and **D.P. Ryan**. Tentative Tomb Protection Priorities. In: **Richard H. Wilkinson** (ed.) *Valley of the Sun Kings: New Explorations in the Tombs of the Pharaohs*. Tuscon: University of Arizona Press, 1995.

Said, R. *The Geology of Egypt*. Amsterdam: Elsevier Publishing Company, 1962.

Skala, R. and **M. Bukovanska**. X-ray Powder Diffraction Examination of Materials from Egypt. Prague: unpublished Report to Theban Mapping Project, 1996.

Survey of Egypt. Geologic Map - Qena Quadrangle. 1946.

Weeks, K. R. The Theban Mapping Project and Work in KV 5. In: **Carl Nicholas Reeves** (ed.) *After Tut'ankhamun: Research and Excavation in the Royal Necropolis at Thebes*. London: Kegan Paul International, 1992.

Weeks, K. R. The Work of the Theban Mapping Project and the Protection of the Valley of the Kings. In: **Richard H. Wilkinson** (ed.) *Valley of the Sun Kings: New Explorations in the Tombs of the Pharaohs*. Tuscon: University of Arizona Press, 1995.

Whittaker, B. N. and **R.C. Frith**. *Tunnelling - Design, Stability and Construction*. London: Institution of Mining and Metallurgy, 1990.

Zipf, R. K. *MULSIM/NL Application and Practitioner's Manual*. Information Circular 9322, U.S. Bureau of Mines. Denver, CO, 1992.

Appendix VI:
KV 5 TOMB STABILITY AND REHABILITATION

John F. Abel, Jr.
Mining Engineer
Colorado P.E. 5642

EXECUTIVE SUMMARY

Rock falls and pillar deterioration started during the original excavation of KV 5, tomb for the sons of Ramesses II, and has continued since then. Visual observation indicates that the location of ceiling deterioration has been controlled by the presence of local fracture intensity, excavation geometry, and depth, in apparent order of importance.

Fracture orientations have been mapped by Michael Bukovansky throughout most of KV 5. The trend (strike) of the primary (most prominent) fracture set mapped in KV 5 is approximately N65°E, ranging from N50°E to N70°E and is near-vertical. Bukovansky measured a secondary near-vertical fracture set that strikes approximately N40°W. Figure V.14 shows the location of the most prominent fractures exposed in KV 5, i.e. continuous and open. Primary fractures were measured at the following ceiling instability and pillar deterioration locations, shown in Figure V.16:

1. The northwest corner of Chamber 3
2. The southeast side of Chamber 3
3. The northeast corner of Chamber 4
4. The central section of Corridor 7
5. The three-way intersection of corridors 7, 10, and 11
6. The north end of Corridor 11

Potentially adverse excavation geometries with respect to ceiling stability and pillar stress concentrations are large rooms and room intersections, i.e. wide ceiling spans are less stable than narrower spans and wide ceiling spans throw heavier loads on interior pillars. Chamber 3 has the widest ceiling span of approximately 15.8 meters by 15.5 meters and highest stability index of 3.91 meters (ceiling area divided by ceiling perimeter), in addition to the most adverse ceiling stability and most severe pillar deterioration of the accessible rooms. Chamber 4, which has a ceiling span of approximately 13.4 meters by 8.8 meters and a stability index of 2.66 meters, is subject to some ceiling instability and significant pillar deterioration. Chamber 2 has a ceiling span of approximately 10.6 meters by 9.7 meters and a stability index of 2.53 meters. Chamber 5 has partially collapsed and is not accessible from underground. The ceiling span of the three-way intersection of corridors 7, 10, and 11 is approximately 11.7 meters by 11.4 meters, with a stability index of 2.89 meters. This intersection has undergone considerable ceiling and pillar deterioration. Normally room stability is inversely related to stability index. However, the collapse of Chamber 5 does not follow this normal geometrically based stability prediction.

The depth of the KV 5 excavations is shown in Figures V.13. Normally, ceiling instability and pillar deterioration increases with depth. Ceiling instability and pillar deterioration in KV 5 is not the most severe at the maximum 36 meter depth. This implies that fracture location and excavation dimensions have controlled ceiling instability and pillar deterioration in KV 5.

Rehabilitation of KV 5 should start with Chamber 3 which has suffered the most ceiling instability and pillar deterioration. The three-way intersection of corridors 7,

10, and 11 should then be rehabilitated. Rehabilitation of Chamber 4 can be safely delayed until later. The deterioration of Chamber 5 is so severe that it probably cannot be safely under-taken from underground, but will have to be recovered from the surface downward. Rehabilitation of Chamber 3 should prevent the expansion of the Chamber 5 collapse into Chamber 3. Rehabilitation of Chamber 3 will necessitate the stabilization of the ceiling in access chambers 1 and 2. Rehabilitation of the three-way intersection of corridors 7, 10, and 11 will necessitate the prior stabilization of Corridor 7.

The most significant recommended stabilization component is the construction of artificial limestone replacement pillars for the badly-damaged and missing pillars in chamber 3 and 4. It is recommended that the replacement pillars be composed of quarried, cut, and dressed 1 meter long by 0.5 meters wide limestone blocks of different thicknesses, depending on the ability to transport the blocks into KV 5 and on the ability to lift the blocks onto the replacement pillar during erection. Minimal gypsum mortar, of the type used to fill open cracks encountered during KV 5 excavation, should be used between block courses to provide the maximum bearing surface.

Figure VI.8 shows the recommended replacement pillar construction. The irregular floor under the limestone block replacement pillars will have to be chiseled level to provide a base for construction. The space between the top course of the replacement pillars and the irregular ceiling will have to be filled with limestone fragments and mortar, much as was done in the case of the original Pillar 3(g) in Chamber 3. Eleven such artificial replacement pillars for missing and badly-damaged originals are recommended for Chamber 3, and four artificial replacement pillars for Chamber 4. The Pillar Inventory following the Summary and Conclusions lists the recommended replacement pillars. Figure VI.1 shows the thirteen missing and damaged pillars that should be replaced. In addition, it is recommended that Pillar 4(d) and Pillar 4(b) in Chamber 4 be replaced as a precautionary measure.

In the area of the three-way intersection between corridors 7, 10, and 11, approximately 43 meters of badly damaged and collapsed doorways and walls will have to be replaced by quarried, cut and dressed 0.4 meter-wide limestone blocks to rehabilitate this area. The floor under these replacement walls will have to be chiseled level and the space between the top of the walls filled in the same way as the replacement pillars.

Pipe jack and beam supports blocked to the ceiling are recommended to reinforce the ceiling in areas where steeply dipping fractures are present and where ceiling falls have occurred in the past. The purpose of these post and beam supports is to reinforce the overlying jointed ceiling. The area immediately under the pipe jacks should be chiseled level and a thin layer of gypsum mortar placed on the chiseled surface to provide a uniform bearing surface for these permanent ceiling supports.

Initially the recommended permanent post and beam supports should be erected and blocked to the ceiling of chambers 1 and 2 to assure long-term stability and safe access during rehabilitation of KV 5. The recommended two or three post and steel beam support in chambers 1 and 2 should be cribbed to the ceiling by cut-to-fit steel cross beams and finally blocked to the ceiling. The beams in the crib should be spot (tack) welded together as they are inserted into the crib to prevent toppling during erection. It is also recommended that the entrance to Chamber 3 from Chamber 2 be braced with vertical angle iron and a horizontal steel beam at the floor and a short pipe jack at the lintel.

It is recommended that replacement pillars for the missing pillars in Chamber 3 be erected first. Temporary pipe jack supports will have to be installed around the missing pillar being replaced to protect the workers as the flash flood debris and pillar fragments are removed and during erection of the replacement pillars. The same procedure should be employed during subsequent replacement of badly damaged pillars. Permanent pipe jack and beam supports should then be erected under deteriorated ceiling along Corridor 7 to the three-way intersection between corridors 7, 10, and 11. Temporary pipe jack supports will have to be installed to protect the workers during removal of collapsed and badly damaged entrance and chamber walls and erection of dressed limestone block replacement walls.

INTRODUCTION

This study of ceiling and pillar conditions in KV 5 and the development of rehabilitation recommendations was undertaken at the direction of Dr. Kent R. Weeks, Theban Mapping Project, The American University in Cairo. The ceiling and pillar conditions were inspected during the week of February 2 - 6, 1998.

The Theban Mapping Project provided plan maps, previous reports concerning geologic conditions, and information about acceptable rehabilitation materials for KV 5. Figure V.1 shows the plan layout of KV 5, as currently known, indicating the major chambers and corridors by number. These include Chamber 1 and Chamber 2 (the entrance rooms), Chamber 3 (the largest room with sixteen pillars), Chamber 5 (the collapsed room to the north), and Chamber 4 (the room in good condition to the south). The main corridors include Corridor 7 (the main east-west access), Corridor 10 (to the south), and Corridor 11 (to the north). Corridors 12 and 20 (declining to the west) are less well explored, still partly filled with flood debris.

GEOMORPHIC SETTING

KV 5 is sited in the lowest limestone unit, Member I, of the Thebes formation, as are most of the other tombs in the Valley of the Kings. Figure V.2 is the stratigraphic column at the Valley of the Kings. The limestone exposed in KV 5 is hard, compact, strong, brittle, and massive. Bedding is indistinct and does not apparently represent a significant weakness plane. Occassional bedding surfaces contain elongate nodules that appear to be chert. The open ceiling fractures exposed in the KV 5 excavations are the most prominent structural feature affecting the stability of KV 5. Michael Bukovansky mapped the most prominent of these fracture features in Figure IV.1. The primary fracture set strikes from N50°E to N70°E, averaging approximately N65°E, and is near-vertical in dip. The secondary fracture set mapped in KV 5 strikes approximately N48°W and is also nearly vertical in dip.

The Valley of the Kings trends very nearly north-south in the vicinity of KV 5. KV 5 was excavated toward the east, under a low ridge extending out from the east wall of the valley, as shown in Figure V.1. This low ridge rises to approximately 30 meters above the valley floor. Figure V.13 shows in cross-section the depth of the various parts of KV 5 below the overlying irregular ground surface. KV 5 is not level, and is inclined downward away from the portal, i.e. the depth of KV 5 does not exactly follow the surface contours. The rooms are level, but many of the corridors are inclined.

The top cross-section in Figure V.13 shows the downward gradient that facilitated the movement of flood debris from the entrance of KV 5 to the east through Chamber 1, Chamber 2, and Chamber 3 to Corridor 7, which while individually level are at progressively lower elevations. The middle cross-section shows the downward gradient that allowed flood debris washed in to the level of Chamber 3 to continue into and through Corridor 12 and Chamber 13 to the level of Chamber 14, and also to continue into Corridor 20. The bottom cross-section shows the downward gradient for finer flood debris to flow from the east end of Corridor 7 downward into corridors 10 and 11.

Limestone Member I of the Thebes formation was evaluated with respect to Bieniawskils Rock Mass Rating (RMR) classification system (1983), N. Barton, Lien, and Lunde's rock mass quality (Q) classification system (1982), and Laubscher's adjusted rock mass rating (ARMR) classification system (1990) rock classification systems. The limestone exposed in KV 5 would be classed as 'Good' rock using the RMR system, yielding a predicted rock load of 0.15 kN/m (70 lb/ft) of tunnel length and recommending local bolting with occasional wire mesh. The limestone would be classed 'Poor' rock using the Barton, et al Q method. The Q recommended support is for bolting,

untensioned, grouted on 1 meter centers. The limestone would be classed as 'Fair' rock using the ARMR classification system. The ARMR recommended support is for local bolts at joint intersections.

CURRENT TOMB CONDITIONS

Ceiling and pillar conditions in KV 5 vary both between and within rooms. Chamber 3, the widest room with a ceiling span of approximately 15.8 meters east-west by 15.5 meters north-south (see Figure VI.1) is typical . A band of deteriorated ceiling and pillars is present along a diagonal trending from the northeast corner to the southwest corner is present. This situation is indicated with respect to pillar deterioration in Figure V.16. The northeast-southwest deterioration trend follows the ceiling fracturing trend mapped by Bukovansky, Figure V.14. In addition, a ceiling fall apparently occurred in the northwest corner of Chamber 3 during excavation. The stability of Chamber 3 may be further jeopardized by the excavations adjacent on all but the south side. The pillars of Chamber 3 are typically 1 meter thick. Chamber 5 to the north, approximately 10.6 meters east-west by 9.7 meters north-south in plan, is severely deteriorated with very limited access and has undergone severe ceiling collapse. Chamber 3 should be the first priority for rehabilitation because the strip pillar between Chamber 5 and Chamber 3 is all that currently protects Chamber 3 from the advance of Chamber 5's collapse to the south.

Chamber 4, to the southwest of Chamber 3, is protected to the east and west by unmined ground. Chamber 4 is approximately 13.4 meters north-south by 8.8 meters east-west in plan (see Figure VI.1). Support is lowest toward the south of Chamber 4 as the plan of KV 5 indicates. Figure V.1, which shows KV 6 to the south overlying KV 5 by approximately 3.7 meters, and KV 55 at the same elevation further to the south, indicates that support from unmined ground to the south is probably about 7 meters further to the south. The ceiling fracturing present in Chamber 3 extends into Chamber 4 (see Figure V.14). However, there is considerably less associated ceiling deterioration in Chamber 4.

The ceiling and wall deterioration in the three-way intersection of corridors 7, 10, and 11 is associated with ceiling fracturing mapped by Bukovansky. The three-way intersection is at a depth of about 27 meters, as compared to a maximum depth of approximately 18 meters for Chamber 3. The ceiling and wall deterioration in the three-way intersection is primarily confined to the approximately 11.7 meters east-west by 11.4 meters north-south plan area.

Laubscher (1990) relates unsupported opening stability to the stability index of the opening (ceiling area divided by ceiling perimeter). Chamber 3 has the widest ceiling span (approximately 15.8 meters by 15.5 meters), the highest stability index of 3.91 meters, the most adverse ceiling stability, and the most severe pillar deterioration of the accessible rooms. Chamber 4, which has a ceiling span of approximately 13.4 meters by 8.8 meters and a stability index of 2.66 meters, is subject to some ceiling instability and significant pillar deterioration. Chamber 5 has a ceiling span of approximately 10.6 meters by 9.7 meters and a stability index of 2.53 meters. Chamber 5 has partially collapsed and is not accessible from underground. The ceiling span of the three-way intersection of corridors 7, 10, and 11 is approximately 11.7 meters by 11.4 meters, with a stability index of 2.89 meters. This intersection has undergone considerable ceiling and pillar deterioration. Laubscher indicates that normally room stability is inversely related to stability index, provided other factors are uniform. However, the collapse of Chamber 5 does not follow this geometrically based stability prediction.

NUMERICAL MODELING OF STRESS AND CLOSURE

Two numerical models were prepared and run to estimate the approximate pillar stresses and opening closures in KV 5 as the result of its original excavation and the pillar and wall deterioration that has taken place over the 3,200-plus years since then.

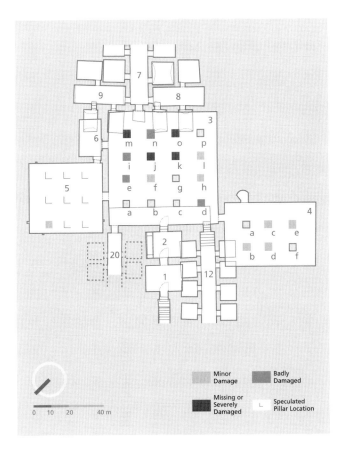

Fig. VI.1: Pillar conditions in chambers 3 and 4

Legend:
- Minor Damage
- Badly Damaged
- Missing or Severely Damaged
- L Speculated Pillar Location

The MULSIM/NL (multiple seams, nonlinear) code employed was developed in FORTRAN by the U.S. Bureau of Mines. MULSIM/NL is a three-dimensional boundary element program for calculating stresses and convergence of thin tabular excavation geometries. The program permits either flat-lying or a uniformly dipping excavation horizon. The irregular and variable inclination of different parts of KV 5 and the variable topography necessitated multiple runs at depths that varied. Runs were made using 5-meter increments of depth, from 5 to 35 meters. After the seven runs were finished the output was composited for depth locations within KV 5 from 0 to 7.5 meters, from 7.5 to 12.5 meters, from 12.5 to 17.5 meters, from 17.5 to 22.5 meters, from 22.5 to 27.5 meters, from 27.5 to 32.5 meters, and from 32.5 to 37.5 meters as indicated by the overburden contours in Figure V.15.

The code permitted the use of strain-softening material properties for the limestone within the height of KV 5. Rock specimens tested in a stiff testing machine and instrumented pillars in mines exhibit this strain-softening behavior. This means that the limestone is assumed to undergo an initial linear stress-strain response up to a limiting maximum stress followed by a linear decrease in stress with increasing strain to a minimum stress after which the material continues to strain without any change in stress. Limestone remote to the KV 5 excavations are subject to more confinement than the limestone exposed at or in close proximity to the room walls and pillars.

It was necessary to use reasonable estimates of the limestone properties because there are no specimen and in situ test results available. In addition, the code requires the assumption that the overlying and underlying rock is a uniform linear elastic material. The result of these necessary assumptions is to call into question the calculated vertical stress and closure values. However, the calculated vertical stresses and closures are valid estimates of relative vertical stresses and closures for locations within KV 5.

The calculated vertical stress estimate at each element represents the average across the 0.6 by 0.6 element. The model mesh is 160 elements long by 115 elements wide, 96 meters long by 69 meters wide. Figure VI.2 shows the calculated vertical stresses at the time KV 5 was excavated, over 3,200 years ago, for the incremental depths taken from Figure V.13. Figure VI.3 shows the calculated stresses that have progressively developed since KV 5 was first excavated, causing the deterioration of the limestone-strength pillars and chamber walls as shown in Figures V.16, VI.1, and VI.2. All rocks progressively deteriorate, or deform, when subjected to a differential stress (deviatoric or shear stress) condition over time. Initially the stress distribution appears to be primarily controlled by depth and secondarily by excavation geometry (room dimensions). As the limestone exposed in the pillars and walls deteriorated, the vertical stress decreased and the unsupportable stress was shed back into the more confined limestone away from the exposed room walls. It was necessary to use reduced-strength and strain-softening properties for the various deterioration conditions that have slowly developed.

Comparison of Figure VI.2 (initial calculated stresses) and Figure VI.3 (current calculated stresses) approximates the pillar load adjustment that has accompanied 3,200-plus years of pillar and wall deterioration in KV 5. The stress calculations indicate that major Chamber 3 stress adjustment has occurred on the east side where the missing and damaged pillars in Chamber 3 and the pillars between Chamber 3 and Corridor 7 and Chamber 8 have shed load to the solid ground to the south. The stress calculations indicate that the wall between Chamber 5 and Chamber 3 has undergone almost no change. The stress calculations further indicate that the stress originally supported by the probably failed pillars in Chamber 5 has been transferred to the solid ground to the east and north. The stress levels on the damaged pillars in Chamber 4 appears to have transferred to the solid ground to the south and east. Similarly, calculations indicate that the stress on the doorways and walls at the three-way intersection of corridors 7, 10, and 11 has decreased as these walls have deteriorated and shed load to the adjacent solid ground to the south and north. The loads in this area have apparently shifted to the solid ground to the east and west. The calculations also indicate that stress increases are moving from this area west toward the front of Corridor 7, south into Corridor 10, and north into Corridor 11. The indication is that the deterioration of the doorways and walls at this intersection will continue to proceed in those directions, as it has in the past, unless the badly-damaged areas are replaced.

The MULSIM/NL numerical model was also used to calculate closures throughout KV 5. It was necessary to perform this set of calculations in two steps. First, the convergence that occurred as the result of overburden load before excavation was calculated and second, the total convergence calculated for the completed KV 5. Figure VI.4 shows the calculated differential ceiling-to-floor convergence (closure) that resulted from the initial excavation of KV 5. Figure VI.5 shows the calculated differential ceiling-to-floor convergence (closure) that resulted from the pillar and wall deterioration that has occurred since initial excavation of KV 5. Initially the calculated closure appears to be primarily controlled by depth and secondarily by excavation geometry (room dimensions), the same as for stress. The calculated closure effects from pillar deterior-

USBM Mulplt of KV 5 Mar. 15. FMD
KV 5, 0.6m Elements, 5-35m Depth, Original
Total Normal Stress - Z Direction

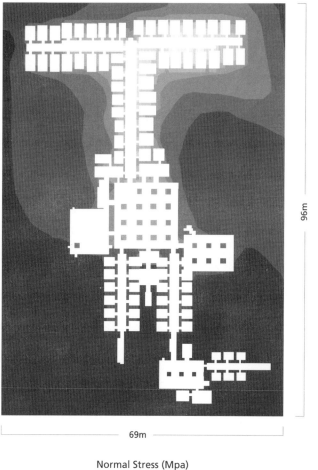

96m

69m

Normal Stress (Mpa)

0.768   0.691   0.614   0.537   0.460   0.384   0.307   0.230   0.153   0.076   0.000

Fig. VI.2: Stress Plot for KV 5 at the time of its original excavation.

USBM Mulplt of KV 5 Mar. 15. FMD
KV 5, 0.6m Elements, 5-35m Depth
Total Normal Stress - Z Direction

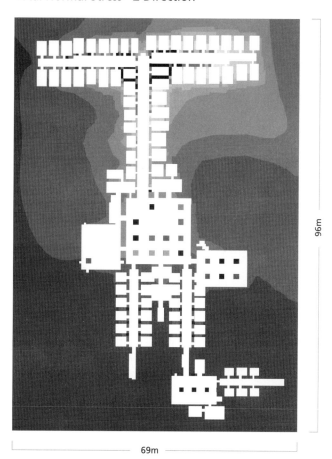

96m

69m

Normal Stress (Mpa)

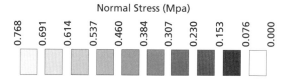

0.768   0.691   0.614   0.537   0.460   0.384   0.307   0.230   0.153   0.076   0.000

Fig. VI.3: Stress Plot for KV 5 after subsequent deterioration.

USBM Mulplt of KV 5 Org3. FMD
KV 5, 0.6m Elements, 5-35m Depth, Original
Delta Closure - Z Direction

USBM Mulplt of KV 5 Mar. 5. FMD
KV 5, Closure. 0.6m Elements, 5-35m Depth

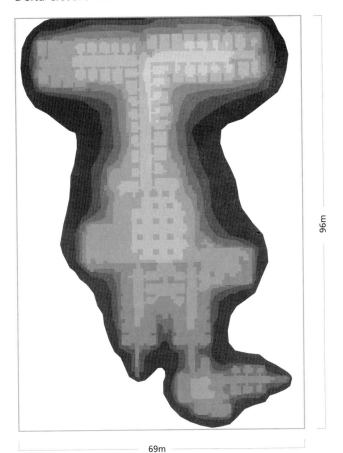

96m

69m

Estimated Excavation Closure (mm)

0.60 0.50 0.40 0.30 0.20 0.10 0.05 0.03 0.02 0.01 0.00

Figure VI.4: Calculated Differential Roof-to-Floor Closure for KV 5 at the time of its original excavation.

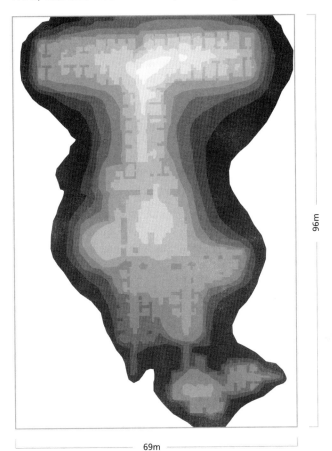

96m

69m

Estimated Excavation Closure (mm)

0.60 0.50 0.40 0.30 0.20 0.10 0.05 0.03 0.02 0.01 0.00

Figure VI.5: Calculated Differential Roof-to-Floor Closure for KV5 after subsequent deterioration.

ation indicate an approximately 50% increase in closure at the three-way intersection of corridors 7, 10 and 11, an approximately 33% increase in closure in Chamber 3, an approximately 50% increase in closure in Chamber 5, and a minor increase in closure in chambers 4, 2, and 1. Calculated ceiling-to-floor closures have increased to the west toward the front of Corridor 7, to the south into Corridor 10, and to the north into Corridor 11. The closure calculation indication is that deterioration of the doorways and walls at this intersection will continue to proceed in those directions, as it has in the past, unless the badly damaged areas are replaced.

The MULSIM/NL numerical model results emphasize the importance of rehabilitating the pillars of Chamber 3 followed by the three-way intersection between corridors 7, 10, and 11. The recommended major rehabilitation of Chamber 3 must be completed first to provide for safe access to the three-way intersection site. The recommended post and beam rehabilitation of chambers 1 and 2 is relatively minor, but is necessary for safety while rehabilitating Chamber 3. Similarly, the recommended post and beam rehabilitation of the Corridor 7 is relatively minor, but is necessary for safety while rehabilitating the three-way intersection of corridors 7, 10, and 11.

ADDITIONAL NUMERICAL MODEL RUNS

A multiple level numerical model was run for KV 5 and the adjacent and overlying tombs KV 6 and KV 55 (see Figure V.1). The overall conclusion is that interaction between the three tombs has no significantly adverse affect on KV 5. Depth appears to be the most important factor with respect to stress concentration and closure, more important than stress concentrations resulting in either adverse opening geometry or interaction with adjacent or overlying tombs. This would not have been the case for the 36-meter KV 5 depth variation if that variation was applied at typical mining depths of over 1,000 feet (305 meters). Basically, the maximum KV 5 pillar and wall stresses develop at the maximum 36-meter depth in Corridor 10 and not in the pillars in Chamber 3, the room with the maximum span but with a depth of only 15 meters, approximately, nor at the adverse intersection of corridors 7, 10, and 11.

The long-term deterioration of room pillars and walls since the original excavation of KV 5, KV 55, and KV 6 has forced the transfer of all or part of their loads to adjacent unmined ground. The loss of support has apparently increased the predicted maximum closure in KV 5 by approximately 25 percent. This could explain the obvious opening of the natural fractures and the collapse of many of the ceiling slabs that has taken place over time. The model suggests that the worst currently active room deterioration should be in the walls of side-chambers 10p, 10o, 10n, and 10d. Generally poor ground conditions should be in the vicinity of the intersection of corridors 7, 10, and 11. Ground conditions should be better at the end of Corridor 10, in side-chambers 10g through 10l, primarily because of support provided on three sides but also because of shielding from the overlying chambers of KV 6.

Excavation Sequence

KV 55 was probably completed more than 60 years before the excavation of KV 5, which means that the initial stress deviations around KV 55 were also complete when the adjacent Chamber 4 of KV 5 at the same elevation was excavated. KV 6 was probably excavated more than 85 years after KV 5. These are certainly significant times on a human scale, but not in the life of the tombs. The deterioration of the strong and brittle Thebes limestone has been significant over the 3,200-year period since excavation.

KV 5 Stress Concentration Predictions

The numerical model indicates a minor stress concentration in the approximately 1.4 meter-thick buttress between KV 55 and Chamber 4 of KV 5. The initial, short-term, stress concentration in the buttress between the two tombs is relatively minor because of the shallow depth of approximately 14 meters. The model indicates that the initial stress concentration in the buttress decreased when KV 6 was excavated

directly overhead. The small side-chamber Ba in KV 6 reduced the stress in Pillar 4(e) in Chamber 4. This agrees with modern-day mining experience, but does not correlate with the present deteriorated condition of the SE pillar, unless it was already deteriorating when KV 6 was excavated.

Further excavations in KV 6 decreased the initial stress concentrations in the underlying side-chambers 10k, 10l, 10m, 10n, 10f, 10g, and 10h of KV 5. However, the load transfer resulting from KV 6 slightly increased the stress concentrations at the intersection of corridors 7, 10, and 11.

The model indicates that the wall deterioration along Corridor 10 forced the transfer of the overburden loading to the adjacent unmined and confined ground, i.e. beyond the corridor's side-chambers. This is exactly what would be expected from our current knowledge of ground response to mining in competent rock, such as Thebes limestone.

KV 5 Opening Closure Predictions

Closure of an underground opening is both an immediate and long-term response to the transfer of the load previously carried by the excavated rock. The load transfer is no further than absolutely necessary. Initially, the KV 5 excavation loads were transferred to the nearest rock walls and pillars. Initial opening closure was restricted by the strength of the rock pillars and walls. The walls of Corridor 10 are subject to the highest stress and the initial maximum closure is generally confined between the corridor walls and centered in the corridor. Initially, the only significant effects of the excavation of KV 6 was to shift both pillar and wall stresses in KV 5 back toward the intersection of corridors 7, 10, and 11. Initially, the maximum closure accompanied the maximum pillar and wall stress transfer locations.

If rock was perfectly elastic, it would not deteriorate over time when subjected to differential stress – i.e. subjected to a high normal stress unrestrained at the pillars and wall ribsides of an excavation. The differential stress magnitude is referred to as the 'deviatoric stress'. Unfortunately, rock is not perfectly elastic. The least restrained parts of any supporting wall or pillar are the corners, referred to as pillar points in mining. Pillar points are unrestrained in two directions, and ribsides in only one direction. Pillar points deteriorate first, followed by the only slightly more restrained exposed ribsides of the walls. As the pillar points and room walls deteriorated over time the loads had to be either transferred to the unmined adjacent rock, or the opening would collapse (possibly – though unlikely – what happened in Chamber 5). Maximum closure has crossed the walls along the west side of Corridor 10 and back into the intersection between corridors 7, 10, and 11. The addition of KV 6 had a minimal effect on the predicted closure in the intersection area.

Stress and Closure Changes from Excavation of KV 6

The initial numerical model calculated KV 5 stress changes as the result of excavating KV 6. All the changes are minor, barely 10% of the maximum stress, but the maximum stress decrease is approximately seven times greater than the maximum stress increase. The stress decreases are logically located where KV 6 overlies Corridor 10 and its side-chambers, and prevents the direct application of most of the overburden loading on KV 5. The lesser magnitude of the stress increases is primarily the result of the greater adjacent area of unmined ground available to accept the transferred load from KV 6.

The predicted decrease in opening closure (rebound) of the underlying rooms in KV 5 due to the excavation of KV 6 probably did not actually reach the indicated magnitudes. Measurements in multiple seam coal mining indicate rebound, but much less than numerical model predictions. It is probable that rock deformations are not as elastic as forced by physical property input restrictions. That is, more of the deformation is non-elastic (permanent) than elastic (recoverable). The properties of the rock pillars and walls used in the numerical model are given in Figure VI.6. The long-term deterioration of KV 5 pillars and walls transferred stress away from KV 6 and resulted in additional rebound (closure decrease) in underlying KV 5 workings. The properties of different pillar conditions are given in Figure VI.7.

KV 6 Numerical Model Predictions

The inclusion of KV 6 in the numerical model analysis permitted prediction of stresses and closure in that tomb and in the adjacent rock in a plane approximately 3 meters above KV 5. The 3 meters represents a gross approximation of the thickness of Thebes limestone between the ceiling of KV 5 and the floor of KV 6. The KV 6 results include the effects of the prior excavation of KV 55 and KV 5. Long-term deterioration increased closure in KV 5 slightly. The closure across that overlying plane above KV 55 and KV 5 was too small to show up in the numerical model output.

REHABILITATION RECOMMENDATIONS

Rehabilitation of KV 5 as an underground mine would be less complicated because of the relatively short design life of underground mine excavations. Stabilization of ceiling fractures in a mine would normally involve tensioned fully resin-grouted rock bolts inserted in drill holes crossing the ceiling fractures, as previously indicated by the three rock classification systems applied. The missing and badly-damaged pillars would most likely be replaced with reinforced concrete pillars. Missing and badly-damaged doorways and chamber walls would very likely be rehabilitated by encasing them in reinforced concrete. Pillars with minor damage could be stabilized by either strapping them with wire rope tensioned with turnbuckles or by applying lateral restraint using channel iron tightened against alternating sides of the pillars with bolts and nuts.

Rock bolting is not an acceptable long-term rehabilitation method for the deteriorated ceiling in KV 5 because of the limited design life of rock bolts. Corrosion limits the service life of rock bolt support to generally more than 50 years (Baxter, 1997). In addition, bolt corrosion takes place unseen within drill holes and could lead to sudden unpredictable ceiling falls in the future.

Concrete has a long, but limited life (Troxell, et al, 1968). However, concrete is not currently an acceptable material for construction of replacement pillars in tomb rehabilitation because of the potential for chemical attack by the minor halite present in the Thebes and Esna formations (Appendix II). Concrete is subject to progressive damage when salt is present. It has also been reported that concrete reacts with the Thebes limestone when the two are in direct contact. This reaction should be studied to determine the magnitude of and damage from the reaction.

Quarried, dressed, and lightly mortared Thebes limestone blocks are recommended for the construction of replacement pillars (see Figure VI.8) for missing and badly-damaged pillars in chambers 3 and 4 and for doorways and walls at the intersection of corridors 7, 10, and 11 in order to provide a long-term stable load bearing structure. The estimated strength of the 1 meter by 1 meter replacement pillars in plan quarried and dressed limestone block pillars is greater than or equal to 1,230 tonnes (1,350 tons). This is based on the conservative assumption that the reduction in limestone strength associated with increase in limestone specimen or pillar size (Jahns, 1966, Pratt, et al, 1972, Bieniawski, 1968, and Abel, 1988) is similar to that for closely jointed coal (Bieniawski, 1968). The estimated Thebes limestone 85 MPa (12,300 psi) uniaxial specimen

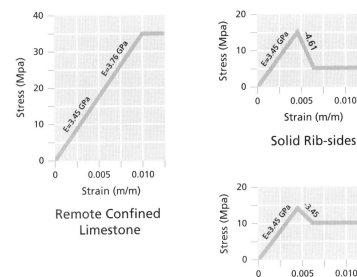

Figure VI.6: Properties of pillars and walls.

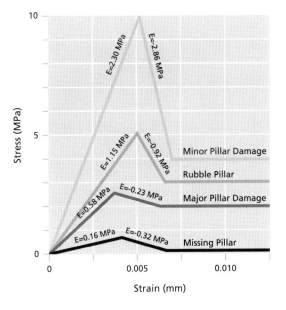

Figure VI.7: Properties of various pillar conditions.

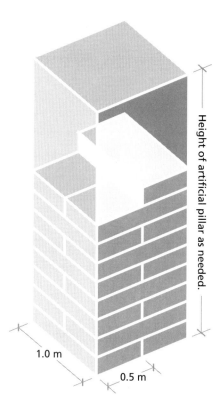

Height of artificial pillar as needed.

1.0 m

0.5 m

Figure VI.8: Construction of replacement pillars.

compression strength was based on the indirect point-load strength test. The estimated 1-meter pillar strength is 12 MPa (1,740 psi). This compares with the Pratt, et al strength/size reduction for massive rocks for the estimated 12,300 psi compressive specimen strength to 21.6 MPa (3,130 psi), and 1-meter pillar strength to 2,210 tonnes (2,430 tons). The more conservative Bieniawski limestone block pillar strength is capable of supporting approximately 13 meters (43 ft) of overlying limestone, more than 2.4 times more than the maximum potential 5.3 meter arch height above Chamber 3. The original Chamber 3 pillars were probably even stronger than the estimated strength of the recommended replacement limestone block pillars. The reason some of the pillars have been crushed into a pile of rubble and others are badly damaged is the time difference involved between specimen rock testing used for mine design and the typical less than 100 year mine opening design life and the greater than 3,200 years that the KV 5 pillars have been supporting compressive stress.

Steel pipe jacks with steel beam supports and cribs are recommended for ceiling support in areas where ceiling fractures are present and where ceiling deterioration has occurred. It is recommended that the steel post and beam support structures be cribbed with steel beams to positions close to the ceiling and then blocked tight to the ceiling with timber blocks and wedges. The timber blocking will have a limited life, somewhat greater than 25 years, and will have to be replaced periodically. The post and beam support structure will, however, be visible for inspection and repair or replacement when necessary. No underground opening has an infinite life when not maintained. The 3,200-plus life of KV 5 is exceptionally long for underground openings that have not been maintained.

The rehabilitation of chambers 1 and 2 with a more permanent post and beam support system should be accomplished first. The current post and timber blocking system provides adequate support for the deteriorated ceiling conditions. However, the present post support partially blocks access to KV 5. It is recommended that the replacement ceiling supports be constructed of post and steel beams. The recommended post and beam units are either two leg or three leg units oriented west to east and erected on each side of the room entrances, providing an unobstructed path through the rooms. The posts placed at the ends of the post and beam unit should be between approximately 0.3 and 0.6 meters from the room walls. The steel beams placed in the saddles at the top of each post should be approximately horizontal and cross braced, referred to as X-bracing, alongside the saddle at each post location unit with lightweight steel angles spot welded from the upper flange of the beam of one unit to the lower flange of the beam of the adjacent parallel unit on the other side of the access corridor. The X-bracing should be reversed, i.e. bottom flange to top flange, on the opposite side of the post saddle. The purpose of the X-bracing is to prevent tipping of the main support beams when loaded. After placing and X-bracing the steel beams in the post saddles, three cross beams are recommended for the next overlying layer of the support crib to progressively fill the irregular space between the X-braced beams and the ceiling. The beams in the crib should be spot (tack) welded together as they are inserted into the crib to prevent toppling during erection. Finally, the steel crib should be blocked to the ceiling with tightly wedged timber blocks and the jacks re-tightened. It will be necessary periodically (at least yearly) to inspect and tighten the blocking and jacks. [Since this report was written, the recommendations for work in chambers 1 and 2 have been completed. -Ed.]

In the area of the three-way intersection between corridors 7, 10, and 11, approximately 43 meters of badly damaged and collapsed doorways and walls will have to be replaced by quarried, cut, and dressed 0.4 meter-wide limestone blocks to rehabilitate this area. The floor under these replacement walls will have to be chiseled level and the space between the top of the walls filled in the same way as the replacement pillars.

It is also recommended that the entrance to Chamber 3 from Chamber 2 be braced with vertical angle iron and a horizontal steel beam at the floor and a short pipe jack at the lintel. This procedure should arrest the deterioration of the entrance.

SUMMARY AND CONCLUSIONS

Rehabilitation is necessary to prevent further deterioration and progressive collapse of certain parts of KV 5, namely Chamber 3 and the three-way intersection of corridors 7, 10, and 11. There is no safe way to safely recover and rehabilitate the already collapsed Chamber 5 from underground. If action is not undertaken to rehabilitate KV 5 in the near future it is predicted that the ceiling above the three-way intersection will collapse, potentially eliminating access to corridors 10 and 11. Chamber 3 is currently at risk because of the loss of four support pillars to deterioration. Replacement of these pillars should prevent further deterioration of the structural stability of KV 5. The north wall of Chamber 3 is actually a strip pillar separating Chamber 3 from Chamber 5. This pillar is currently in good condition, but it is apparent that this strip pillar is a critical support member with respect to the advance of the Chamber 5 collapse into Chamber 3. The recommended replacement pillars are 1 meter by 0.5 meter quarried limestone blocks installed at the locations of missing and badly-damaged pillars. The thickness, or thicknesses, of the blocks should be dependent on the efficient movement of the blocks to the pillar replacement site and placement of the blocks to the necessary height. Replacement of the four missing pillars with quarried, dressed, and lightly mortared limestone blocks in Chamber 3 will add major support to the ceiling, estimated as greater than 4,910 tonnes (5,400 tons).

Access to Chamber 3, and beyond to the three-way intersection between corridors 7, 10, and 11, for rehabilitation, is dependent on the installation of light ceiling support in areas of deterioration over the narrow corridors that currently provide access to KV 5. The post and steel beam support system recommended should prevent localized ceiling deterioration from dropping a slab into these corridors.

Structural failure of the three-way intersection between corridors 7, 10, and 11 is dependent on the replacement of the approximately 43 meters of the entrance and rear walls. The recommended support replacements are 0.4-meter wide walls of quarried, dressed, and lightly mortared limestone blocks. The length and thickness, or lengths and thicknesses, of the blocks should be dependent on the efficient movement of the blocks to the wall replacement site and placement of the blocks to the necessary height.

PILLAR INVENTORY FOR CHAMBERS 3 AND 4

See Figure VI.1 for pillar designations. The observed conditions of exposed pillars and detailed recommendations for stabilization are given below:

Chamber 3

3(a) Extremely minor vertical splitting. Strap pillar on 0.5 m spacing top to bottom, set of two posts with beam and blocking to ceiling between pillar and both north and west walls.
Minor restraint.

3(b) Buried in flash flood debris with no portion of pillar visible.
None possible.

3(c) Numerous near-vertical stress splits. Replace pillar with quarried and dressed limestone blocks, 1 m by 0.5 m in plan, with minimal gypsum mortar between courses. Short-term rehab with steel pillar straps on 0.3 m spacing top to bottom, set of two posts with beam and blocking to ceiling between pillar and west wall, and diagonally between Pillar 3(c) and Pillar 3(h) to southeast.
Replace pillar.

3(d) Numerous near-vertical and inclined stress splits. Replace pillar with quarried and dressed limestone blocks, 1 m by 0.5 m in plan, with minimal gypsum mortar between courses. Set of two posts with beam and blocking to ceiling between Pillar 3(d) and both west and south walls, between Pillar 3(d) and badly-damaged Pillar 3(h) to east, and along the southeast diagonal between Pillar 3(d) and south wall of Chamber 3 (across near-vertical, northeast striking jointing in ceiling).
Replace pillar.

3(e) More than half of pillar has failed toward west. East side of pillar is in deceptively good condition. Replace pillar with quarried and dressed limestone blocks, 1 m by 0.5 m in plan, with minimal gypsum mortar between courses. Set of two posts with beam and blocking to ceiling between pillar and north wall.
Replace pillar.

3(f) Exposed top, approximately 0.7 m of pillar, has been crushed. Replace pillar with quarried and dressed limestone blocks, 1 m by 0.5 m in plan, with minimal gyp-

sum mortar between courses. Set of two posts with beam and blocking to ceiling between Pillar 3(f) and badly-damaged Pillar 3(e) to north, between Pillar 3(f) and missing Pillar 3(j) to east, between Pillar 3(f) and missing Pillar 3(k) to southeast (across pronounced near-vertical, northeast striking jointing in ceiling), and between Pillar 3(f) and artificial Pillar 3(g) to south.
Replace pillar.

3(g) This artificial pillar is composed of irregular shaped blocks and fragments of limestone enclosed in gypsum mortar. Minor near-vertical stress fractures visible on exposed pillar faces. Strap pillar on 0.5 m spacing top to bottom, set of two posts with beam and blocking to ceiling between Pillar 3(g) and badly-damaged Pillar 3(f) to north, between Pillar 3(g) and missing Pillar 3(k) to east, between Pillar 3(g) and relatively undamaged Pillar 3(l) to southeast (across pronounced near-vertical, northeast striking jointing in ceiling), and between Pillar 3(g) and badly-damaged Pillar 3(h) to south.
Minor restraint.

3(h) Cross section of exposed top, approximately 0.9 m of pillar, has been reduced to about two-thirds. Replace pillar with quarried and dressed limestone blocks, 1 m by 0.5 m in plan, with minimal gypsum mortar between courses. Set of two posts with beam and blocking to ceiling between Pillar 3(h) and Pillar 3(d) to west, diagonally between Pillar 3(h) and Pillar 3(c) to northwest, between Pillar 3(h) and artificial Pillar 3(g) to north, between Pillar 3(h) and relatively undamaged Pillar 3(l) to east (across pronounced near-vertical, north-east striking jointing in ceiling), between Pillar 3(h) and the south wall of Chamber 3, and along the southeast diagonal between Pillar 3(h) and south wall of Chamber 3 (across pronounced near-vertical, northeast striking jointing in ceiling).
Replace pillar.

3(i) More than half of pillar has failed in exposed upper part of pillar. An inclined open fracture cuts completely across exposed upper part of pillar. Replace pillar with quarried and dressed limestone blocks, 1 m by 0.5 m in plan, with minimal gypsum mortar between courses. Set of two posts with beam and blocking to ceiling between pillar and north wall of Chamber 3, between Pillar 3(i) and missing Pillar 3(m) to east, between Pillar 3(i) and badly-damaged Pillar 3(n) to southeast (across pronounced near-vertical, northeast striking jointing in ceiling), and between Pillar 3(i) and missing Pillar 3(j) to south.
Replace pillar.

3(j) Pillar 3(j) is missing and must be replaced. Replace pillar with quarried and dressed limestone blocks, 1m by 0.5m in plan, with minimal gypsum mortar between courses. Set of two posts with beam and blocking to ceiling between Pillar 3(j) and Pillar 3(i) to north, between Pillar 3(j) and badly-damaged Pillar 3(n) to east, between Pillar 3(j) and missing Pillar 3(o) to southeast (across pronounced near-vertical, north-east striking jointing in ceiling), and between Pillar 3(j) and missing Pillar 3(k) to south.
Replace pillar.

3(k) Pillar 3(k) is missing and must be replaced. Replace pillar with quarried and dressed limestone blocks, 1 m by 0.5 m in plan, with minimal gypsum mortar between courses. Set of two posts with beam and blocking to ceiling between Pillar 3(k) and Pillar 3(j) to north, between Pillar 3(k) and badly-damaged Pillar 3(o) to east, between Pillar 3(k) and relatively undamaged Pillar 3(p) to southeast (across pronounced near-vertical, northeast striking jointing in ceiling), and between Pillar 3(k) and relatively undamaged Pillar 3(l) to south.
Replace pillar.

3(l) Relatively undamaged pillar. Strap pillar on 0.5 m spacing top to bottom, set of two posts with beam and blocking to ceiling between pillar and south wall of Chamber 3, between Pillar 3(l) and Pillar 3(h) to west, between Pillar 3(l) and Pillar 3(g) to northwest, and between Pillar 3(l) and Pillar 3(k) to north.
Minor restraint.

3(m) Pillar 3(m) is missing and must be replaced with quarried and dressed limestone blocks, 1 m by 0.5 m in plan, with minimal gypsum mortar between courses. Set of two posts with beam and blocking to ceiling between Pillar 3(m) and badly-damaged Pillar 3(i) to west, between Pillar 3(m) and north wall of Chamber 3 across entrance to Chamber 6 north of badly-damaged Pillar 3(i) and across pronounced near-vertical, northeast striking jointing in ceiling (avoid post placement over Side-chamber 9c), between Pillar 3(m) and north wall of Chamber 3 (avoid post placement over Side-chamber 9c), between Pillar 3(m) and east wall of Chamber 3, between Pillar 3(m) and the east wall of Chamber 3 immediately south of entrance to Corridor 7, and between Pillar 3(m) and badly-damaged Pillar 3(n) to south.
Replace pillar.

3(n) The upper approximately 1 m of pillar is severely fractured, including one inclined fracture cutting completely across the exposed top of the pillar. Pillar must be replace with quarried and dressed limestone blocks, 1 m by 0.5 m in plan, with minimal gypsum mortar between courses. Set of two posts with beam and blocking to ceiling between Pillar 3(n) and missing Pillar 3(j) to west (across pronounced near-vertical, northeast striking jointing in ceiling), between Pillar 3(n) and badly-damaged Pillar 3(i) to northwest (across pronounced near-vertical, northeast striking jointing in ceiling), between Pillar 3(n) and missing Pillar 3(m) to north, between Pillar 3(n) and east wall of Chamber 3 (avoid post placement over Side-chamber 8c), and between Pillar 3(n) and missing Pillar 3(o) to south (avoid post placement over Side-chamber 8c).
Replace pillar.

3(o) Pillar 3(o) is missing and must be replaced. Replace pillar with quarried and dressed limestone blocks, 1 m by 0.5 m in plan, with minimal gypsum mortar between courses. Set of two posts with beam and blocking to ceiling between Pillar 3(o) and missing Pillar 3(k) to west (across pronounced near-vertical, northeast striking jointing in ceiling), between Pillar 3(o) and missing Pillar 3(j) to northwest (across pronounced near-vertical, northeast striking jointing in ceiling), between Pillar 0 and badly-damaged Pillar 3(n) to north (avoid post placement over Side-chamber 8c), between Pillar 3(o) and east wall of Chamber 3 (avoid post placement over Side-chamber 8b), and between Pillar 3(o) and relatively undamaged Pillar 3(p) to south (avoid post placement over Side-chamber 8b).
Replace Pillar.

3(p) Relatively undamaged pillar. Strap pillar on 0.5 m spacing top to bottom, set of two posts with beam and blocking to ceiling to southeast between Pillar 3(p) and southeast corner of Chamber 3 (across near-vertical open fracture in ceiling striking northeast), between Pillar 3(p) and missing Pillar 3(o) to north (avoid post placement over Side-chamber 8b), and between Pillar 3(p), and missing Pillar 3(k) to northwest.
Minor restraint.

Chamber 4

4(a) Diagonal shear fracture angles completely across exposed upper approximately 0.8 m of pillar. Replace pillar with quarried and dressed limestone blocks, 1 m by 0.5 m in plan, with minimal gypsum mortar between courses. Set of two posts with beam and blocking to ceiling between Pillar 4(a) and north wall of Chamber 4 on west side of entrance, between Pillar 4(a) and east wall and between Pillar 4(a) and Pillar 4(c) to the south, and between Pillar 4(a) and Pillar 4(b) to west.
Replace pillar.

4(c) Pillar 4(c) has lost about 25% of east-west width to spalling to east. Remainder of Pillar 4(c) is intact. Strap pillar on 0.5 m spacing top to bottom. Set of two posts with beam and blocking to ceiling between Pillar 4(c) and Pillar 4(a), between Pillar 4(c) and east wall of Chamber 4, between Pillar 4(c) and Pillar 4(d), and between Pillar 4(c) and Pillar 4(b) under northeast striking ceiling fracture along northwest diagonal. Long-term stabilization can be accomplished by replacing pillar with quarried and dressed limestone blocks, 1 m by 0.5 m in plan, with minimal gypsum mortar between courses.
Minor restraint.

4(e) Over half of exposed pillar cross-section has been lost to spalling toward east. Replace pillar with quarried and dressed limestone blocks, 1 m by 0.5 m in plan, with minimal gypsum mortar between courses. Set of two posts with beam and blocking to ceiling between Pillar 4(e) and Pillar 4(c), between Pillar 4(e) and east wall of Chamber 4, between Pillar 4(e) and Pillar 4(f), and between Pillar 4(c), Pillar 4(e), and Pillar 4(d) under a northeast striking ceiling fracture over the northwest diagonal. Long-term stabilization can be accomplished by replacing pillar with quarried and dressed limestone blocks, 1 m by 0.5 m in plan, with minimal gypsum mortar between courses.
Replace pillar.

4(f) Extremely minor vertical splitting. Strap pillar at one-third distances from ceiling and floor. Set posts with beam and blocking to ceiling between Pillar 4(f) and Pillar 4(e), and between Pillar 4(f) and Pillar 4(d).
Minor restraint.

4(d) The load carrying capacity of about 25% of pillar has been lost because of spall on east side of exposed pillar. Numerous near-vertical and inclined fractures cut across pillar faces. Pillar could be temporarily stabilized by strapping at 0.5 m intervals. Long-term stabilization will require replacing pillar with quarried and dressed limestone blocks, 1 m by 0.5 m in plan, with minimal gypsum mortar between courses. Set of two posts with beam and blocking to ceiling between Pillar 4(d) and Pillar 4(f), between Pillar 4(d) and Pillar 4(f), and between Pillar 4(d) and Pillar 4(e) along southeast diagonal under northeast striking ceiling fracture.
Replace Pillar.

4(b) About one-third of exposed pillar cross section may have been lost due to spall toward west. Pillar contains several vertical stress fractures but is otherwise in relatively good condition. Pillar could be temporarily stabilized by strapping at 0.5 m intervals. Long-term stabilization will require replacing pillar with quarried and dressed limestone blocks, 1 m by 0.5 m in plan, with minimal gypsum mortar between courses. Set of two posts with beam and blocking to ceiling between Pillar 4(b) and Pillar 4(d), between Pillar 4(b) and west wall of Chamber 4 where a large block has fallen from ceiling, between Pillar 4(b) and Pillar 4(a), angled between Pillar 4(b) and north wall of Chamber 4 (avoid placement of post over underlying side-chambers in Corridor 12 complex), and between Pillar 4(b) and Pillar 4(c) along southeast diagonal under northeast striking ceiling fracture.
Replace Pillar.

REFERENCES

Abel, Jr., J.F. Soft rock pillar design. *International Journal of Mining & Geological Engineering*, v. 6 (1988): 215-248

Barton, N., R. Lien and **J. Lunde.** Rock reinforcement. In: **W. A. Hustrulid** (ed.) *Underground mining methods handbook.* SME, 1982. Pp. 1540-1555.

Baxter, D.A. Rockbolt corrosion under scrutiny. *Tunnels & Tunnelling International*, July (1997): 35-38.

Bieniawski, Z.T. The effect of specimen size on the compressive strength of coal. *International Journal of Rock Mechanics & Mineral Science*, v. 5, no. 4 (1968): 325-335.

Bieniawski, Z.T. and **W.L. van Heerden.** The significance of in situ tests on large rock specimens. *International Journal of Rock Mechanics & Mineral Science*, v. 12 (1975): 101-113.

Bieniawski, Z.T. *Rock mechanics design in mining and tunneling.* Rotterdam: A.A. Balkema, 1983. P. 454.

Brauner, G. *Subsidence due to underground mining, Part 2. Ground movements and mining damage.* USBM IC8572, 1973. P. 53.

Coates, D.F. *Rock mechanics principles.* Monograph 874 (Revised). CANMET Energy Mines & Resources Canada, 1981. P. 446.

Curtis, G. *The geology of the Valley of the Kings.* Unpublished report, Brooklyn Museum Theban Expedition, 1979.

Deere, D.U., R.B. Peck, J.E. Monsees and **B. Schmidt.** *Design of tunnel liners and support systems.* Report of the U.S. Dept. of Transportation, NTIS PB 183 799, 1969. P. 287.

Jahns, H. Measuring the strength of rock in situ at an increasing scale. *Proceedings, First International Symposium on Rock Mechanics, Lisbon, Portugal.* v. 1 (1966): 477-482.

Laubscher, D.H. A geomechanics classification system for the rating of rock mass in mine design. *Journal of the South African Institute of Min. & Met.*, Oct (1990): 257-272.

National Coal Board (British). *Subsidence Engineers' Handbook.* National Coal Board, Mining Dept, 1975. P. 111.

Piggott, R.J. and **P. Eynon.** Ground movements from the presence of abandoned mine workings. In: **J.D. Geddes** (ed.) *Proceedings, Conference on Large Ground Movements and Structures.* Wiley, 1977. Pp. 749-780.

Pratt, H.R., A.D. Black, W.S. Brown and **W.F. Brace.** The effect of specimen size on the mechanical properties of unjointed diorite. *International Journal of Rock Mechanics & Mineral Science*, v. 9 (1972): 513-529.

Smith, W.C. *Ceiling control strategies for underground coal mines.* USBM Info Circ 9351, 1993. P. 17.

Troxell, G.E., H.E. Davis and **J.W. Kelly.** *Composition and properties of concrete, 2nd Edition.* New York: McGraw-Hill, 1968. P. 529.

Whittaker, B.N. & R.C. Firth. *Tunnelling: design, stability and construction.* London: Institution Mining & Met., 1990. P. 460.

Wilson, A.H. Research into the determination of pillar size, Part 1, An hypothesis concerning pillar stability. *The Mining Engineer*, Trans. Inst. Mining Engineers, Jun (1972): 409-417.

Zipf, R.K., Jr. *MULSIM/NL application and practitioner's manual.* USBM Info Circ 9322, 1992. P. 48.

ACKNOWLEDGMENTS

Amoco Foundation, Inc.
Mr. Bruce L. Ludwig
Mobil Corporation
National Geographic Society
Pfizer Egypt S.A.E.
Sante Fe International (Egypt)

At the American University in Cairo:
  President John Gerhart
  Provost Tim Sullivan
  Dean Cynthia Nelson
  Chair Nicholas Hopkins

At the American University in Cairo Press:
  Mr. Mark Linz
  Mr. Neil Hewison
  Ms. Andrea Al-Akshar

At the Supreme Council of Antiquities:
  Dr. Gaballa A. Gaballa
  Dr. Abdel Halim Nour Eddin
  Dr. Zahi Hawass
  Dr. Mohammed Sughayer
  Dr. Mohammed Nasr
  Dr. Sabry Abd el Aziz
  Mr. Ibrahim Soliman
  Mr. Mohammed Bially
  Mr. Fathy Salim
  Mr. Ahmed Ezz